DEATH BY

Chocolate *Cakes*

DEATH BY
Chocolate *Cakes*

An Astonishing Array of Chocolate Enchantments

MARCEL DESAULNIERS

*Recipes with Ganache Hill Test Kitchen
Chef Brett Bailey and The Trellis Pastry
Chef Kelly Bailey*

Photography by DUANE WINFIELD

WM

WILLIAM MORROW
An Imprint of HarperCollinsPublishers

HarperCollins books may be purchased for educational, business, or sales promotional use. For information please write: Special Markets Department, HarperCollins Publishers Inc., 10 East 53rd Street, New York, NY 10022.

FIRST EDITION

Prop styling by Robyn Glazer

Printed on acid-free paper

Library of Congress Cataloging-in-Publication Data

Desaulniers, Marcel.
  Death by chocolate cakes : an astonishing array of chocolate enchantments / Marcel Desaulniers ; recipes with Brett Bailey and Kelly Bailey; photography by Duane Winfield.—1st ed.
    p. cm.
  Includes bibliographical references and index.
  ISBN 0-688-16297-5
  1. Cake. 2. Cookery (Chocolate) I. Bailey, Brett. II. Bailey, Kelly. III. Title.

TX771 .D44 2000
641.8'653—dc21

00—056247

00 01 02 03 04 / RRD 10 9 8 7 6 5 4 3 2 1

Other Books by Marcel Desaulniers

The Trellis Cookbook
Death by Chocolate
The Burger Meisters
Desserts to Die For
An Alphabet of Sweets
Death by Chocolate Cookies
Salad Days

Dedication

To my mom, Mrs. D, and to all the moms, including my friend Penny Seu

Acknowledgments

Thank you to everyone who helped make yet another book on delicious demise with chocolate a reality.

Connie Desaulniers

Brett Bailey

Kelly Bailey

Dan Green

Harriet Bell

Justin Schwartz

Carrie Weinberg

Duane Winfield

Leah Carlson-Stanisic

Michael Calabrese

John and Julia Curtis

Michael Holdsworth

Steve Francisco

Robert Cappetta

Michele Montano

Jason Wade

Erick Fisher

The students, instructors, and staff at the Culinary Institute of America

Contents

Introduction

DEATH BY CHOCOLATE? Not according to the Harvard School of Public Health, which stated that, in a recent study of 7,841 Harvard male graduates, chocolate eaters—regardless of how voracious their appetites—live almost a year longer than those who abstain.

So how much more encouragement do we need to yield to our passion for chocolate? Probably not much if you are reading this book. I would guess that like me, you have probably been a lifelong chocolate lover. My obsession with chocolate started at an early age: Teething with unfettered abandon on my mother's dark chocolate fudge was followed by the voracious sinking of newly emerged teeth into her absurdly chocolaty caramels. More serious and texturally engaging treats followed as mom tried to keep her rambunctious, chocolate-loving brood under control (under her chocolate spell may be more accurate). As my five sisters and I maneuvered through the vicissitudes of being kids, our behavior was constantly being tempered by homemade chocolate confections.

Now, I'm not saying that chocolate is the answer to solidifying family values, but I'm also not saying it isn't. I shall leave it up to you, my fellow chocophile, to decide whether or not Chocolate Heart of Darkness Cakes (page 5) will mend a wounded psyche, or whether a Chocolate Chip Goober Gobble Cupcake (page 23) will get an ants-in-the-pants kid stuck to the dining room table. But who knows?

After all, they're not just cakes; they're *Death by Chocolate Cakes*.

BABY CAKES

DIMINUTIVE BUT DEVASTATINGLY DELICIOUS CHOCOLATE NIBBLES

CHOCOLATE HEART *of* DARKNESS CAKES

MAKES 12 CAKES

Make the Dark Chocolate Truffle Hearts
Place 8 ounces chopped semisweet chocolate in a small bowl. Heat ¾ cup heavy cream in a small saucepan over medium heat. Bring to a boil. Pour the boiling cream over the chopped chocolate. Set aside for 5 minutes and then stir with a whisk until smooth. Pour the mixture (called ganache) onto a nonstick baking sheet and use a rubber spatula to spread the ganache in a smooth, even layer to within about 1 inch of the inside edges. Place the ganache in the freezer for 15 minutes, or in the refrigerator for 30 minutes, until very firm to the touch.

Line a 10- to 12-inch dinner plate with parchment paper or wax paper. Remove the firm ganache from the freezer or the refrigerator. Portion 12 heaping tablespoons (a bit more than 1 ounce each) of ganache onto the paper. Wearing a pair of disposable vinyl (or latex) gloves, individually roll each portion of ganache in your palms in a circular motion, using just enough gentle pressure to form a smooth orb. This is a traditional truffle. You should refrain from indulging in them now, since absence of a truffle in a cake will make the heart grow darker. Return each formed truffle to the paper-lined plate, and place in the freezer while preparing the cake batter.

Make the Chocolate Cocoa Cakes
Preheat the oven to 325°F. Lightly coat the inside of each of 12 individual nonstick muffin cups (3 inches in diameter) with some of the 2 teaspoons melted butter. Set aside until needed.

In a sifter, combine ⅔ cup flour and ½ cup cocoa powder. Sift onto a large piece of parchment paper (or wax paper), and set aside until needed.

Melt 8 ounces chopped semisweet chocolate and 5 ounces of butter in the top half of a double boiler, or in a microwave oven (see pages 197–98 for more details), and stir until smooth.

Place 3 eggs, 2 egg yolks, and ½ cup sugar in the bowl of an electric mixer fitted with a paddle. Beat on medium-high speed for 2 minutes until the mixture is slightly frothy. Add the melted chocolate and butter and mix on low speed to combine, about 15 seconds. Continue to operate the mixer on low while gradually adding the sifted dry ingredients. Once they have been incorporated, stop the mixer and scrape down the sides of the bowl. Add 1 teaspoon vanilla extract and mix on medium to combine, about 15 seconds. Remove the bowl from the mixer and use a rubber spatula to finish mixing the batter until thoroughly combined.

Portion 3 heaping tablespoons (about 2½ ounces) of the cake batter into each muffin cup. Place the muffin tin on the center rack of the preheated oven. Bake for 5 minutes. Remove the truffles from the freezer.

DARK CHOCOLATE TRUFFLE HEARTS
8 ounces semisweet baking chocolate, coarsely chopped
¾ cup heavy cream

CHOCOLATE COCOA CAKES
5 ounces unsalted butter, cut into ½-ounce pieces; plus 2 teaspoons (melted)
⅔ cup all-purpose flour
½ cup unsweetened cocoa powder
8 ounces semisweet baking chocolate, coarsely chopped
3 large eggs
2 large egg yolks
½ cup granulated sugar
1 teaspoon pure vanilla extract

Remove the muffin tin from the oven and, moving quickly, place a single frozen truffle in the center of each portion of cake batter, pressing the truffle about halfway down into the batter. Immediately return the muffin tin to the center rack of the oven and bake until a toothpick inserted into a cake (not the truffle) comes out clean, 17 to 18 minutes.

Remove the cakes from the oven and cool at room temperature for 20 minutes. To remove the cakes from the muffin cups, hold the top edge of a cake, and give the cake a slight jiggle to loosen it from inside the cup. Then insert the pointed tip of a knife into an outside edge of the top of the cake and loosen it so that you can gently pull the baked cake out of the cup. Serve immediately while still warm.

THE CHEF'S TOUCH

You are undoubtedly aware that chocolate has not only pleased palates but also increased libido since the Aztec emperor Montezuma quaffed a cold, spiced cocoa drink before engaging in corporeal activities of a passionate nature. In Montezuma's day, only the elite had the privilege of chocolate, and indeed, drinking it from a golden goblet was de rigueur. The masses remained uninformed about chocolate's virtues until the seventeenth century, when English Quakers popularized sweetened hot chocolate as an alternative to demon gin. Ever since that time, chocolate lovers have had a warm spot in their hearts for hot chocolate (even though gin has remained one of the more popular sins).

Which brings me to Chocolate Heart of Darkness. This warm, molten chocolate cake is so sensual it could be the eighth deadly sin. How appropriate that it was created by my sister Denise Yocum, a psychologist in Massachusetts. Whose lust was she analyzing when she developed this recipe?

If the racks in your oven slide out easily and are stable, instead of removing the muffin tin from the oven, slide the center rack out and quickly insert the truffles. Then return the rack to its place and finish the baking.

After the Chocolate Heart of Darkness Cakes have cooled to room temperature, you may keep them covered with plastic wrap for up to 24 hours at room temperature, or in the refrigerator for 3 to 4 days. Being a purist who is stuck in his ways, here is a revelation I hate to admit: The cakes may be rewarmed in a microwave oven, and they are extraordinary. Make sure the cakes are at room temperature, then heat them one or two at a time for 30 to 40 seconds in a microwave oven set on defrost power. The cake will be warm and moist, and the truffle center will be a hot ooze of ecstasy.

CHOCOLATE PEANUT BUTTER SOME MORE CAKES (*Please*)

MAKES 12 CAKES

Make the Graham Cracker Crust Bottom
Preheat the oven to 325°F. Place the graham cracker pieces in the bowl of a food processor fitted with a metal blade. Pulse until all the crackers are in crumbs, about 30 seconds. Add ¼ pound melted butter and 2 tablespoons dark brown sugar; pulse until thoroughly combined, about 10 to 15 seconds. Transfer the cracker mixture to a 9 × 13 × 2-inch nonstick pan. Use your fingertips to press the mixture onto the bottom of the pan and into the corners and sides, creating an even layer. Place the pan on the center rack of the preheated oven and bake for 5 minutes. Remove the pan from the oven and set aside at room temperature while preparing the cake batter.

Prepare the Cocoa Milk Chocolate Chip Cake
Keep the oven temperature at 325°F. In a sifter combine 2 cups flour, ½ cup cocoa powder, ½ teaspoon baking powder, and ¼ teaspoon salt. Sift onto a large piece of parchment paper (or wax paper) and set aside until needed.

Place 1 cup dark brown sugar and ½ pound butter in the bowl of an electric mixer fitted with a paddle. Mix on low speed for 30 seconds, then beat on medium for 4 minutes until soft and thoroughly combined. Scrape down the sides of the bowl and the paddle.

Add 3 eggs, one at a time, beating on medium for 1 minute after each addition, and scraping down the sides of the bowl once all the eggs have been incorporated.

Operate the mixer on low while gradually adding the sifted dry ingredients. Mix until incorporated, about 45 seconds. Add ½ cup milk and 1 tablespoon vanilla extract, and mix on low speed to combine, about 20 seconds. Add 2 cups milk chocolate chips and mix on low for 10 seconds. Remove the bowl from the mixer and use a rubber spatula to finish mixing the ingredients until thoroughly combined.

Transfer the batter to the cracker crumb crust in the pan, using a rubber spatula to spread evenly. Bake on the center rack of the preheated oven until a toothpick inserted in the center of the cake comes out clean, 43 to 45 minutes. Remove the cake from the oven and cool in the pan at room temperature for 20 minutes. Invert the cake onto a baking sheet and refrigerate for 10 minutes. Turn the cooled cake out onto a cutting board, crust side down. Using a sharp cook's knife, cut away about ¼ inch of the edges of the cake to form a rectangle approximately 12 inches long and 8 inches wide. Cut the rectangle in half lengthwise; then make five cuts crosswise on each half to create 6 rectangles (a total of 12 for both halves) measuring approximately 4 × 2 inches. Place the cake

GRAHAM CRACKER CRUST BOTTOM

One 5½-ounce package graham crackers (11 double crackers), broken into 2- to 3-inch pieces
¼ pound (1 stick) unsalted butter, melted
2 tablespoons (1 ounce) tightly packed dark brown sugar

COCOA MILK CHOCOLATE CHIP CAKE

2 cups all-purpose flour
½ cup unsweetened cocoa powder
½ teaspoon baking powder
¼ teaspoon salt
1 cup (8 ounces) tightly packed dark brown sugar
½ pound (2 sticks) unsalted butter, cut into ½-ounce pieces
3 large eggs
½ cup whole milk
1 tablespoon pure vanilla extract
2 cups milk chocolate chips (one 11½-ounce package)

CREAMY PEANUT BUTTER FILLING

1½ cups creamy peanut butter
½ cup confectioners' sugar

FLUFFIE'S NUTTY MERINGUE TOPPING

½ cup unsalted dry roasted peanuts
¼ cup granulated sugar
¼ cup light corn syrup
¼ cup water
4 large egg whites

portions, evenly spaced, onto a baking sheet and set aside at room temperature until needed.

Make the Creamy Peanut Butter Filling

Place 1½ cups peanut butter and ½ cup confectioners' sugar in the bowl of an electric mixer fitted with a paddle. Mix on low speed for 20 seconds. Use a rubber spatula to scrape down the sides of the bowl, then beat on medium-high for 3 minutes until shiny and slightly fluid in texture. Set aside at room temperature until needed.

Make Fluffie's Nutty Meringue Topping

Preheat the oven to 450°F. Finely chop ½ cup peanuts in the bowl of a food processor fitted with a metal blade, about 20 seconds (or finely chop by hand using a cook's knife). Set aside.

Heat ¼ cup granulated sugar, ¼ cup light corn syrup, and ¼ cup water in a small saucepan over medium-high heat, stirring to dissolve the sugar. Bring to a boil. Continue to boil, stirring often, until the temperature of the syrup reaches 240°F, about 3 minutes. Remove the saucepan from the heat.

Immediately place 4 egg whites in the bowl of an electric mixer fitted with a balloon whip. Whisk on high speed until soft peaks form, about 1 minute. Lower the mixer speed to medium. Carefully and slowly pour the hot syrup into the egg whites and whisk until all of the syrup has been added; then increase the speed to high and continue whisking the egg whites until stiff, but not dry, about 2 minutes. Remove the bowl from the mixer. Use a rubber spatula to fold the ground peanuts into the meringue. Transfer the meringue to a pastry bag fitted with a medium star tip.

Top, Toast, and Serve the Cakes

Pipe a ½-inch-wide border of meringue around the top edge of each of the cakes. Fill the center of the meringue border on each cake with 1 heaping tablespoon of the creamy peanut butter filling. Pipe the remainder of the meringue, lengthwise, onto the cakes, completely covering the creamy peanut butter filling and the meringue border. Place the baking sheet on the center rack in the preheated oven and toast the meringue tops until they begin to turn golden brown, about 3½ minutes. Remove from the oven and serve.

THE CHEF'S TOUCH

As an inveterate outdoor camper and fisherman, Brett Bailey, the Ganache Hill test kitchen chef, knows his s'mores. He also knows that folks get a bit jittery when you mess with a classic. But Brett takes his "license" as test kitchen chef seriously, and transformed the familiar Girl Scout version of the treat into sophisticated and sassy s'mores that are sure to please campers and serious diners alike.

These cakes may be prepared over 2 days. DAY 1: Make the Graham Cracker Crust Bottom. Prepare the Cocoa Milk Chocolate Chip Cake. Transfer the cake batter to the pan with the crust and bake the cake. Cut the cake into 12 individual cakes. Cover the cakes with plastic wrap, and refrigerate until ready to top with meringue and filling (the cakes may be kept covered in the refrigerator for several days before assembly, or frozen for 2 to 3 weeks). DAY 2: Make the Creamy Peanut Butter Filling and Fluffie's Nutty Meringue Topping. Top, toast, and serve the cakes.

After assembling and toasting, you may keep the Chocolate Peanut Butter Some More Cakes covered in a large, tightly sealed plastic container for up to 24 hours at room temperature, but they are best eaten within 1 hour after the meringues have been toasted in the oven.

Rather than recommending an adult beverage with this already idiosyncratic recipe, I think it would be more appropriate to go with a mug of hot cocoa. Now, you could float a marshmallow on that, if you like!

CHOCOLATE PISTACHIO MADELEINES

**CHOCOLATE PISTACHIO
MADELEINES**

⅓ cup (about 1½ ounces) shelled
   natural pistachios

¼ pound (1 stick) unsalted butter,
   cut into ½-ounce pieces; plus
   1 tablespoon (melted)

1 cup all-purpose flour

½ teaspoon salt

⅔ cup granulated sugar

3 large eggs

1 teaspoon pure vanilla extract

½ cup semisweet chocolate mini-
   morsels

CHOCOLATE COATING

3 ounces semisweet baking
   chocolate, coarsely chopped

Make the Madeleines

Preheat the oven to 375°F. Place ⅓ cup shelled pistachios in the mini-bowl of a food processor fitted with a metal blade. Pulse the pistachios until coarsely chopped, about 25 to 30 seconds (or coarsely chop by hand using a cook's knife). Reserve 1 tablespoon of chopped pistachios to garnish the baked madeleines. The remaining ¼ cup will be added to the madeleine batter.

Using the 1 tablespoon of melted butter, lightly coat the inside of each of 24 individual madeleine molds. Make sure that all of the indentations in each mold are coated. Flour the insides of the molds using ¼ cup of the flour. Shake any excess flour out of the molds. (This can be untidy, so I recommend shaking the flour out onto an open section of the *National Enquirer* and then tossing the whole mess into the trash.) Set aside until needed.

In a sifter combine the remaining ¾ cup flour and ½ teaspoon salt. Sift onto a large piece of parchment paper (or wax paper) and set aside until needed. Place ¼ pound butter in a small glass bowl in a microwave oven set at medium power for 50 seconds. Remove from the microwave oven, and use a rubber spatula to stir the butter until melted, smooth, and creamy.

Place ⅔ cup of sugar and 3 eggs in the bowl of an electric mixer fitted with a paddle. Beat on medium-high speed for 3 minutes until light in color and thickened. Operate the mixer on low while gradually adding the sifted dry ingredients. Once they have been incorporated, 35 to 40 seconds, stop the mixer and scrape down the sides of the bowl. Slowly add the melted ¼ pound butter and mix on low speed for 40 to 50 seconds until combined. Scrape down the sides of the bowl. Add 1 teaspoon vanilla extract and mix on low speed to combine, about 10 seconds. Add ¼ cup coarsely chopped pistachios and ½ cup mini-morsels and mix on low to combine, about 10 seconds. Remove the bowl from the mixer and use a rubber spatula to finish mixing the batter until thoroughly combined.

Portion 2 level tablespoons (1 ounce) of the batter into each of the molds (the batter will spread on its own in the oven). Place the unit(s) of madeleine molds on the center rack in the preheated oven and bake until a toothpick inserted into the center of a madeleine comes out clean, 15 to 16 minutes. Remove the madeleines from the oven.

Immediately invert the unit and firmly tap one side of an inverted edge (holding the edge of the opposite side with a dry towel in both hands) against a clean, dry work surface to release the individual madeleines (they should drop right out). Transfer the madeleines to a wire cooling rack and cool to room temperature.

Make the Chocolate Coating

Melt 3 ounces chopped semisweet chocolate in a double boiler or a microwave oven. (See pages 197–98 for more details.)

Finish the Madeleines with Chocolate and Pistachios

One at a time, dip about 1 inch of the rounded end of the indented side of each madeleine into the melted chocolate. Let the excess chocolate drip into the top half of the double boiler or the glass bowl before placing the madeleine, smooth side down, onto a baking sheet. Once all of the madeleines have been dipped in the chocolate, sprinkle ⅛ teaspoon of the remaining chopped pistachios over the chocolate coating on each madeleine. Refrigerate the madeleines for a few minutes to firm the chocolate before serving.

THE CHEF'S TOUCH

With so much reverence heaped on to a diminutive cake called a "madeleine," I have always wondered why it makes so few appearances at the table. Perhaps we will change that with our version, which tends to be a wee bit more buttery and far more pleasurable than most, and perhaps more memorable than Proust's legendary "petite madeleine."

What a sexy and prolific little nut, the pistachio. The typical pistachio grove has one male tree pollinating ten female trees. But it was not sex education that I had on my mind when I tried to engage my son Marc in shelling pistachios in the kitchen at The Trellis many years ago. I was trying to keep a twelve-year-old out of trouble and hoped picking open the tan shells of the toothsome green nuts would entertain him. Instead of the normal ratio of ⅓ cup shelled nuts from each ⅔ cup of unshelled nuts, only a few remained after Marc's job. Although Marc was not enamored of kitchen work like I was, he certainly was attuned to tasteful food.

In testing this recipe, I found the microwave better for melting butter into an emulsified, creamy, and viscous liquid, which is preferable to the separated milk fat, water, and milk solids typical of the stovetop method. A saucelike consistency is important in enhancing the buttery flavor of the madeleine without making it greasy to the touch. If too much time lapses between melting and using the butter in the batter, the butter may solidify. If it becomes too thick to pour, you may return it to the microwave for a few seconds, or warm it over slightly hot water (not simmering) for a few moments, and then stir until smooth and cohesive.

These delicate madeleines are at their optimum within a few hours of being baked.

PAM'S BLUEBERRY CHOCOLATE CHIP GOSSIP CAKES *with* "SMASHED" BLUEBERRIES

MAKES 12 CAKES

Make the Blueberry Chocolate Chip Cakes

Preheat the oven to 325°F. Lightly coat the inside of each of 12 individual nonstick mini–fluted tube pans (each cup is 3½ × 1¾ inches) with the 1 tablespoon of melted butter, making sure that all of the indentations in each of the pans are coated.

In a sifter combine the 2 cups flour, 1 teaspoon baking powder, ½ teaspoon baking soda, and ½ teaspoon salt. Sift onto a large piece of parchment paper (or wax paper) and set aside until needed.

Place the ¼ pound butter, ½ cup light brown sugar, and ½ cup granulated sugar in the bowl of an electric mixer fitted with a paddle. Mix on low speed for 1 minute, and then beat on medium for 2 minutes until soft. Scrape down the sides of the bowl and the paddle. Add 2 eggs, one at a time, beating on medium for 1 minute after each addition, and scraping down the sides of the bowl once all the eggs have been incorporated.

Operate the mixer on low while gradually adding the sifted dry ingredients. Once they have been incorporated, about 30 seconds, add ½ cup sour cream and ½ teaspoon vanilla extract and mix on low speed to combine, about 15 seconds. Remove the bowl from the mixer, add the coarsely chopped pecans, 1 cup blueberries, and 1 cup mini-morsels and use a rubber spatula to mix until thoroughly combined.

Portion 3 heaping tablespoons of the cake batter into each individual mini–fluted non-stick tube pan. Spread the batter evenly. Place the 2 units of mini–fluted tube pans on the top and center racks of the preheated oven, and bake until a toothpick inserted in the center of the cake comes out clean, about 40 minutes. (Rotate the units from top to center halfway through the baking time and turn each 180 degrees.) Remove the cakes from the oven and cool at room temperature for 20 minutes. Invert the units to release the cakes. Turn the cakes baked top facing up and set aside at room temperature while preparing the "Smashed" Blueberries.

Make the "Smashed" Blueberries

Heat ¼ cup granulated sugar and ¼ cup orange juice in a small saucepan over medium-high heat. When hot, stir to dissolve the sugar. Bring to a boil, then adjust the heat and allow to simmer for 4 minutes until thickened to the consistency of pancake syrup. Remove from the heat. Add ¼ cup Triple Sec and ¼ cup vodka; stir to incorporate. Add 1 cup blueberries and stir. The

BLUEBERRY CHOCOLATE CHIP CAKES
- ¼ pound (1 stick) unsalted butter, cut into ½-ounce pieces; plus 1 tablespoon (melted)
- 2 cups all-purpose flour
- 1 teaspoon baking powder
- ½ teaspoon baking soda
- ½ teaspoon salt
- ½ cup (4 ounces) tightly packed light brown sugar
- ½ cup granulated sugar
- 2 large eggs
- ½ cup sour cream
- ½ teaspoon pure vanilla extract
- 1 cup pecan halves, toasted (page 199) and coarsely chopped
- 1 cup fresh blueberries, stemmed and washed
- 1 cup semisweet chocolate mini-morsels

"SMASHED" BLUEBERRIES
- ¼ cup granulated sugar
- ¼ cup orange juice
- ¼ cup Triple Sec
- ¼ cup vodka
- 1 cup fresh blueberries, stemmed and washed

"Smashed" Blueberries may be served immediately, or cooled and refrigerated for up to 24 hours before using.

To Serve

Place the Gossip Cakes on individual plates; then spoon an equal amount of "Smashed" Blueberries over each cake. Serve immediately.

THE CHEF'S TOUCH

Pam Sullivan is the self-proclaimed gossip maven of Bedford, New Hampshire. Pam, a graduate of Cornell University's School of Human Ecology and a registered dietitian (she is also the sister of Ganache Hill test kitchen chef Brett Bailey), learned long ago that the more agreeable the goodies she serves her lady friends, the longer they stay and the juicier the gossip! She found that these cakes elicit news as plump and juicy as the blueberries that adorn the tasty morsels.

If you don't have Triple Sec in your liquor cabinet, how about other orange-flavored liqueurs such as curaçao, Grand Marnier, or Cointreau? Any of these will put a sparkle in the cakes and the conversation. If you prefer to abstain, you can substitute orange juice for the Triple Sec.

Today, thanks to the global market, blueberries can be enjoyed year-round. I do offer a caveat regarding their availability: Long-term travel and storage cause berries to lose their texture and flavor. If the package contains shriveled or moldy berries, I suggest choosing another berry (raspberries would work particularly well in this recipe), or another recipe (can you imagine the tittle-tattle if Pam offered the ladies Death by Chocolate?).

After the Gossip Cakes have cooled to room temperature, you may keep them, covered with plastic wrap, for up to 24 hours at room temperature, or in the refrigerator for 2 to 3 days. To avoid permeating the cakes with refrigerator odors, place them in a large, tightly sealed plastic container.

No matter the time of the day for your coffee and conversation, I would recommend serving the same orange liqueur on the side that you used for the cakes.

For quicker and more efficient portioning of the Blueberry Chocolate Chip Gossip Cake batter use a #12 ice cream scoop rather than a tablespoon, and portion a level scoop per individual mini–fluted tube pan.

CHOCOLATE CHUNK COOKIE CAKES

MAKES 16 CAKES

Preheat the oven to 350° F. Lightly coat the inside of each of 16 individual nonstick petite loaf pans with the 1 tablespoon of melted butter. Flour the insides of the individual loaf pans with the 1 tablespoon of flour. Shake out and discard the excess flour.

In a sifter combine the remaining 2¼ cups flour, 1 teaspoon baking powder, and ¼ teaspoon salt. Sift onto a large piece of parchment paper (or wax paper) and set aside until needed.

Place ½ pound butter, 1 cup light brown sugar, and ¾ cup granulated sugar in the bowl of an electric mixer fitted with a paddle. Mix on low speed for 1 minute, then beat on medium for 3 minutes, until soft. Scrape down the sides of the bowl and the paddle. Beat for an additional 3 minutes on medium until very soft and lighter in color. Scrape down the sides of the bowl. Add 3 eggs, one at a time, beating on medium for 30 seconds after each addition, and scraping down the sides of the bowl once all the eggs have been incorporated. Beat on medium for an additional 2 minutes until fluffy. Operate the mixer on low while gradually adding the sifted dry ingredients. Once they have been incorporated, about 1 minute, add ½ cup sour cream and 1 tablespoon vanilla extract and mix on low to combine, about 20 seconds. Remove the bowl from the mixer, add 12 ounces chocolate chunks, and use a rubber spatula to finish mixing the batter until thoroughly combined.

Portion 4 slightly heaping tablespoons of the cake batter into each individual petite loaf pan. Spread the batter evenly. (If you are into a more tactile experience, you may use your well-washed index finger to spread the batter; otherwise use a rubber spatula.)

Place the units of petite loaf pans on the top and center racks of the preheated oven, and bake until a toothpick inserted in the center of one cake comes out clean, about 25 minutes. (Rotate the units from top to center halfway through the baking time, and turn each 180 degrees.) Remove the cakes from the oven and cool in the pans for 10 minutes at room temperature.

Invert the units to release the cakes. (If the cakes do not pop out of the pans by simply inverting them, use a small plastic knife to "cut" around the edges of each cake to free them from the pans without tearing the cakes.)

You don't have to ask permission to have a cookie cake, so you may reward yourself and enjoy one immediately. Or, invite the gang over and dispense with them forthwith. If the cakes are not immediately gobbled up, wrap each one individually in plastic wrap once it has cooled to room temperature. The cakes are good to go wherever and just about whenever at this point.

½ pound (2 sticks) unsalted butter, cut into ½-ounce pieces; plus 1 tablespoon (melted)

2¼ cups plus 1 tablespoon all-purpose flour

1 teaspoon baking powder

¼ teaspoon salt

1 cup (8 ounces) tightly packed light brown sugar

¾ cup granulated sugar

3 large eggs

½ cup sour cream

1 tablespoon pure vanilla extract

12 ounces semisweet baking chocolate, chopped into ½-inch chunks

THE CHEF'S TOUCH

The plan here was for an unpretentious-looking cake that could withstand the rigors of being plopped into a lunch pail, squished in a brown paper bag, packed in a knapsack, or even stuffed in a tackle box. The cake would need to deliver an immediate, palate-pleasing reaction whether it was eaten moments after exiting the oven or several days later, when extricated from its lair to please a youngster at recess or reward the fanatic fisherman for perseverance and good luck. And, of course, this little cake would provide a chocolaty taste and texture that, although reminiscent of a favorite cookie, would actually transcend the genre of round and flat. I say, Mission Accomplished.

Although the recipe calls for the chocolate to be chopped into ½-inch chunks, I would suggest a nimble touch with the knife so as not to shatter the chocolate into small shards. Use a serrated cook's knife for this task, work carefully, and you will be rewarded with chunks that are distinctly obvious in the baked cake.

For quicker and more efficient portioning of the Chocolate Chunk Cookie Cake batter, use a #12 ice cream scoop rather than a tablespoon, and portion a level scoop into each individual petite loaf pan.

After the Chocolate Chunk Cookie Cakes have cooled to room temperature, individually wrap each cake with plastic wrap. They will stay remarkably fresh, for up to 4 days at room temperature, or for 1 week in the refrigerator. To avoid permeating the cakes with refrigerator odors, place the plastic-wrapped cakes in a large, tightly sealed plastic container. Allow refrigerated Chocolate Chunk Cookie Cakes to come to room temperature before serving.

Depending on the time of the year and the locale in which the cakes will be polished off, a chocolate-infused beverage—chocolate milk or hot chocolate—will make the break "a piece of cake."

COCOA HAZELNUT BITES
with BARK

MAKES 24 BITES

Make the Cocoa Hazelnut Cakes

Preheat the oven to 325°F. Lightly coat the inside of each of 24 individual nonstick miniature muffin cups with the 1 teaspoon of melted butter. Flour the inside of the cups with the 2 tablespoons of the flour. Shake any excess flour out of the cups. Set aside.

In a sifter combine the remaining ½ cup flour, 2 tablespoons cocoa powder, ¼ teaspoon baking powder, and ¼ teaspoon salt. Sift onto a large piece of parchment paper (or wax paper) and set aside until needed.

Place ½ cup sugar and 2 ounces butter in the bowl of an electric mixer fitted with a paddle. Mix on low speed for 1 minute, then beat on medium until soft, about 2 minutes. Scrape down the sides of the bowl and the paddle. Beat on medium for an additional 2 minutes, until very soft. Add 2 egg yolks and beat on medium for 1 minute until slightly fluffy. Scrape down the sides of the bowl. Add ¼ cup sour cream and beat on medium for 20 seconds. Operate the mixer on low while gradually adding the sifted dry ingredients; mix until incorporated, about 45 seconds. Add 2 tablespoons buttermilk and 1 teaspoon vanilla extract and mix on low speed for 15 seconds. Remove the bowl from the mixer, add the chopped hazelnuts, and then use a rubber spatula to finish mixing the ingredients until thoroughly combined.

Portion 1 slightly heaping tablespoon of the cake batter into each muffin cup. Place the muffin tins on the center rack of the preheated oven and bake until a toothpick inserted in the center of the cake comes out clean, 17 to 18 minutes.

Remove the cakes from the oven and cool at room temperature for 10 minutes. Invert the pans to release the cakes. (If the cakes do not release from the cups, use the tip of a plastic knife to "cut" around the edges of each cake to free them from the pans without tearing the cakes.) Set aside at room temperature while making the Red Raspberry Tease.

Make the Red Raspberry Tease

Place 3 ounces cream cheese, ½ cup raspberries, and 2 tablespoons sugar in the bowl of a food processor fitted with a metal blade. Pulse the ingredients for 15 seconds, and then process for 1 minute.

Top each cake with 1 scant teaspoon of the Red Raspberry Tease. Set aside at room temperature while preparing the Chocolate Hazelnut Bark.

Prepare the Chocolate Hazelnut Bark

Use a cook's knife to cut each toasted hazelnut in half. Set aside until needed.

Temper 4 ounces chopped semisweet chocolate: Melt the chocolate in a small glass bowl in a microwave oven set at medium power for 1 minute and 20 seconds. (For more details, see pages 197–98.) Remove the chocolate from the microwave oven, and use a

COCOA HAZELNUT CAKES

2 ounces unsalted butter, cut into
    ½-ounce pieces; plus 1 teaspoon
    (melted)

½ cup plus 2 tablespoons all-
    purpose flour

2 tablespoons unsweetened cocoa
    powder

¼ teaspoon baking powder

¼ teaspoon salt

½ cup granulated sugar

2 large egg yolks

¼ cup sour cream

2 tablespoons buttermilk

1 teaspoon pure vanilla extract

½ cup skinned hazelnuts, toasted
    (page 199) and finely chopped

RED RASPBERRY TEASE

3 ounces cream cheese

½ cup fresh red raspberries

2 tablespoons granulated sugar

CHOCOLATE HAZELNUT BARK

1 ounce skinned hazelnuts, toasted
    (page 199)

4 ounces semisweet baking
    chocolate, coarsely chopped

rubber spatula to stir the chocolate until smooth. Transfer the melted chocolate to a piece of parchment paper (or wax paper). Use an offset spatula (or a cake spatula) to spread the chocolate into an ⅛-to-¼-inch-thick 4 × 6-inch rectangle. Sprinkle the hazelnuts evenly over the surface of the chocolate. Set the chocolate aside at room temperature for 10 minutes, until firm.

Use a cook's knife to cut the bark into 24 portions: Cut the bark in half lengthwise across the center. Then cut each half lengthwise in half again. Now make five cuts crosswise on each section to make equal sixths. Place a piece of bark, hazelnut side up, onto the Red Raspberry Tease on each cake, and serve immediately.

THE CHEF'S TOUCH

These tantalizing confectionery morsels take a measure of their inspiration from the famed Austrian confection called linzertorte. The more familiar white linzertorte contains no chocolate; however, a lesser known brown linzertorte does. As we tend to be nonconformists, we didn't see why we shouldn't work our favorite ingredient into the traditional matrix of ground nuts and red raspberries, and create a mouthful that would transmogrify the venerable classic into a bite with a bit of bark.

You can simplify things by transferring the Red Raspberry Tease to a pint-size Ziploc bag. Then snip the tip from a bottom corner of the bag, and pipe about 1 teaspoon of the Red Raspberry Tease on top of each Cocoa Hazelnut Cake.

These cakes may be prepared over 2 days. DAY 1: Bake the individual Cocoa Hazelnut Cakes. Once they have cooled, cover with plastic wrap and refrigerate until ready to assemble. (The cakes may be kept covered in the refrigerator for 2 to 3 days before assembly, or frozen for 2 to 3 weeks.)

DAY 2: A couple of hours before serving, make the Red Raspberry Tease and the Chocolate Hazelnut Bark. Assemble as directed in the recipe. The Red Raspberry Tease will discolor and get sticky in a relatively short period of time, so the bites should be served within 2 to 3 hours of preparation.

While we are breaking some of the rules for classic linzertorte, let's stray from the norm and offer a raspberry liqueur. The velvety smooth Royale Chambord liqueur, with its unrestrained raspberry flavor and redolent perfume would allow for painless consumption of Bites with Bark.

CHOCOLATE CHIP GOOBER GOBBLE CUPCAKES

MAKES 18 CAKES

Make the Peanut Chocolate Chip Cupcakes

Preheat the oven to 325°F. Line each of the 18 individual muffin tin cups with the 2½-inch foil-laminated bake cups. Set aside.

In a sifter combine 1 cup flour, ½ teaspoon baking powder, ½ teaspoon baking soda, and ½ teaspoon salt. Sift onto a large piece of parchment paper (or wax paper) and set aside until needed.

Place 1 cup light brown sugar, ½ cup unsalted peanuts, ½ cup peanut butter, 2 ounces butter, and 2 ounces cream cheese in the bowl of an electric mixer fitted with a paddle. Mix on low speed for 1 minute, and then beat on medium for 3 minutes until combined.

Use a rubber spatula to scrape down the sides of the bowl. Add 3 eggs, one at a time, beating on medium for 30 seconds after each addition, and scraping down the sides of the bowl once all the eggs have been incorporated. Operate the mixer on low while gradually adding the sifted dry ingredients; mix until incorporated, about 30 seconds. Scrape down the sides of the bowl.

Add the ¼ cup sour cream and 2 teaspoons vanilla extract and mix on medium to combine, about 15 seconds. Remove the bowl from the mixer, add ½ cup chocolate chips, and use a rubber spatula to finish mixing the ingredients until thoroughly combined.

Portion 3 heaping tablespoons (about 2¼ ounces) of the cupcake batter into each bake cup. Place the muffin tins on the top and center racks of the preheated oven, and bake until a toothpick inserted in the center of the cupcake comes out clean, about 30 minutes. (Rotate the units from top to center halfway through the baking time, and turn each 180 degrees.) Remove the cupcakes from the oven and cool at room temperature in the tins for 10 minutes. Remove the cupcakes from the muffin tins (but not from the foil bake cups), and cool at room temperature for an additional 20 minutes prior to preparing the Chocolate Goober Gobble.

Make the Chocolate Goober Gobble

Place 1 cup peanut butter and 2 ounces melted semisweet chocolate in the bowl of an electric mixer fitted with a balloon whip. Whisk on medium-high speed to combine, about 30 seconds. Scrape down the sides of the bowl. Whisk on high for an additional 30 seconds until very smooth and shiny.

Assemble the Cupcakes and Serve

Using a paring knife, make a 2-inch-in-diameter, circular cutout from the top of each Peanut Chocolate Chip Cupcake. To do this, insert the knife at a slight, inward angle about ½ inch away from the outside edge, and to a depth of about 1 inch, and cut all the way

---

PEANUT CHOCOLATE CHIP CUPCAKES

1 cup all-purpose flour

½ teaspoon baking powder

½ teaspoon baking soda

½ teaspoon salt

1 cup (8 ounces) tightly packed light brown sugar

½ cup unsalted dry-roasted peanuts

½ cup Skippy creamy peanut butter

2 ounces (½ stick) unsalted butter, cut into ½-ounce pieces

2 ounces cream cheese

3 large eggs

¼ cup sour cream

2 teaspoons pure vanilla extract

½ cup semisweet chocolate chips

CHOCOLATE GOOBER GOBBLE

1 cup peanut butter

2 ounces semisweet baking chocolate, coarsely chopped and melted (pages 197–98)

around the cupcake. Remove the cutout. (Wonder what the fate of those scrumptious cupcake scraps will be?) Portion a slightly heaping tablespoon of Chocolate Goober Gobble into each cupcake hollow. Serve immediately.

THE CHEF'S TOUCH

If the name Goober Gobble tickles your funny bone, wait until this peanut butter–chocolate duo tickles your palate. Somehow the Jerry Lewis and Dean Martin of confections couldn't be called something as mundane as "For Peanut Butter Lovers Only."

My mom (aka Mrs. D) has enjoyed Skippy brand creamy peanut butter since the early 1940s and started serving it to me shortly thereafter. (I arrived on the scene in 1945.) This may sound like an endorsement, but we tried two other well-known brands for this cupcake with not-so-delightful results.

Mom knows best: Stick with Skippy for this one.

No need to chop the peanuts in this recipe if you use a table-model electric mixer. However, if you mix the cupcake batter by hand using a whisk, or if you use a hand-held electric mixer, coarsely chop the peanuts before adding.

I hesitate to suggest further embellishment of the Goober Gobble, but what the heck. To turn these fun cupcakes into a carnival, sprinkle one or more of the following over the Goober Gobble: chocolate chips, chocolate chunks, raisins, chopped peanuts, chocolate-covered peanuts, or peanut M&M's.

After assembly, you may keep the Chocolate Chip Goober Gobble Cupcakes covered in a tightly sealed plastic container for up to 48 hours at room temperature.

I can't imagine another liquid as effective in transporting the Gobble down the tummy as milk, and lots of it! That's what Mrs. D served the fledgling Guru of Ganache.

CHOCOLATE-DIPPED ORANGE FRY CAKES *with* COFFEE *and* CREAM

MAKES 8 FRY CAKES

Make the Coffee Ice Cream

Heat 4 ounces white chocolate and 1 cup of the heavy cream together in the top half of a double boiler, or in a microwave oven (see pages 197–98 for more details), and stir until smooth. Set aside.

Heat the remaining 1 cup heavy cream, ¼ cup of the sugar, and 2 tablespoons coffee liqueur in a medium saucepan over medium-high heat. When hot, stir to dissolve the sugar. Bring to a boil.

While the cream mixture is heating, place 4 egg yolks and the remaining ¼ cup sugar in the bowl of an electric mixer fitted with a paddle. Beat on high speed for 2 minutes until thoroughly combined; then use a rubber spatula to scrape down the sides of the bowl and the paddle. Beat on high for an additional 2 minutes until slightly thickened and pale yellow. If at this point the cream mixture has not yet started to boil, adjust the mixer speed to low and continue to mix until it does boil; otherwise, undesirable lumps may form when the boiling cream mixture is added. Gradually pour the boiling cream mixture into the beaten egg yolk and sugar mixture, and mix on medium to combine, about 30 seconds. (To avoid splattering the boiling cream mixture, use a pouring shield attachment, or place a towel or plastic wrap over the top of the mixer and down the sides of the bowl.) Add 1 tablespoon instant espresso powder and mix on medium to combine, about 10 seconds.

Return the combined mixture to the saucepan, using a rubber spatula to facilitate transferring all of the mixture; then heat over medium heat, stirring constantly. Bring to a temperature of 185°F, about 3 minutes. Remove from the heat and transfer to a large stainless steel bowl. Add the melted white chocolate and cream mixture and 2 teaspoons vanilla extract and stir to combine. Cool in an ice-water bath to a temperature of 40° to 45°F.

When the mixture is cold, freeze in an ice cream freezer following the manufacturer's instructions. Transfer the semifrozen ice cream to a 2-quart plastic container. Cover the container securely, then place in the freezer for several hours before serving.

Make the Irish Cocoa Cream Sauce

Heat ½ cup heavy cream, ¼ cup sugar, 2 teaspoons cocoa powder, and ½ teaspoon espresso powder in a medium saucepan over medium-high heat. When hot, stir to dissolve the sugar, cocoa, and espresso powder. Bring to a boil, then adjust the heat and simmer the mixture for 6 minutes, until slightly thickened. Remove from the heat and transfer to a medium stainless steel bowl. Add ¼ cup Baileys Original Irish Cream and stir to combine. Cool in an ice-water bath to a temperature of 40° to 45°F. Refrigerate until needed.

COFFEE ICE CREAM

4 ounces white chocolate, coarsely chopped

2 cups heavy cream

½ cup granulated sugar

2 tablespoons coffee liqueur

4 large egg yolks

1 tablespoon instant espresso powder

2 teaspoons pure vanilla extract

IRISH COCOA CREAM SAUCE

½ cup heavy cream

¼ cup granulated sugar

2 teaspoons unsweetened cocoa powder

½ teaspoon instant espresso powder

¼ cup Baileys Original Irish Cream

ORANGE FRY CAKES

6 cups vegetable oil

2¼ cups all-purpose flour

½ teaspoon salt

¼ teaspoon baking soda

¼ teaspoon cream of tartar

½ cup granulated sugar

1 large egg

1 large egg yolk

2 tablespoons minced orange zest

½ teaspoon orange extract

½ cup sour cream

CHOCOLATE DIP

6 ounces semisweet baking chocolate, coarsely chopped

Make the Orange Fry Cakes

Heat 6 cups vegetable oil in a deep fryer (or high-sided, heavy-duty, 4- to 5-quart saucepan) to a temperature of 365° to 375°F.

In a sifter combine 1¾ cups of the flour, ½ teaspoon salt, ¼ teaspoon baking soda, and ¼ teaspoon cream of tartar. Sift onto a large piece of parchment paper (or wax paper) and set aside until needed.

Place ½ cup sugar, 1 egg, 1 egg yolk, 2 tablespoons orange zest, and ½ teaspoon orange extract in the bowl of an electric mixer fitted with a paddle. Beat on medium-high speed for 3 minutes until combined and thickened. Scrape down the sides of the bowl and the paddle. Add ½ cup sour cream and beat on medium speed for 10 seconds, until combined. Scrape down the sides of the bowl. Operate the mixer on low while gradually adding the sifted dry ingredients. Mix until a dough is formed, about 1 minute. Remove the dough from the mixer.

Transfer the dough to a clean, dry, well-floured work surface. Use the palms of your hands to gently press the dough (using the extra ½ cup of flour as necessary to prevent sticking) into a rectangle approximately 9½ inches long, 7 inches wide, and ½ inch thick. Cut the dough into 6 fry cakes using a 3-inch doughnut cutter. (Dip the cutter in flour after making each cut to prevent sticking.) Form the remaining dough into a ball. Press the dough into a rectangle approximately 7 inches long, 3½ inches wide, and ½ inch thick. Cut the dough into 2 fry cakes using the doughnut cutter (again dipping the cutter in flour after making each cut to prevent sticking).

Fry the fry cakes 4 at a time in the hot oil for 1½ to 1¾ minutes on each side until uniformly golden brown. Use a skimmer (or a slotted spoon) to remove the fry cakes from the oil and transfer to a baking sheet lined with paper towels. Set the fry cakes aside at room temperature while preparing the Chocolate Dip.

Prepare the Chocolate Dip

Melt 6 ounces semisweet chocolate in the top of a double boiler or in a microwave oven. (See pages 197–98 for details.)

Dip the Orange Fry Cakes and Serve

One at a time, hand dip the fry cakes in the melted chocolate to cover the top surface and about ½ inch of the curved sides of each fry cake. Set on wax paper.

Flood the bases of eight 9- to 10-inch white china soup or pasta plates with ¼ cup each of the Irish Cocoa Cream Sauce. Place an Orange Fry Cake, chocolate side up (of course), into the center of the sauce on each plate. With a #20 scoop, top each fry cake with Coffee Ice Cream and serve immediately.

THE CHEF'S TOUCH

For the best ice cream flavor and texture, use the same satin-smooth coffee liqueur we cook and bake with at Ganache Hill, Kahlúa. Select Medaglia D'Oro instant espresso powder from your specialty grocer or supermarket. You'll find it near the instant coffee. I favor this brand for its almost freshly made taste.

Be certain to choose orange extract and not orange oil for this recipe. I find the flavor of the oil to be too intense for the volume of this fry cake recipe.

Lacking a doughnut cutter, use a 3-inch biscuit cutter to cut the dough into 8 pieces, then use a 1-inch biscuit cutter to cut the hole out of the center of each 3-inch-in-diameter piece of dough.

Although alcoholic beverages were seldom, if ever, served in the diners of yesteryear, I can't help but suggest a snifter of coffee liqueur straight up as an affable accompaniment. Now where did I put that bottle of Kahlúa?

This dessert may be prepared over 2 days. DAY 1: Make and freeze the Coffee Ice Cream. Make and refrigerate the Irish Cocoa Cream Sauce. DAY 2: Make the Orange Fry Cakes. Dip the fry cakes into the Chocolate Dip and serve with ice cream and sauce as directed in the recipe.

CHOCOLATE HAZELNUT HYSTERIA CAKES *with* WHITE CHOCOLATE TIPSY TANGERINE ICE CREAM

MAKES 6 CAKES

Make the White Chocolate Tipsy Tangerine Ice Cream

Heat together 7 ounces chopped white chocolate and 1 cup of the heavy cream in the top half of a double boiler over medium-low heat, or in a medium glass bowl in a microwave oven (see pages 197–98 for more details), and stir until smooth.

Heat the remaining ½ cup heavy cream, ½ cup half-and-half cream, ¼ cup of the sugar, and 2 tablespoons tangerine zest in a medium saucepan over medium-high heat. When hot, stir to dissolve the sugar. Bring to a boil.

While the cream mixture is heating, place 2 egg yolks and the remaining ¼ cup sugar in the bowl of an electric mixer fitted with a paddle. Beat on high speed for 2 minutes, until combined, and then use a rubber spatula to scrape down the sides of the bowl and the paddle. Beat on high for an additional 2 minutes until slightly thickened and pale yellow. If at this point the cream mixture has not yet started to boil, adjust the mixer speed to low and continue to mix until it does boil; otherwise, undesirable lumps may form when the boiling cream mixture is added.

Gradually pour the boiling cream mixture into the beaten egg yolk and sugar mixture and mix on medium to combine, about 1 minute. (To avoid splattering the boiling cream and milk mixture, use a pouring shield attachment, or place a towel or plastic wrap over the top of the mixer and down the sides of the bowl.) Return the combined mixture to the saucepan, using a rubber spatula to transfer all of the mixture, including the tangerine zest, from the bottom of the bowl.

Heat over medium heat, stirring constantly. Bring to a temperature of 185°F, about 2 minutes. Remove from the heat and transfer to a large stainless steel bowl. Add the melted white chocolate and cream mixture, and 2 tablespoons Cointreau, and stir to combine. Cool in an ice-water bath to a temperature of 40° to 45°F. Freeze in an ice cream freezer following the manufacturer's instructions. Transfer the semifrozen ice cream to a 2-quart plastic container, cover the container securely and then place in the freezer for several hours before serving.

Prepare the Tangerine Hysteria

Combine the tangerine pieces and ½ cup of Cointreau in a small glass bowl. Cover the top of the bowl with plastic wrap and refrigerate until needed.

WHITE CHOCOLATE TIPSY TANGERINE ICE CREAM

7 ounces white chocolate, coarsely chopped
1½ cups heavy cream
½ cup half-and-half cream
½ cup granulated sugar
2 tablespoons thin julienne of tangerine zest
2 large egg yolks
2 tablespoons Cointreau

TANGERINE HYSTERIA

4 tangerines, peeled, sectioned, seeded, and cut into ½-inch pieces
½ cup Cointreau

DARK CHOCOLATE HAZELNUT CAKES

¼ pound (1 stick) unsalted butter, cut into ½-ounce pieces; plus 2 teaspoons (melted)
¾ cup all-purpose flour
1 tablespoon unsweetened cocoa powder
½ teaspoon baking powder
3 ounces semisweet baking chocolate, coarsely chopped
1 ounce unsweetened baking chocolate, coarsely chopped
3 large eggs
⅓ cup granulated sugar
½ cup skinned hazelnuts, toasted (page 199) and coarsely chopped
¼ cup hazelnut liqueur
1 teaspoon pure vanilla extract

Make the Dark Chocolate Hazelnut Cakes

Preheat the oven to 375°F. Lightly coat the inside of each of 6 individual nonstick mini–angel food cake pans with the 2 teaspoons of melted butter. Set aside until needed.

In a sifter combine ¾ cup flour, 1 tablespoon cocoa powder, and ½ teaspoon baking powder. Sift onto a large piece of parchment paper (or wax paper) and set aside until needed.

Melt 3 ounces chopped semisweet chocolate, 1 ounce unsweetened chocolate, and ¼ pound butter in the top half of a double boiler, or in a glass bowl in a microwave oven (see pages 197–98 for more details) and stir until smooth.

Place 3 eggs and ⅓ cup sugar in the bowl of an electric mixer fitted with a paddle. Beat on medium-high speed for 2 minutes until slightly thickened. Add the melted chocolate and butter mixture and mix on medium to combine, about 15 seconds. Operate the mixer on low while gradually adding the sifted dry ingredients. Once they have been incorporated, stop the mixer and scrape down the sides of the bowl. Add ½ cup hazelnuts, ¼ cup hazelnut liqueur, and 1 teaspoon vanilla extract and mix on low for 30 seconds. Remove the bowl from the mixer and use a rubber spatula to finish mixing the batter until thoroughly combined.

Divide the batter evenly into each individual mini–angel food cake pan (exactly ½ cup in each pan), spreading the batter evenly. Place the unit of mini–angel food cake pans on the center rack of the preheated oven and bake until a toothpick inserted in the center of the cakes comes out clean, about 15 minutes. Remove the cakes from the oven and cool at room temperature for 10 minutes. Invert the pans to release the cakes. (If the cakes do not pop out of the pans by simply inverting, use a small plastic knife to "cut" around the edges of each cake to free them from the pans without tearing the cakes.)

To Serve

Serve each Dark Chocolate Hazelnut Cake while still warm with a scoop or two of the White Chocolate Tipsy Tangerine Ice Cream, and then spoon 3 to 4 tablespoons of the Tangerine Hysteria over the cake and ice cream.

THE CHEF'S TOUCH

Warning: Do not share these cakes, or you will risk widespread hysteria over the intense flavor and sublime texture packed into their small size. If the chocolate-laden treasure doesn't put you over the edge, the silken embrace of the ice cream surely will. Be further advised that these Hysteria Cakes are not for those who suffer from guilt by indulgence. If the snake had given Eve a bite of this dessert, the two of them would have left Adam under the tree alone.

If you choose temperance, you can eliminate the Cointreau from the ice cream and from the Tangerine Hysteria without adjusting the recipe. The hazelnut liqueur may also be eliminated. (The alcohol does evaporate during baking.) The dessert will still be delicious, although not as hysterical.

Tangerines are the most widely available mandarin orange family members in the United

States. My favorite variety of these loose-skinned, lavishly perfumed citrus fruits is the clementine, which is practically seedless and is smaller, thinner-skinned, and more succulently sweet than the average tangerine. It is also unfortunately more difficult to find at the market. Not to give the tangerine an inferiority complex, but if you find clementines, it is worth the upgrade. You will need 8 to 10 clementines if you do make this substitution.

The Chocolate Hazelnut Cakes may be cooled to room temperature, then refrigerated for 3 to 4 days. To avoid permeating the cakes with refrigerator odors, store them in a tightly sealed plastic container. The cakes are best eaten warm, so if you refrigerated them, heat them in the microwave on defrost power for 40 to 60 seconds before serving.

This dessert may be prepared over 2 days. DAY 1: Make and freeze the White Chocolate Tipsy Tangerine Ice Cream. Prepare and refrigerate the Tangerine Hysteria. DAY 2: Make the Dark Chocolate Hazelnut Cakes. Serve the cakes warm with the ice cream and tangerines as directed in the recipe.

HAPPY ALL *the* TIME CAKES

MAKES 12 CAKES

Make the Cocoa Bourbon Cakes

Preheat the oven to 325°F. Lightly coat the inside of each of 12 individual nonstick muffin cups (3 inches in diameter) using the 2 teaspoons of melted butter. Set aside until needed.

In a sifter combine 1 cup flour, 2 tablespoons cocoa powder, 1 teaspoon baking soda, and ¼ teaspoon salt. Sift onto a large piece of parchment paper (or wax paper) and set aside until needed.

Place ¾ cup light brown sugar and ¼ pound butter in the bowl of an electric mixer fitted with a paddle. Mix on low speed for 1 minute; then beat on medium for 2 minutes until soft. Scrape down the sides of the bowl and the paddle. Beat on medium for an additional 2 minutes until very soft. Add 1 egg and beat on medium for 30 seconds to incorporate. Add the egg white and beat on medium for 30 seconds to incorporate. Scrape down the sides of the bowl and the paddle. Now beat on medium-high for 1 minute until slightly fluffy. Scrape down the sides of the bowl.

Operate the mixer on low while gradually adding the sifted dry ingredients; mix until incorporated, about 45 seconds. Add 2 ounces cream cheese and beat on medium for 30 seconds. Add ¼ cup bourbon and mix on low speed for 15 seconds. Remove the bowl from the mixer. Add ½ cup of the chopped pecans and ½ cup of the chopped walnuts (reserving the remaining nuts to decorate the cakes); then use a rubber spatula to finish mixing the ingredients until thoroughly combined. Portion ¼ cup of the cake batter into each muffin cup.

Place the muffin tin on the center rack of the preheated oven and bake until a toothpick inserted in the center of the cake comes out clean, 21 to 22 minutes. Remove the cakes from the oven and cool at room temperature for 10 minutes. Invert the pan to release the cakes. (They should pop right out.)

Place the cakes, baked tops down and evenly spaced, onto a cooling rack set on a baking sheet with sides. Refrigerate the cakes while preparing the glaze.

Prepare the Chocolate Honey Bourbon Glaze

Place 6 ounces chopped semisweet chocolate and 2 ounces chopped unsweetened chocolate in a medium bowl.

Heat ½ cup heavy cream, ¼ cup bourbon, 3 tablespoons butter, and 2 tablespoons honey in a small saucepan over medium-high heat. When hot, stir to dissolve the honey. Bring to a boil. Pour the boiling cream mixture over the chopped chocolate. Set aside for 5 minutes, and then stir with a whisk until smooth.

Coat the Cakes with Glaze and Nuts

Remove the cakes from the refrigerator. Spoon about 2 tablespoons of glaze over each

COCOA BOURBON CAKES

- ¼ pound (1 stick) unsalted butter, cut into ½-ounce pieces; plus 2 teaspoons (melted)
- 1 cup all-purpose flour
- 2 tablespoons unsweetened cocoa powder
- 1 teaspoon baking soda
- ¼ teaspoon salt
- ¾ cup (6 ounces) tightly packed light brown sugar
- 1 large egg
- 1 large egg white
- 2 ounces cream cheese, cut into ½-ounce pieces
- ¼ cup bourbon
- 1¼ cups pecan halves, toasted (page 199) and coarsely chopped
- 1¼ cups walnut halves, toasted (page 199) and coarsely chopped

CHOCOLATE HONEY BOURBON GLAZE

- 6 ounces semisweet baking chocolate, coarsely chopped
- 2 ounces unsweetened chocolate, coarsely chopped
- ½ cup heavy cream
- ¼ cup bourbon
- 3 tablespoons unsalted butter
- 2 tablespoons clover honey

cake, allowing the flowing glaze to coat the top and sides of the cake. Before returning the glazed cakes to the refrigerator, scrape the glaze from the baking sheet and return it to the same medium bowl, stirring gently until smooth. Set aside. Refrigerate the cakes for 20 minutes. Remove from the refrigerator. Spoon about 1 tablespoon of glaze over each cake, once again allowing the glaze to flow over the top and sides of the cake.

Refrigerate the cakes for an additional 20 minutes. Remove from the refrigerator. Press an equal amount of the remaining chopped walnuts and pecans into the sides of each cake, coating evenly. Refrigerate for 10 minutes before serving.

THE CHEF'S TOUCH

For internationally acclaimed artist Nancy Thomas, being "happy all the time" was sometimes incongruous with her life as a working mother with three children. The whimsy and energy of her beloved paintings and sculptures belied the fact that she occasionally needed to seek solitude and solace in her kitchen, where she liked to bake. It was there, one day several years ago, that an inadvertent spill of bourbon into a cake batter made "Happy All the Time" cake a reality. Best not to ask the whys and wherefores on this one; just believe in happiness, as Nancy does.

For quicker and more effective portioning of the Cocoa Bourbon Cake batter, use a #20 ice cream scoop rather than a measuring cup, and portion a slightly heaping scoop into each muffin cup.

Feeling a bit parsimonious after splurging on a bottle of bourbon? Use chopped cookie crumbs instead of the chopped pecans and walnuts as a coating on the sides of the cakes.

To up the ante on the chocolate flavor in the Chocolate Honey Bourbon Glaze, you may substitute 2 tablespoons Chocolate Honey (see page 180) for the 2 tablespoons of clover honey in the recipe.

These cakes may be prepared over 2 days. DAY 1: Bake the individual Cocoa Bourbon Cakes. Once cooled, cover with plastic wrap and refrigerate. DAY 2: Make the Chocolate Honey Bourbon Glaze. Coat the cakes with glaze and chopped nuts as directed in the recipe. Refrigerate for 10 minutes before serving.

After assembly, you may keep the Happy All the Time Cakes in the refrigerator for 2 to 3 days before serving. To avoid permeating the cakes with refrigerator odors, place them in a large, tightly sealed plastic container.

The errant splash of bourbon in Nancy's kitchen was Jim Beam, a classic Kentucky sour mash whiskey. Depending on how "accident prone" you may be, I suggest using a similar quality whiskey for the recipe and for the happiness quotient.

COCOA-CRUSTED ESSENCE *of* ESPRESSO CHEESECAKES

MAKES 9 MINI CAKES

Make the Cocoa Crust

In a sifter, combine 1 cup of the flour and 2 tablespoons cocoa powder. Sift onto a large piece of parchment paper (or wax paper) and set aside until needed.

Place 3 ounces butter and ⅓ cup confectioners' sugar in the bowl of an electric mixer fitted with a paddle. Mix on low speed for 1 minute; then beat on medium-high for 3 minutes until soft and thoroughly combined. Use a rubber spatula to scrape down the sides of the bowl and the paddle. Add 2 egg yolks, one at a time, beating on medium for 20 seconds after each addition, and scraping down the sides of the bowl once both yolks have been incorporated. Operate the mixer on low while gradually adding the sifted dry ingredients. Mix until the dough comes together, about 1 minute.

Remove the dough from the mixer and form it into a smooth, round ball. Place the dough onto a clean, dry, lightly floured work surface. Use a rolling pin to roll the dough to a thickness of ¼ inch. (Sprinkle the remaining 2 tablespoons of flour on the rolling pin and work surface, as necessary, to prevent sticking.) Cut 6 round pieces out of the dough, using a 3¼-inch biscuit cutter. Form the remaining dough into a ball. Roll the dough again to a thickness of ¼ inch, and cut out 2 more round pieces. Repeat the process in order to cut 1 more round piece from the rolled dough. Place each round dough piece into one of 9 individual nonstick muffin cups (3 inches in diameter). One cup at a time, use your fingers to press the dough into a crust of even thickness lining the bottom and sides of the cup. (The dough should reach the rim of the cup.) Set aside while preparing the cheesecake batter.

Prepare the Espresso Cheesecakes

Preheat the oven to 250°F. Place 8 ounces cream cheese and ⅓ cup granulated sugar in the bowl of an electric mixer fitted with a paddle. Mix on low for 30 seconds; then beat on medium-high speed for 2 minutes until soft and thoroughly combined. Use a rubber spatula to scrape down the sides of the bowl and the paddle. Beat the mixture on medium-high for an additional 3 minutes until very soft and smooth. Add 2 eggs, one at a time, beating on medium for 20 seconds after each addition, and scraping down the sides of the bowl once both eggs have been incorporated. Add ½ teaspoon espresso powder and beat on medium to combine, about 15 seconds. Add the melted chocolate and ½ teaspoon vanilla extract and mix on medium to combine, about 10 seconds.

Portion 3 tablespoons of batter into each cocoa dough–lined cup.

Place the muffin tin on the center rack of the preheated oven, and bake until the batter rises to the top edge of the dough and is fairly firm to the touch, about 45 minutes.

COCOA CRUST

1 cup plus 2 tablespoons all-purpose flour

2 tablespoons unsweetened cocoa powder

3 ounces unsalted butter, cut into ½-ounce pieces

⅓ cup confectioners' sugar

2 large egg yolks

ESPRESSO CHEESECAKES

8 ounces cream cheese, cut into 1-ounce pieces

⅓ cup granulated sugar

2 large eggs

½ teaspoon instant espresso powder

2 ounces semisweet baking chocolate, coarsely chopped and melted (pages 197–98)

½ teaspoon pure vanilla extract

COFFEE LIQUEUR CREAM CHEESE TOPPING

8 ounces cream cheese, cut into 1-ounce pieces

½ cup confectioners' sugar

1 tablespoon coffee liqueur

Remove the cheesecakes from the oven and cool at room temperature in the muffin tin for 20 minutes. (While cooling, the top of the baked batter will collapse very slightly, creating a small recession; this area will be filled with the cream cheese topping.) Remove the cheesecakes from the muffin tin and set aside at room temperature while making the topping.

Make the Coffee Liqueur Cream Cheese Topping

Place 8 ounces cream cheese and ½ cup confectioners' sugar in the bowl of an electric mixer fitted with a paddle. Mix on low speed for 30 seconds; then beat on medium-high for 2 minutes until soft and thoroughly combined. Scrape down the sides of the bowl. Add 1 tablespoon coffee liqueur and mix on low for 10 seconds; then beat on medium high for 2 minutes, until very smooth.

Top and Serve

Portion 1 big heaping tablespoon of topping into the recession on each cheesecake. Use a small spatula or a dinner knife to spread the topping to the inside edges of the cocoa crust. Serve immediately.

THE CHEF'S TOUCH

I am attracted to this confection for two reasons: I love smooth and creamy cheesecake, and I adore smooth and creamy cheesecake that takes only 45 minutes to bake. Even with the bantam size and brief baking time, these cakes wield such maximum taste and texture that you'd think you were eating the Joe Louis of Cheesecakes.

Instant espresso powder itself packs a powerful punch in a dessert, especially when teamed with chocolate. I don't, however, recommend it for use as a beverage. Instant espresso can usually be found near the instant coffee display at the supermarket.

Gild the lily by adorning each mini-cheesecake with a chocolate-covered espresso bean. These lilliputian candies with a jolt are sold at specialty grocery stores or espresso bars.

After assembly, you may keep the Cocoa-Crusted Essence of Espresso Cheesecakes in the refrigerator for 2 days before serving. Avoid exposing the cakes to competing refrigerator odors by placing them in a large, tightly sealed plastic container.

Now if someone were to offer me a Kahlúa-and-cream as a beverage accompaniment to these cheesecakes, I would say that he or she was quite knowledgeable about "smooth and creamy."

MY LITTLE KUMQUAT CAKES

MAKES 6 CAKES

Make the Ginger Macadamia Nut Cake

Preheat the oven to 325°F. Lightly coat the inside of a 10¾ × 7 × 1½-inch nonstick biscuit/brownie pan with some of the 1 teaspoon of melted butter. Line the bottom of the pan with parchment paper (or wax paper), then lightly coat the paper with more melted butter. Set aside.

In a sifter combine 1 cup flour, 1 teaspoon ground ginger, ¼ teaspoon baking powder, and ¼ teaspoon baking soda. Sift onto a large piece of parchment paper (or wax paper). Set aside

Place ¼ pound butter and ½ cup sugar in the bowl of an electric mixer fitted with a paddle. Mix on low speed for 1 minute; then beat on medium for 2 minutes until soft. Use a rubber spatula to scrape down the sides of the bowl; then beat on medium for an additional 2 minutes until very soft. Scrape down the sides of the bowl. Add the egg and beat on medium for 30 seconds to combine. Operate the mixer on low while gradually adding half of the sifted dry ingredients; mix until incorporated, about 20 seconds. Add ½ cup sour cream and mix on medium to combine, about 10 seconds. Gradually add the remaining dry ingredients while mixing on low until combined, about 20 seconds. Remove the bowl from the mixer. Add ¾ cup of the chopped toasted macadamia nuts. (The remaining ¼ cup chopped nuts will be used to garnish the tops of the cakes.) Use a rubber spatula to finish mixing the ingredients until thoroughly combined.

Transfer the cake batter to the prepared biscuit/brownie pan, spreading evenly to the edges. Bake on the center rack in the preheated oven until a toothpick inserted in the center of the cake comes out clean, 26 to 27 minutes. Remove the cake from the oven and cool in the biscuit/brownie pan for 15 minutes at room temperature. Invert the cake onto a baking sheet. Carefully peel the paper away from the bottom of the cake. Refrigerate the cake until needed.

Prepare the Chocolate Kumquat Mousse

Trim about ⅛ inch from each end of the kumquats. Cut each kumquat into ¼-inch-thick slices. (The ½ pound should yield about 1½ cups sliced.) Pick out and discard the occasional seed from the kumquat slices. Set aside.

Heat ¾ cup of the sugar and ¼ cup water in a medium saucepan over medium-high heat. When hot, stir to dissolve the sugar. Bring to a boil. Add the sliced kumquats and stir to incorporate. Bring to a boil again; then adjust the heat to allow the mixture to cook at a slow boil for 12 minutes until the kumquat slices are tender and sweet. Strain the kumquats and discard the cooking syrup. Transfer the kumquat slices to a baking sheet or large plate and spread evenly. Place, uncovered, in the refrigerator to cool.

GINGER MACADAMIA NUT CAKE

- ¼ pound (1 stick) unsalted butter, cut into ½-ounce pieces; plus 1 teaspoon (melted)
- 1 cup all-purpose flour
- 1 teaspoon ground ginger
- ¼ teaspoon baking powder
- ¼ teaspoon baking soda
- ½ cup granulated sugar
- 1 large egg
- ½ cup sour cream
- 1 cup whole raw unsalted macadamia nuts, toasted (page 199) and finely chopped

CHOCOLATE KUMQUAT MOUSSE

- ½ pound small fresh kumquats, washed and dried
- 1 cup granulated sugar
- ¼ cup water
- 1 cup heavy cream
- 4 ounces unsweetened baking chocolate, coarsely chopped and melted (pages 197–98)

Reserve 6 kumquat slices to garnish the cakes. Finely chop the remaining kumquats with a cook's knife. Set aside while preparing the mousse.

Place 1 cup heavy cream and the remaining ¼ cup sugar in the bowl of an electric mixer fitted with a balloon whip. Whisk on medium-high for 2 minutes until firm, but not stiff, peaks form. Add about ¾ cup of the whipped cream to the bowl of melted unsweetened chocolate, and use a rubber spatula to fold together until thoroughly combined. Add the combined whipped cream and chocolate to the remaining whipped cream, and use a rubber spatula to fold together until smooth and thoroughly combined. Transfer ¼ cup of the chocolate mousse to a pastry bag fitted with a medium star tip. Add the chopped kumquats to the remaining mousse, and use a rubber spatula to fold them in together until the mixture is thoroughly combined. Refrigerate the mousse in the pastry bag and the Chocolate Kumquat Mousse for a few minutes while beginning the assembly of the cakes.

Assemble the Cakes

Cut a 12 × 3½-inch strip of parchment paper (or wax paper) crosswise into 6 equal pieces. Use the paper to line the insides of 6 sections of PVC pipe 2½ inches high with a 3-inch opening. Place the paper-lined pipes on a baking sheet. (The paper should extend over the top of each pipe.)

Remove the Ginger Macadamia Nut Cake from the refrigerator and place on a clean, dry work surface. Use a 3-inch biscuit cutter to cut the cake into six 3-inch cake circles. (The remaining cake "scraps" can be fed to your favorite pet. Can you hear me purring?) As if placing a coin into a paper coin wrapper, place the cake circles into the paper-lined pipes (one for each pipe), gently pressing the cakes to the bottom.

Spoon about ⅓ cup Chocolate Kumquat Mousse on top of each cake portion, spreading evenly. Sprinkle 2 teaspoons of the remaining chopped macadamia nuts over the entire surface of the mousse on each cake. Pipe a chocolate mousse star onto the center of each cake, then top each star with a kumquat slice. Refrigerate the cakes in the pipes for 1 hour before serving.

To Serve

Remove the cakes from the refrigerator. Slip the PVC pipe up, up, and away from the outside of each cake. (Yes, the pipes really do slip right off.) Gently peel the parchment paper off each cake. Serve immediately.

THE CHEF'S TOUCH

"Mmmm . . . you are my little kumquat. I will prepare this delectable baby cake just for you." Using "kumquat" as a term of endearment for my wife, Connie, dates back several years.

Kumquat season peaks during winter months, just like citrus. (Although many think kumquats are a citrus fruit, they are classed in the *Fortunella* group.) But thanks to a global market, kumquats can be located sporadically throughout the year. I favor small, oval-shaped kumquats, about 80 fruit per pound (fruit size: approximately 1¼ inches long and ¾ inch wide). At the supermarket, kumquats are usually sold by the pint, which weighs about 12 ounces.

PVC (polyvinyl chloride) piping can be purchased at almost any hardware store across the land. The PVC used for My Little Kumquat Cakes set us back about 50 cents per 2½-inch-high pipe at our local Ace Hardware store.

Instead of spooning the Chocolate Kumquat Mousse onto the cakes inside the PVC pipes, you may find it easier to pipe the mousse. Fill a pastry bag, fitted with a large straight tip, with the mousse, then pipe about ⅓ cup of mousse onto each cake. After all the mousse has been dispensed, pick up the baking sheet holding the six PVC pipes, hold it 6 to 8 inches above the work surface, and then allow it to drop. Do this 3 to 4 times, or until the mousse has settled evenly inside the PVC.

When my little kumquat and I partake of delicate confections, our thoughts (other than those *other* thoughts) turn to bubbles. Need I say more?

LEMON POPPY SEED CAKELETTES *with* CHOCOLATE LEMON DROP TOPS

MAKES 24 CAKELETTES

Make the Lemon Poppy Seed Cakelettes

Preheat the oven to 325°F. Using the 1 teaspoon of melted butter, lightly coat the insides of two 12-cup nonstick miniature muffin tins.

In a sifter combine 1 cup flour and ¼ teaspoon baking powder. Sift onto a large piece of parchment paper (or wax paper) and set aside until needed.

Place 6 ounces butter and ¾ cup granulated sugar in the bowl of an electric mixer fitted with a paddle. Mix on low speed for 1 minute; then beat on medium until soft, about 2 minutes. Scrape down the sides of the bowl and the paddle. Beat on medium for an additional 2 minutes, until very soft. Add 2 eggs, one at a time, beating on medium for 30 seconds after each addition, and scraping down the sides of the bowl after both eggs have been incorporated.

Operate the mixer on low while gradually adding the sifted dry ingredients; mix until incorporated, about 45 seconds. Add 1 tablespoon minced lemon zest, 1 tablespoon fresh lemon juice, 1 tablespoon poppy seeds, and ½ teaspoon vanilla extract and mix on low speed for 15 seconds. Scrape down the sides of the bowl, and then mix on medium for 20 seconds. Remove the bowl from the mixer; then use a rubber spatula to finish mixing the ingredients until thoroughly combined.

Portion 2 level tablespoons of the cakelette batter into each miniature muffin cup. Place the muffin tins on the center rack of the preheated oven and bake until a toothpick inserted in the center of each cakelette comes out clean, 18 to 20 minutes. Remove the cakelettes from the oven and cool at room temperature for 10 minutes. Invert the pans to release the cakelettes. (If the cakelettes do not release from the cups, use the tip of a plastic knife to "cut" around the edges of each cakelette to free them from the pans without tearing the cakelettes.) Set aside at room temperature while making the Chocolate Lemon Drop Tops.

Make the Chocolate Lemon Drop Tops

Sift ½ cup of confectioners' sugar onto a piece of parchment paper (or wax paper). Set aside.

Place 8 ounces cream cheese, 2 tablespoons lemon juice, and 2 tablespoons lemon zest in the bowl of an electric mixer fitted with a paddle. Mix on low speed for 1 minute; then beat on medium-high for 2 minutes until soft. Scrape down the sides of the bowl and the paddle. Operate the mixer on low while gradually adding the sifted confectioners' sugar; mix until incorporated, about 30 seconds. Beat the mixture on medium-high for 1 minute. Scrape down the sides of the bowl. Add the melted chocolate and beat on medium-high for 30 seconds. Scrape down

LEMON POPPY SEED CAKELETTES

6 ounces (1½ sticks) unsalted butter, cut into ½-ounce pieces; plus 1 teaspoon (melted)

1 cup all-purpose flour

¼ teaspoon baking powder

¾ cup granulated sugar

2 large eggs

1 tablespoon minced lemon zest

1 tablespoon fresh lemon juice

1 tablespoon poppy seeds

½ teaspoon pure vanilla extract

CHOCOLATE LEMON DROP TOPS

½ cup confectioners' sugar

8 ounces cream cheese, cut into 1-ounce pieces

2 tablespoons fresh lemon juice

2 tablespoons minced lemon zest

4 ounces semisweet baking chocolate, coarsely chopped and melted (pages 197–98)

the sides of the bowl; then beat for an additional 45 seconds on medium-high until light in texture. Remove the bowl from the mixer. Transfer the icing to a pastry bag fitted with a small straight tip.

Pipe several "drops" (about 1 tablespoon each) of the Chocolate Lemon Drop Tops onto the top of each cakelette. Refrigerate until ready to serve.

To Serve

Remove the cakelettes from the refrigerator and keep at room temperature for 15 to 20 minutes before serving.

THE CHEF'S TOUCH

In case the reader conjectures that a contrived name like "cakelette" was used to bring significance to something having none, I assure them that even though the term may be whimsical, the diminutive cakelette delivers a magical mouthful of exciting citrus flavor.

For the minced lemon zest, use a sharp vegetable peeler to remove the colored part of the skin of the lemon, not the bitter white pith underneath. Once the colored skin has been removed, use a very sharp cook's knife to cut it into as thin a julienne as possible; then mince the julienne strips.

The most commonly available poppy seeds are dark slate-blue in color, although brown and yellow seeds also exist. The seeds bring texture and a subtle nutty flavor, especially when toasted. In this recipe, the poppy seeds do not need toasting since they will develop their flavor while the cakelettes bake.

For a burst of color, sprinkle a fine julienne of lemon zest over the Chocolate Lemon Drop Top on each cakelette.

The cakelettes may be prepared over 2 days. DAY 1: Bake the individual Lemon Poppy Seed Cakelettes. Once cooled, cover with plastic wrap and refrigerate. DAY 2: Make the Chocolate Lemon Drop Tops. Pipe the icing "drops" onto the cakelettes as directed in the recipe. Refrigerate until ready to serve.

After assembly, you may keep the Lemon Poppy Seed Cakelettes with Chocolate Lemon Drop Tops in the refrigerator for 2 to 3 days before serving. To avoid permeating the cakelettes with refrigerator odors, place them in a large, tightly sealed plastic container.

Your perspicaciousness in serving our cakelettes with tea would earn you as many kudos as there are poppy seeds in a jar.

CHOCOLATE CARAWAY ON-THE-ROCKS TRIFLES

MAKES 4 ON-THE-ROCKS TRIFLES

Prepare the Pear Compote

Heat 3 tablespoons sugar, 1 tablespoon chocolate-flavored vodka, and 1 tablespoon water in a medium saucepan over medium-high heat. When hot, stir to dissolve the sugar. Bring to a boil, and then allow to boil for 1 to 1½ minutes until syrupy. Remove the vodka syrup from the heat and set aside while preparing the pears.

Wash and dry 2 Bartlett pears. Peel, core, quarter, and then dice the pears into ½-inch pieces. Immediately place the diced pears into the saucepan with the vodka syrup. Stir to thoroughly coat each piece of pear with the syrup. (This will prevent them from discoloring.) Return the saucepan to medium-high heat and cook the pears, while constantly stirring, for 1½ to 2 minutes until they are cooked, but still firm. Place the pears in a colander to drain for about 1 minute. Transfer them to a baking sheet with sides, spreading them evenly. Refrigerate, uncovered, to cool.

Make the Chocolate Caraway Cake

Preheat the oven to 350°F. Lightly coat the inside of a 10 × 15-inch nonstick baking sheet using some of the 2 teaspoons of melted butter. Line the bottom and sides of the baking sheet with a single sheet of parchment paper (or wax paper) and then lightly coat the paper with more melted butter. Set aside.

In a sifter, combine the 1 cup flour, 1 tablespoon cocoa powder, and 1 teaspoon baking powder. Sift onto a large piece of parchment paper (or wax paper) and set aside until needed.

Place ½ cup sugar and 2 ounces butter in the bowl of an electric mixer fitted with a paddle. Mix on low speed for 1 minute; then beat on medium until soft, about 2 minutes. Use a rubber spatula to scrape down the sides of the bowl and the paddle. Beat on medium for an additional 2 minutes until softer. Add 1 egg and 1 egg white, one at a time, beating on medium for 30 seconds after each addition, and scraping down the sides of the bowl once the egg and the egg white have been incorporated. Add 3 ounces melted semisweet chocolate and beat on medium for 20 seconds until combined. Operate the mixer on low while gradually adding the sifted dry ingredients; mix until incorporated, about 45 seconds. Scrape down the sides of the bowl.

Add ⅓ cup chocolate-flavored vodka, ⅓ cup sour cream, and 1 tablespoon caraway seeds and mix on the lowest speed ("stir") for about 30 seconds; then beat on medium for 15 seconds. Remove the bowl from the mixer and use a rubber spatula to finish mixing the batter until thoroughly combined. Transfer the batter to the prepared baking sheet; use an offset spatula (or a cake spatula) to spread the batter evenly to the edges.

Bake on the center rack of the preheated oven until a toothpick inserted in the center of the cake layer comes out clean, about 12

PEAR COMPOTE

3 tablespoons granulated sugar

1 tablespoon Kremlyovskaya chocolate-flavored, triple-distilled vodka

1 tablespoon water

2 large green Bartlett pears

CHOCOLATE CARAWAY CAKE

2 ounces (½ stick) unsalted butter, cut into ½-ounce pieces; plus 2 teaspoons (melted)

1 cup all-purpose flour

1 tablespoon unsweetened cocoa powder

1 teaspoon baking powder

½ cup granulated sugar

1 large egg

1 large egg white

3 ounces semisweet baking chocolate, coarsely chopped and melted (pages 197–98)

⅓ cup Kremlyovskaya chocolate-flavored, triple-distilled vodka

⅓ cup sour cream

1 tablespoon whole caraway seeds

SEMISWEET CHOCOLATE MOUSSE

¾ cup heavy cream

1 tablespoon granulated sugar

4 ounces semisweet baking chocolate, coarsely chopped and melted (pages 197–98)

ON-THE-ROCKS GARNISH

1 pint fresh red raspberries

1 cup Kremlyovskaya chocolate-flavored, triple-distilled vodka

minutes. Remove the cake layer from the oven and cool in the baking sheet for 15 minutes at room temperature. Use a 3¼-inch biscuit cutter to cut 12 individual circles of cake from the cake layer in the baking sheet. Transfer the cake circles, baked top facing up, to a baking sheet lined with parchment paper (or wax paper) and refrigerate until ready to assemble.

Make the Semisweet Chocolate Mousse

Place ¾ cup heavy cream and 1 tablespoon sugar in the bowl of an electric mixer fitted with a balloon whip. Whisk on medium-high for 1½ minutes until firm, but not stiff, peaks form. Add about half the amount of the whipped cream to the bowl of 4 ounces melted semisweet chocolate, and use a rubber spatula to mix together until thoroughly combined. Add the combined whipped cream and chocolate to the remaining whipped cream and use a rubber spatula to fold together until smooth and thoroughly combined. Refrigerate until needed.

Assemble the On-the-Rocks Trifles

Place ½ cup fresh red raspberries into each of four 14- to 16-ounce double old-fashioneds. Pour ¼ cup chocolate-flavored vodka over the berries in each glass. One at a time, place a cake circle (baked top facing up), in a similar fashion to placing a coin into a coin wrapper, into each glass, gently pressing down until the cake is resting on top of the raspberries and vodka. Top each of these cake circles with 2 slightly heaping tablespoons of pear compote, and use a teaspoon to push the pear to the

sides of the glass, leaving an open space about 1¼ inches in diameter in the center of each cake circle. Spoon 2 slightly heaping tablespoons of chocolate mousse in the open space on each cake. Place a second layer of cake in each glass, gently pressing it into place, and repeat the procedure with the pear compote and chocolate mousse. Place the third circle of cake into place in each glass, again pressing down gently. Top each last cake circle with 1 tablespoon of the chocolate mousse. Sprinkle the remaining raspberries onto the mousse and serve immediately.

THE CHEF'S TOUCH

A trifle is one of America's most traditional desserts, having arrived by way of England. Typically, a trifle is a grand composition of custard and liquor-soaked cake or biscuits layered in a deep glass dish. Although the eighteenth century was considered to be the golden age of such desserts, today's pastry chefs are producing new and exciting interpretations of classic confections like trifle.

When I arrived in Williamsburg, Virginia, in 1970, some five years after graduating from the Culinary Institute of America, I had much to learn about American cooking. Up to that point my culinary education—both formal and on the job in New York City—was concentrated on the principles of French cuisine. In Williamsburg, much of the food that was served in the restaurants operated by Colonial Williamsburg took its cue from dishes popular in eighteenth-century America. Soon I was making peanut soup, roasting rockfish, cooking Smithfield hams, and assembling trifles for such diverse guests as the Japanese cabinet, the Shah of Iran, and Gerald Ford.

Kremlyovskaya chocolate-flavored, triple-distilled vodka is one of several chocolate-flavored vodkas available nationwide. The Kremlyovskaya has a remarkably distinctive chocolate aroma and flavor, lending a specific nuance to the pear compote and the cake. The "on-the-rocks" portion of the assembled dessert wouldn't be the same without it. If satisfaction is not achieved with that bottom layer, then I suggest a small side pour of the Kremlyovskaya directly from the freezer.

MOM'S CAKES

WHY WOULD YOU EVER LEAVE HOME AND MOM'S CHOCOLATE?

MOM BAILEY'S CHOCOLATE ICEBOX CAKE

SERVES 10

Make Ruth's Pound Cake

Preheat the oven to 325°F. Lightly coat the inside of a 9 × 5 × 3-inch nonstick loaf pan with the 1 teaspoon of melted butter. Set aside.

In a sifter combine 2½ cups cake flour, ¼ teaspoon baking soda, and ½ teaspoon salt. Sift onto a large piece of parchment paper (or wax paper). Set aside until needed.

Place 1½ cups sugar and ½ pound butter in the bowl of an electric mixer fitted with a paddle. Mix on low speed for 2 minutes; then beat on medium for 3 minutes. Scrape down the sides of the bowl and the paddle. Beat for an additional 3 minutes on medium speed. Scrape down the sides of the bowl, and then beat for 2 minutes on high speed until soft and slightly fluffy. Scrape down the sides of the bowl. Add 3 eggs, one at a time, beating on medium for 30 seconds after each addition, and scraping down the sides of the bowl once all the eggs have been incorporated. Now beat on medium for 4 minutes until very fluffy. Scrape down the sides of the bowl.

Operate the mixer on low while gradually adding one-third of the milk followed by one-third of the sifted dry ingredients. Once these ingredients have been incorporated, about 30 seconds, gradually add another one-third of the milk, followed by one-third of the sifted dry ingredients, and mix on low until

incorporated for about 30 seconds. Now gradually add the remaining milk followed by the remaining sifted dry ingredients, and mix on low until incorporated, about 30 seconds. Add 1 teaspoon vanilla extract and beat on medium for 15 seconds until combined. Remove the bowl from the mixer and use a rubber spatula to finish mixing the batter until thoroughly combined. Transfer the batter to the prepared loaf pan using a rubber spatula and spread the batter evenly.

Bake on the center rack of the preheated oven until a toothpick inserted in the center of the cake comes out clean, about 1 hour and 15 minutes to 1 hour and 20 minutes. Remove the cake from the oven and cool in the pan at room temperature for 15 to 20 minutes. Turn the cake out of the pan onto a baking sheet. Turn the cake top side up, then refrigerate for 1 hour.

Prepare the Cake for Assembly

Place the cake on a clean, dry work surface. Cut off the top of the cake in one piece by using a serrated slicer to slice the cake horizontally ¼ inch below the rim. Set the top aside, being careful to keep it in one piece. Turn the cake over, cut top down, on the work surface, and cut a ½-inch-thick horizontal slice off the bottom of the cake. Place the bottom slice (baked bottom side down) into a

GRANDMA RUTH'S POUND CAKE LEGACY

½ pound (2 sticks) unsalted butter, cut into ½-ounce pieces; plus 1 teaspoon (melted)
2½ cups cake flour
¼ teaspoon baking soda
½ teaspoon salt
1½ cups granulated sugar
3 large eggs
⅓ cup whole milk
1 teaspoon pure vanilla extract

CREAMY CHOCOLATE CENTER

10 ounces semisweet baking chocolate, coarsely chopped
1½ cups heavy cream
¼ cup granulated sugar

LAZY VANILLA CREAM

1 cup heavy cream
2 tablespoons confectioners' sugar
1 teaspoon pure vanilla extract

clean, dry 9 × 5 × 3-inch loaf pan. Now slice ½-inch-thick slices, first from each end of the cake, followed by each long side of the cake. Place the cut sides and ends back into the loaf pan as they were prior to being sliced. (If I have to suggest to you what to do with the leftover center section of this scrumptious cake, you probably should be reading a novel.) Set aside the cake slices while preparing the Creamy Chocolate Center.

Make the Creamy Chocolate Center

Place 10 ounces semisweet chocolate in a medium bowl. Heat ¾ cup of the heavy cream in a small saucepan over medium-high heat. Bring to a boil.

Pour the boiling cream over the chopped chocolate. Set aside for 5 minutes; then stir with a whisk until smooth. Set this ganache aside for a few moments.

Place the remaining ¾ cup heavy cream and ¼ cup sugar in the bowl of an electric mixer fitted with a balloon whip. Whisk on medium-high speed for 1½ minutes until firm peaks form. Add the ganache to the whipped cream and whisk on medium for 30 seconds until combined. Remove the bowl from the mixer and use a rubber spatula to fold the mixture together until smooth (we prepared the Creamy Chocolate Center at least ten times when testing this book, and it always came out ever so smoo-ooth) and thoroughly combined.

Assemble the Icebox Cake

Transfer the Creamy Chocolate Center mixture into the cutout center of the pound cake, using a rubber spatula to spread it evenly to the top inside edges of the cake. Place the cut top back onto the cake, pressing it down gently into place. Refrigerate the cake for 2 to 3 hours, until the Creamy Chocolate Center is firm, before slicing.

Make the Lazy Vanilla Cream

Place 1 cup heavy cream, 2 tablespoons confectioners' sugar, and 1 teaspoon vanilla extract in the bowl of an electric mixer fitted with a balloon whip. Whisk the mixture on medium-high speed until thickened but not stiff (no peaks), about 1 minute and 20 seconds. Cover with plastic wrap and refrigerate until needed.

To Serve

Remove the cake from the refrigerator, and invert it onto a clean, dry work surface. Turn the cake top side up. Heat the blade of a serrated slicer under hot running water and wipe the blade dry before cutting a ¾- to 1-inch-thick slice from each end of the cake. (Cut enough away to fully expose the Creamy Chocolate Center.) Then cut the cake crosswise into 10 approximately ¾-inch-thick pieces. Place each slice onto a serving plate, top with a large dollop of Lazy Cream, and serve immediately.

THE CHEF'S TOUCH

Phyllis Bailey, mother of Ganache Hill test kitchen chef Brett Bailey, had a difficult culinary relationship with her mother-in-law, Ruth Bailey. By all accounts, Ruth was an accomplished cook. She took great pride in her kitchen expertise, and delighted in pleasing her family at the dinner table. However, Ruth had a dark side: She refused to reveal her secret recipes, even to her family.

Brett's dad, John, didn't make things easy for his new bride when he insisted that she acquire the recipe for his favorite cake. Because Ruth was not forthcoming, Phyllis was reduced to snooping around her mother-in-law's kitchen in search of a written recipe. She came up empty-handed. Exasperated, Phyllis began looking over Ruth's shoulder during the preparation of the desired cake, and after several such opportunities, she, no slouch in the kitchen herself, was able to re-create her own version of the cake, using her husband as recipe arbiter. Fortunately for us, Phyllis's largess is such that not only does she please friends and family with this admired confection—crisp-baked exterior, delicate, vanilla-accented interior, and rich creamy chocolate center—she now generously offers the recipe to all. Brett thinks his grandmother would secretly be proud.

Although you will find icebox cookie or icebox pie recipes included in many culinary lexicons, icebox cake doesn't seem to be noted anywhere. The fact is, this rubric was attached to the cake by Brett's grandmother. The cake was always kept refrigerated because Ruth's original recipe for the Creamy Chocolate Center called for a puddinglike custard that needed to be kept refrigerated. Bless Grandma Ruth, now that all her secrets are being revealed—well, almost all.

The provenance of pound cake suggests a recipe that includes one pound of each primary ingredient in the mix. In fact, that's the way pound cake was prepared for decades. If most pound cake recipes share a commonality, what separates the *extraordinary* pound cake from the ordinary is technique. The most important technique is creaming, a lengthy blending of key ingredients. Brett's mom advises, "Cream, cream, then cream some more." Specifically, in this case, "creaming" means combining the butter and sugar until the mixture is smooth as silk, then adding the eggs one at a time (don't be impatient) to the butter-sugar mixture until it is pure silk charmeuse. The result is a baked cake with a fine crumb texture that belies the use of the word "crumb" in the same sentence.

AUNT CECIL'S COCOA WALNUT CRUNCH CAKE

SERVES 10

Make the Cocoa Walnut Sponge Cake

Preheat the oven to 350°F. Lightly coat the insides of two 9 × 1½-inch nonstick cake pans with some of the 2 teaspoons of melted butter. Line the bottom of the pans with parchment paper (or wax paper), then lightly coat the paper with more melted butter. Set aside.

In a sifter combine ½ cup cake flour, ¼ cup cocoa powder, 2 teaspoons baking powder, and ¼ teaspoon salt. Sift onto a large piece of parchment paper (or wax paper) and set aside until needed.

Place 5 egg yolks and ¼ cup of the sugar in the bowl of an electric mixer fitted with a paddle. Beat on medium-high for 3 minutes until combined and slightly thickened. Use a rubber spatula to scrape down the sides of the bowl; then beat on medium-high for an additional 2 minutes until very thick. Scrape down the sides of the bowl.

Operate the mixer on low while adding the sifted dry ingredients; mix until incorporated, about 45 seconds. Add ¼ cup hot water and 1 teaspoon vanilla extract and mix on low to combine, about 45 seconds. Scrape down the sides of the bowl. Add the chopped walnuts and mix on medium to thoroughly combine, about 10 seconds. Transfer the batter to a large bowl and set aside at room temperature while whisking the egg whites.

Place 5 egg whites and the remaining ¼ cup sugar in the bowl of an electric mixer fitted with a balloon whip. Whisk on high speed for 2 minutes until soft peaks form. Add about one-third of the whisked egg whites to the batter in the large bowl and use a rubber spatula to quickly fold together until thoroughly combined. Add the remaining whisked egg whites to this mixture and use a rubber spatula to fold together until thoroughly combined.

Immediately divide the cake batter into the prepared pans (about 2½ cups of batter in each pan), spreading it evenly. Bake on the center rack in the preheated oven until a toothpick inserted in the center of each cake layer comes out clean, about 20 minutes. Remove the layers from the oven and cool in the pans for 10 minutes at room temperature. Invert the cake layers onto cake circles (or onto cake plates). Carefully peel the paper away from the bottom of the cakes. Refrigerate the cakes until needed.

Make the Walnut Crunch

Place the toasted walnuts on a baking sheet and set aside.

COCOA WALNUT SPONGE CAKE

2 teaspoons unsalted butter, melted

½ cup cake flour

¼ cup unsweetened cocoa powder

2 teaspoons baking powder

¼ teaspoon salt

5 large eggs, separated

½ cup granulated sugar

¼ cup hot water

1 teaspoon pure vanilla extract

1 cup walnut halves, toasted (page 199) and coarsely chopped

WALNUT CRUNCH

1½ cups walnut halves, toasted (page 199) and coarsely chopped

2 cups granulated sugar

1 teaspoon fresh lemon juice

CHOCOLATE WALNUT FROSTING

8 ounces semisweet baking chocolate, coarsely chopped

¾ cup heavy cream

¾ pound (3 sticks) unsalted butter, cut into ½-ounce pieces

1 teaspoon pure vanilla extract

Place 2 cups sugar and 1 teaspoon lemon juice in a large saucepan. Stir with a whisk to combine (the sugar will resemble moist sand).

Caramelize the sugar for about 10 minutes over medium-high heat, stirring constantly with a whisk to break up any lumps. The sugar will first turn clear as it liquefies, then light brown as it caramelizes. Remove the saucepan from the heat. Immediately pour the caramelized sugar over the walnuts on the baking sheet and place in the freezer to harden, about 10 minutes. (If you are short on room in your freezer, you may harden the Walnut Crunch in the refrigerator for about 20 minutes, or at air-conditioned room temperature for about 30 minutes.)

Use your hands to break the hardened Walnut Crunch into irregular pieces measuring 2 to 3 inches in width. Place the broken pieces in the bowl of a food processor fitted with a metal blade and process for 5 seconds until coarsely chopped (or coarsely chop by hand using a cook's knife). Sift the chopped Walnut Crunch in a medium-gauge strainer. Discard the finely sifted sugar residue, or use it as a beverage sweetener. Store the sifted, coarsely chopped Walnut Crunch (about 2 cups) in a tightly sealed plastic container until ready to use in the frosting.

Prepare the Chocolate Walnut Frosting

Place 8 ounces chopped semisweet chocolate in a medium bowl.

Heat ¾ cup heavy cream in a small saucepan over medium-high heat. Bring to a boil. Pour the boiling cream over the chopped chocolate. Set aside for 5 minutes, then stir with a whisk until smooth. Pour the mixture (now called ganache) onto a baking sheet with sides and refrigerate until thoroughly chilled, about 30 minutes.

Place ¾ pound butter in the bowl of an electric mixer fitted with a paddle. Mix on low speed for 1 minute, then increase the speed to medium-high and beat for 2 minutes until soft. Scrape down the sides of the bowl and the paddle. Beat on medium for 2 more minutes until very soft. Add the chilled ganache and beat on medium-high speed for 2 minutes until incredibly fluffy. Scrape down the sides of the bowl and the paddle.

Add the coarsely chopped and sifted Walnut Crunch and 1 teaspoon vanilla extract and mix on low for 5 seconds; then increase the speed to medium and beat for an additional 10 seconds until thoroughly combined.

Assemble the Cake

Remove the cakes from the refrigerator. Turn over one of the inverted cakes and return it to the cake circle (or cake plate) crust side up. Use a cake spatula to evenly and smoothly spread 2 cups of the Chocolate Walnut Frosting over the top and to the edges of the cake layer. Invert the second cake layer onto the frosting-coated cake layer and gently press into place. Spread the remaining 4 cups of frosting evenly and smoothly on the top and sides of the cake. Refrigerate the cake for 1 hour before slicing and serving.

To Serve

Heat the blade of a serrated slicer under hot running water and wipe the blade dry before cutting each slice. Place each one onto a dessert plate and keep at room temperature for 10 to 15 minutes before serving. (While the cake is good cold, it is heavenly after a few minutes at room temperature.)

THE CHEF'S TOUCH

In many families, baking recipes are regarded with the same respect as precious heirlooms. They are treasured and handed down to subsequent generations as symbols of the joyous events at which they were served. The Trellis's dining room manager, Geralyn Butler, was the fortunate recipient of her Aunt Cecil's Cocoa Walnut Crunch Cake, which brought so much pleasure at family gatherings when she was a child. Now, as a mom, Geri revels in the traditions related to baking this special cake for her own children.

For an outrageously dramatic decoration, prepare an extra batch of the Walnut Crunch. After the crunch hardens, break it into approximately 2- to 3-inch-wide irregular pieces. Garnish the top of each slice of cake with these wicked pieces of crunch.

This cake may be prepared over 2 days. DAY 1: Bake the Cocoa Walnut Sponge Cake layers. Once cooled, cover each layer with plastic wrap and refrigerate until the next day. Make the Walnut Crunch. Once cooled, chop in the food processor as directed, then store in a tightly sealed plastic container at air-conditioned room temperature until the next day. DAY 2: Prepare the Chocolate Walnut Frosting, then frost the cake. Refrigerate the cake for 30 minutes before slicing and serving.

Make a festive celebration out of the next family gathering by serving the elegant Iron Horse Brut Rosé with this cake. Its lively citrus flavor is certain to bring harmony to the palate and the occasion.

MARTHA'S CHOCOLATE FRECKLES FRESH BLUEBERRY ICE CREAM CAKE

SERVES 12

Make the Blueberry Ice Cream

Place 1½ cups blueberries, 6 ounces cream cheese, ¾ cup sugar, ⅓ cup light corn syrup, and ½ cup sour cream in the bowl of an electric mixer fitted with a paddle. Mix on low speed for 30 seconds to combine. Now beat on medium-high for 2 minutes; then use a rubber spatula to scrape down the sides of the bowl. To avoid splattering the ingredients outside of the bowl, use a pouring shield attachment, or place a towel or plastic wrap over the top of the mixer and down the sides to the bowl. Continue beating the mixture on medium-high for an additional 3 minutes until very smooth. (The mixture may have some very small white lumps of cream cheese; no need to worry, these lumps will not be noticeable in the ice cream.) Scrape down the sides of the bowl. Operate the mixer on medium while slowly pouring in ½ cup milk, ¼ cup heavy cream, 2 tablespoons lemon juice, and 2 teaspoons vanilla extract; mix until thoroughly combined and smooth, about 1 minute.

Freeze this mixture in an ice cream freezer following the manufacturer's instructions. Transfer the semifrozen ice cream to a 2-quart plastic container. Cover the container securely, and then place in the freezer for 1 hour before assembling the cake.

Make the Chocolate Freckles Cake

Preheat the oven to 350°F. Lightly coat the insides of two 9 × 1½-inch nonstick cake pans with some of the 2 teaspoons of melted butter. Line the bottoms of the pans with parchment paper (or wax paper), then lightly coat the paper with more melted butter. Set aside.

In a sifter combine 1 cup flour, ½ teaspoon baking soda, ¼ teaspoon baking powder, and ¼ teaspoon salt. Sift onto a large piece of parchment paper (or wax paper), and set aside until needed.

Place ¾ cup sugar and ¼ pound butter in the bowl of an electric mixer fitted with a paddle. Mix on low speed for 1 minute; then beat on medium for 2 minutes until soft. Use a rubber spatula to scrape down the sides of the bowl and the paddle; then beat on medium for an additional 2 minutes until a little softer. Scrape down the sides of the bowl.

Add 2 eggs, one at a time, beating on medium for 15 seconds after each addition, and scraping down the sides of the bowl once both eggs have been incorporated. Operate the mixer on low while gradually adding the sifted dry ingredients; mix until incorporated, about 30 seconds.

Gradually add ¼ cup buttermilk and mix on low until incorporated, about 20 seconds. Add ¼ cup sour cream and 1 teaspoon vanilla

BLUEBERRY ICE CREAM

1½ cups fresh blueberries, stemmed and rinsed

6 ounces cream cheese, cut into 2-ounce pieces

¾ cup granulated sugar

⅓ cup light corn syrup

½ cup sour cream

½ cup whole milk

¼ cup heavy cream

2 tablespoons fresh lemon juice

2 teaspoons pure vanilla extract

CHOCOLATE FRECKLES CAKE

¼ pound (1 stick) unsalted butter, cut into ½-ounce pieces; plus 2 teaspoons (melted)

1 cup all-purpose flour

½ teaspoon baking soda

¼ teaspoon baking powder

¼ teaspoon salt

¾ cup granulated sugar

2 large eggs

¼ cup buttermilk

¼ cup sour cream

1 teaspoon pure vanilla extract

1 ounce semisweet baking chocolate, coarsely grated

WHIPPED CREAM TOPPING

2 cups heavy cream

½ cup confectioners' sugar

1 tablespoon pure vanilla extract

BLUEBERRY CROWN

½ cup fresh blueberries, stemmed and rinsed

extract and beat on medium for 20 seconds to incorporate. Remove the bowl from the mixer. Add 1 ounce grated chocolate and use a rubber spatula to finish mixing the batter until thoroughly combined. Immediately divide the cake batter into the prepared pans (a bit more than 1½ cups of batter in each pan), spreading evenly.

Bake on the center rack in the preheated oven until a toothpick inserted in the center of each cake layer comes out clean, about 18 to 20 minutes. Remove the cake layers from the oven and cool in the pans for 15 minutes at room temperature. Invert the layers onto cake circles (or directly onto cake plates). Very carefully (yes, *very,* as this cake is delicate), peel the paper away from the bottoms of the layers. Refrigerate the cake layers for 30 minutes before assembling the cake.

Begin Assembling the Cake

Remove the cake layers from the refrigerator, and the ice cream from the freezer. Turn over one of the inverted cake layers, and place it, crust side up, into a clean and dry 9 × 1½-inch nonstick cake pan. Portion about half of the ice cream on top of the cake layer. Use a rubber spatula to spread the ice cream evenly over the cake. In another clean and dry cake pan, repeat this procedure with the second cake layer and remaining half of the ice cream. Cover the top of each pan with plastic wrap and place in the freezer for at least 12 hours, until the ice cream is solid to the touch.

Continue the Assembly

Remove the 2 pans with the cake and ice cream layers from the freezer. Remove and discard the plastic wrap. Use a paring knife to cut all around the frozen cake and ice cream in each of the two pans, inserting the knife between the outside edges of the cake and the inside edges of the cake pan. Invert one of the frozen cake and ice cream sections onto a cake circle (or cake plate), then turn it over onto another cake circle (the ice cream layer should be facing up). Invert the remaining cake and ice cream section in the pan onto the ice cream layered cake on the cake circle, pressing down gently on the top cake layer to set the two sections into place. Use a cake spatula to smooth the ice cream evenly around the sides of the cake. Return the cake to the freezer while preparing the Whipped Cream Topping.

Prepare the Whipped Cream Topping

Place 2 cups heavy cream and ½ cup confectioners' sugar in the bowl of an electric mixer fitted with a balloon whip. Mix on low speed for 30 seconds; then increase speed to medium-high, and whisk for 1½ minutes until firm peaks form. Add 1 tablespoon vanilla extract and whisk on medium for 10 seconds.

Crown the Cake and Serve

Remove the ice cream cake from the freezer. Use a cake spatula to spread the Whipped Cream Topping evenly over the top and sides of the cake. Place the blueberries in a ring around the outside edge of the top of the cake. Return the cake to the freezer for 1 hour before cutting and serving.

Heat the blade of a serrated slicer under hot running water and wipe the blade dry before making each slice. Serve immediately.

THE CHEF'S TOUCH

Even though some time had passed since her training wheels had been removed from her bicycle, certain biking rules were strictly enforced for young Kelly Seroczynski: Mainly, never ever cross the highway. Martha, The Trellis's pastry chef Kelly Seroczynski Bailey's mom, was vigilant about many aspects of Kelly's upbringing, from biking to baking. So Kelly was thrilled at age ten when Mom gave her the green light and a wooden spoon, and let her go solo on her father's birthday cake. Out of sight of her mother's watchful eye, Kelly did fine until she got to the Whipped Cream Topping, which she overwhipped and turned into butter. On her own, she made a judgment call. Across the forbidden highway she ventured on the bicycle to buy more whipped cream at the grocery store. And who was there but Mom and Dad. After all was said and done, the cake was completed, and the birthday was happily celebrated. Needless to say, Kelly has crossed many highways and baked many cakes since then.

If the cake is in the freezer for several days, it will harden and become difficult to cut. So about a half hour or so before serving, transfer the cake to the refrigerator until it softens enough (but doesn't melt) and can be easily cut into servings.

Although blueberries are thankfully available year-round, check the berries closely for mold and moisture loss when they are not in season.

Grating a small square of baking chocolate with a box grater can be a knuckle-shredding job. For a less grating experience, purchasing a 2- to 3-pound block of chocolate gives you a lot of room to work with and plenty of leftover chocolate to use for other desserts. Grating chocolate in the food processor is a messy experience. My advice is to stick with the box grater and watch your fingers.

If you use a 2- to 3-pound block of chocolate for grating, grate a few extra ounces to decorate inside the Blueberry Crown on top of the cake or use a vegetable peeler to shave long, thin chocolate shavings from the block for the top of the cake.

MRS. D'S CHOCOLATE CRUNCHY CORN FLAKE, PEANUT *and* GRAPE DOUBLE LAYER NO-BAKE CAKE

SERVES 10 TO 12

Prepare the Chocolate Crunchy Corn Flake Layer

Assemble a 9 × 2¾-inch nonstick springform pan with the bottom insert turned over (the lip of the insert facing down).

Place 4 cups of corn flakes and 1 cup chopped peanuts in an extra-large bowl and set aside.

Melt together 16 ounces of chopped semisweet chocolate and ½ pound butter (see page 198 for more details).

Pour the melted chocolate and butter mixture over the corn flakes and peanuts. Use a rubber spatula to stir the ingredients until thoroughly coated with the chocolate mixture (the corn flakes will be crushed in the process). Transfer the chocolate-covered corn flakes and peanut mixture into the springform pan; firmly and evenly spread to the inside edges using a rubber spatula. Refrigerate while preparing the top layer.

Make the Chocolate Peanut and Grape Layer

Place 8 ounces chopped semisweet chocolate in a medium bowl.

Heat 1¼ cups heavy cream, 2 tablespoons butter, and 2 tablespoons sugar in a small saucepan over medium-high heat. When hot, stir to dissolve the sugar. Bring to a boil. Pour the boiling cream over the chopped chocolate. Set aside for 5 minutes; then stir with a whisk until smooth. Add 2 cups red seedless grapes and 1 cup of the peanuts and stir to combine. Pour the mixture over the Chocolate Crunchy Corn Flake Layer in the springform pan, spreading evenly. Sprinkle the remaining ¼ cup peanuts over the surface of the top layer. Refrigerate the cake for 12 hours before cutting.

To Serve

Remove the cake from the refrigerator. Using a thin-bladed paring knife, cut around the inside edges of the pan, then release the cake from the sides of the springform pan (leave the cake on the bottom of the pan). Heat the blade of a serrated slicer under hot running water and wipe the blade dry before cutting each slice. Keep the slices at room temperature for 20 to 30 minutes before serving.

THE CHEF'S TOUCH

When you are a single working mom with six children, you can bet on plenty of corn flakes in the cupboard. If you are like my mom, Mrs. D, you will also have lots of chocolate

---

CHOCOLATE CRUNCHY CORN FLAKE LAYER

4 cups corn flakes

1 cup unsalted dry roasted peanuts, coarsely chopped

16 ounces semisweet baking chocolate, coarsely chopped

½ pound (2 sticks) unsalted butter, cut into ½-ounce pieces

CHOCOLATE PEANUT AND GRAPE LAYER

8 ounces semisweet baking chocolate, coarsely chopped

1¼ cups heavy cream

2 tablespoons unsalted butter, cut into 1-tablespoon pieces

2 tablespoons granulated sugar

2 cups red seedless grapes, stemmed, washed, and thoroughly dried

1¼ cups unsalted dry roasted peanuts

and peanuts at the ready to whip up a "happy and out of trouble" treat. So when the household chores loom higher than the Rockies, you will be as pleased as Mrs. D to have a no-bake cake in your repertoire.

My penchant for peanuts seems preposterous at times. My favorites are the freshly roasted Virginia peanuts from the Peanut Shop of Williamsburg. (If you use the Virginia peanuts for this recipe, toast the nuts in a 325°F oven for 10 to 12 minutes and allow to cool to room temperature before adding to the recipe.) However, to continue on a harmonious no-bake path with this recipe, I suggest using Planters unsalted dry roasted peanuts. Use them directly from the jar (no need to toast).

Mrs. D used raisins in her original recipe for the no-bake cake. Grapes were not financially feasible for her when we were kids. Now that she does not have to be quite as frugal, she loves the juicy surprise that fresh seedless grapes provide in their chocolate interment.

Turning over the bottom insert of the springform pan (the lip of the bottom insert facing down) before assembling the pan will make it easier to remove the cut portions from the bottom insert.

Mrs. D has a much more interesting variety of liquids in the refrigerator these days than when her children were in the growing-up-to-be-big-and-strong stage. Although my own tastes have changed, I still choose milk to go with the no-bake cake; otherwise, milk gets paired only with cereal at my house.

VIRGINIA'S COCOA POUND CAKE *with* WARM BUTTERED BRANDY BERRIES

SERVES 14

Make Virginia's Cocoa Pound Cake

Preheat the oven to 325°F. Liberally coat the inside of a 9½ × 4-inch nonstick angel food cake pan with the 2 teaspoons of melted butter. Set aside.

In a sifter combine 2¼ cups flour, ½ cup cocoa powder, ½ teaspoon baking powder, and ½ teaspoon salt. Sift onto a large piece of parchment paper (or wax paper). Set aside until needed.

Place 2¼ cups sugar and ¾ pound butter in the bowl of an electric mixer fitted with a paddle. Mix on low speed for 2 minutes; then beat on medium for 3 minutes until soft. Scrape down the sides of the bowl and the paddle. Beat for an additional 3 minutes on medium until softer. Scrape down the sides of the bowl; then beat for 2 minutes on high speed until even softer and slightly fluffy. Scrape down the sides of the bowl again. Add 5 eggs, one at a time, beating on medium for 30 seconds after each addition, and scraping down the sides of the bowl once all the eggs have been incorporated. Now beat on medium for 4 minutes. (The batter should have the texture of dense pastry cream.) Scrape down the sides of the bowl. Operate the mixer on low while gradually adding about half of the sifted dry ingredients followed by about half of the milk. Once these ingredients have been incorporated, about 1 minute, gradually add the remaining sifted dry ingredients, followed by the remaining milk, and mix on low until incorporated, about 1 minute. Add 1 teaspoon vanilla extract and beat on medium for 15 seconds until combined. Remove the bowl from the mixer and use a rubber spatula to finish mixing the batter until thoroughly combined.

Transfer the batter to the prepared angel food cake pan, using a rubber spatula to spread it evenly. Bake on the center rack of the preheated oven until a toothpick inserted in the center of the cake comes out with a few slightly moist, beadlike crumbs, about 1 hour and 6 minutes. (This baking time results in a cake that is moist throughout and fudgey under the baked crown; if you prefer a more traditional pound cake texture, bake for a total of 1 hour and 22 minutes.)

Remove the cake from the oven and cool in the pan at room temperature for 15 to 20 minutes. Turn the cake out of the pan onto a cardboard cake circle (or a cake plate). Now turn the cake baked top facing up. Set aside at room temperature.

Make the Buttered Brandy Berries

Place 3 pints whole fresh strawberries in a colander and spray them with lukewarm water.

COCOA POUND CAKE
- ¾ pound (3 sticks) unsalted butter, cut into ½-ounce pieces; plus 2 teaspoons (melted)
- 2¼ cups all-purpose flour
- ½ cup unsweetened cocoa powder
- ½ teaspoon baking powder
- ½ teaspoon salt
- 2¼ cups granulated sugar
- 5 large eggs
- ¾ cup whole milk
- 1 teaspoon pure vanilla extract

WARM BUTTERED BRANDY BERRIES
- 3 pints whole fresh strawberries
- ½ cup brandy
- ⅓ cup granulated sugar
- 4 tablespoons (½ stick) unsalted butter, cut into ½-ounce pieces

Gently shake the colander to remove excess water from the berries. Stem and then cut the berries crosswise into ½-inch-thick slices. Place the berries in an extra-large noncorrosive bowl. Pour ½ cup of brandy over the berries. Sprinkle ⅓ cup sugar over the berries, then toss gently to combine. Cover the top of the bowl with plastic wrap and set aside at room temperature to macerate for 30 to 60 minutes.

Strain the liquid from the bowl of strawberries into a large nonstick sauté pan, and set aside the berry slices. Heat the liquid over medium-high heat. Bring to a boil, then adjust the heat and simmer for 5 minutes until slightly syrupy. Add the berry slices and stir to combine. Heat for only 1 minute, then remove from the heat; add 4 tablespoons butter and stir until the butter has melted and blended with the syrup.

To Serve

Heat the blade of a serrated slicer under hot running water and wipe the blade dry before making each slice. Spoon an equal amount (about ⅓ cup) of Warm Buttered Brandy Berries onto each plate; then place a slice of cake on each portion of berries and serve immediately.

THE CHEF'S TOUCH

My mother-in-law, Virginia Warren, taught her three daughters a thing or two about striking a young man's fancy. But one of her best tricks of the trade was this Cocoa Pound Cake. For the Warren girls, learning to make Cocoa Pound Cake ranked up there with other rites of passage, like being allowed to wear lipstick. According to my wife, Connie, special boyfriends who were invited home for a slice usually wanted more—cake, of course. And for maximum reaction, all the Warrens recommend baking it "sorry" (translation: slightly underdone), since the resulting fudge ribbon of chocolate has aphrodisiac qualities. It certainly won me over.

Virginia's cake may also be prepared using cake flour instead of all-purpose flour. The end result with cake flour is a baked cake with a finer crumb. For the record, I prefer the all-purpose version.

"Woe is I," you say after reading the seemingly unending mixing of the batter. Be assured that the multiple mixings deliver a superior product.

I recommend heating the berries just prior to serving. They will warm in about 1 minute and, once removed from the heat source, the berries will continue to heat internally. So don't heat them too long, or they will lose texture, color, and much of their appeal.

If buttered brandy berries are not your bag, you may serve Virginia's Cocoa Pound Cake with ice cream, whipped cream, chocolate sauce, or alone (but preferably with a friend).

MARGIE'S GOLDEN RAISIN HEAVY FUDGE CAKE

SERVES 10

Make the Heavy Fudge Icing

Heat 2 cups dark brown sugar, 1¼ cups heavy cream, 1 cup half-and-half cream, and 8 ounces chopped unsweetened chocolate in a medium saucepan over medium heat. When hot, stir to dissolve the sugar and melt the chocolate. Bring to a boil. Adjust the heat to medium-low, and simmer the mixture for 25 minutes, stirring frequently, until thick and smooth. Remove the saucepan from the heat. Add 3 ounces butter, ½ ounce at a time, stirring to incorporate the butter before adding the next piece. Transfer the fudge mixture to a baking sheet with sides, spreading it evenly. Refrigerate for 1 hour until firm.

While the fudge mixture is chilling out in the fridge, make the Cocoa Golden Raisin Cake layers.

Make the Cocoa Golden Raisin Cake

Preheat the oven to 325°F. Lightly coat the insides of two 9 × 1½-inch nonstick cake pans with some of the 2 teaspoons of melted butter. Line the bottom of the pans with parchment paper (or wax paper), then lightly coat the paper with more melted butter. Set aside.

Place 1 cup golden raisins in a small bowl. Sprinkle the 1 teaspoon of flour over the raisins. Using your hands, toss the raisins to lightly cover them with the flour. (The light dusting of flour will help prevent the raisins from sinking to the bottom of the cake layers during baking.)

In a sifter, combine 1¾ cups flour, 2 tablespoons cocoa powder, 1 teaspoon baking soda, and ¼ teaspoon salt. Sift onto a large piece of parchment paper (or wax paper) and set aside until needed.

Place 6 ounces unsalted butter and 1 cup sugar in the bowl of an electric mixer fitted with a paddle. Mix on low speed for 1 minute; then beat on medium for 2 minutes until soft. Scrape down the sides of the bowl and the paddle. Add 2 eggs, one at a time, beating on medium for 30 seconds after each addition, and scraping down the sides of the bowl once both eggs have been incorporated.

Operate the mixer on low while gradually adding half of the sifted dry ingredients; mix until incorporated, about 30 seconds. Add ¼ cup of the apple juice and mix on low to combine, about 15 seconds. Gradually add the remaining dry ingredients while mixing on low until combined, about 20 seconds. Add the remaining ¼ cup apple juice and mix on low to combine, about 15 seconds. Scrape down the sides of the bowl. Add ½ cup sour cream and mix on medium to combine, about 15 seconds. Remove the bowl from the mixer, add the flour-dusted golden raisins, and then use a rubber spatula to finish mixing the batter until thoroughly combined. Imme-

HEAVY FUDGE ICING

- 2 cups (1 pound) tightly packed dark brown sugar
- 1¼ cups heavy cream
- 1 cup half-and-half cream
- 8 ounces unsweetened baking chocolate, coarsely chopped
- 3 ounces unsalted butter, cut into ½-ounce pieces

COCOA GOLDEN RAISIN CAKE

- 6 ounces (1½ sticks) unsalted butter, cut into ½-ounce pieces; plus 2 teaspoons (melted)
- 1 cup golden raisins
- 1¾ cups plus 1 teaspoon all-purpose flour
- 2 tablespoons unsweetened cocoa powder
- 1 teaspoon baking soda
- ¼ teaspoon salt
- 1 cup granulated sugar
- 2 large eggs
- ½ cup 100 percent pure apple juice
- ½ cup sour cream

diately divide the cake batter into the prepared pans (about 2½ cups of batter in each one), spreading it evenly.

Bake on the center rack in the preheated oven until a toothpick inserted in the center of each cake layer comes out clean, about 28 minutes. Remove the layers from the oven and cool in the pans for 15 minutes at room temperature. Invert the cake layers onto cake circles (or cake plates) that are covered with plastic wrap. (This keeps the cake layers from sticking.) Carefully peel the paper away from the bottoms of the cake layers. Refrigerate the cake layers until needed.

Assemble the Cake

Place the chilled fudge in the bowl of an electric mixer fitted with a paddle. Beat on medium speed for 1 minute until thoroughly combined. Scrape down the sides of the bowl and the paddle. Beat on medium for 30 more seconds until slightly fluffy.

Remove the cake layers from the refrigerator. Use a cake spatula to spread 2 cups of icing evenly and smoothly over the top and to the edges of one of the inverted cake layers. Place a second cake layer, inverted side up, onto the icing-coated cake layer and gently press it into place. Spread the remaining 3¾ cups of icing over the top and sides of the cake.

Refrigerate the cake for 2 hours before slicing and serving.

To Serve

Heat the blade of a serrated slicer under hot running water and wipe the blade dry before cutting each slice. Serve immediately.

THE CHEF'S TOUCH

It seems natural that Marjorie Poore, the producer of such popular public television programs as *Cookoff America*, *Cooking Secrets of the CIA*, and *Home Cooking with Amy Coleman*, would have an impressive repertoire of her own recipes. Despite all the travel, anxiety, and rigors of on-the-road television production work, Margie still finds time to enchant her family, and sometimes her production crews, with an irresistible confection.

The Golden Raisin Heavy Fudge Cake recipe is one that Margie adapted from a cake that her mom would make frequently. Margie explains that often the completed cake "would never make it out of the kitchen," as the family was deft at "sneaking in and cutting slices and slivers" until there was no more. Nowadays, with only husband Alec and daughter Jennifer at home, the cake has a higher survival rate, and sometimes a few pieces make it to the studio, to the delight of her crew.

Golden raisins are produced from Thompson seedless grapes that have been treated with sulfur dioxide to prevent their darkening.

This cake may be prepared over 2 days. DAY 1: Bake the Cocoa Golden Raisin Cake layers. Once cooled, cover each layer with plastic wrap and refrigerate until the next day. DAY 2: Make the Heavy Fudge Icing, then ice and assemble the cake as directed in the recipe. Refrigerate the cake for 2 hours before slicing and serving.

Taking a cue from one of the Cocoa Golden Raisin Cake ingredients, cold 100 percent pure apple juice is an excellent beverage to quench the crew's thirst when polishing off Margie's cake.

CELEBRATION CAKES

ENTERTAINING CHOCOLATE CREATIONS FOR SPECIAL OCCASIONS

GOLDEN ANNIVERSARY CHOCOLATE CHIP BROWNIE CAKE

SERVES 12

Make the Brownie Cake

Preheat the oven to 325°F. Lightly coat the insides of two 9 × 1½-inch nonstick cake pans with some of the 2 teaspoons of melted butter. Line the bottoms of the pans with parchment paper (or wax paper); then lightly coat the paper with more melted butter. Set aside.

In a sifter combine 2 cups flour, ½ teaspoon baking powder, and ¼ teaspoon salt. Sift onto a large piece of parchment paper (or wax paper) and set aside until needed.

Place 2 cups light brown sugar and ½ pound butter in the bowl of an electric mixer fitted with a paddle. Mix on low speed for 1 minute, then on medium-high for 4 minutes until soft. Use a rubber spatula to scrape down the sides of the bowl; then beat on medium-high for 2 more minutes. Scrape down the sides of the bowl again. Add 3 eggs, one at a time, beating on medium for 1 minute after each addition, and scraping down the sides of the bowl once all the eggs have been incorporated. Operate the mixer on low while gradually adding the sifted dry ingredients. Once they have been incorporated, about 45 seconds, add ½ cup sour cream and 2 teaspoons vanilla extract and mix on low speed to combine, about 20 seconds. Add 1 cup chocolate chips and combine on low for 10 seconds. Remove the bowl from the mixer

and use a rubber spatula to finish mixing the ingredients until thoroughly combined.

Immediately divide the cake batter into the prepared pans (about 3 cups of batter in each pan), spreading the batter evenly. Bake on the center rack in the preheated oven until a toothpick inserted in the center of each cake layer comes out clean (spearing a chocolate chip doesn't count), about 40 minutes. Remove the cake layers from the oven and cool in the pans for 20 minutes at room temperature. Invert the cake layers onto cake circles or cake plates. (The cakes should readily release from the pans; if not, use a paring knife to cut around the inside edges of the pan before inverting.) Carefully peel the paper away from the bottoms of the cake layers and set aside at room temperature until needed.

Make the Golden Sugar

Place 2 cups sugar and 1 teaspoon lemon juice in a large saucepan. Stir with a whisk to combine. (The sugar will resemble moist sand.)

Caramelize the sugar for about 10 minutes over medium-high heat, stirring constantly with a whisk to break up any lumps. The sugar will first turn clear as it liquefies, then light brown as it caramelizes. Remove the saucepan from the heat. Immediately pour the caramelized sugar onto a nonstick

BROWNIE CAKE

½ pound (2 sticks) unsalted butter, cut into ½-ounce pieces; plus 2 teaspoons (melted)

2 cups all-purpose flour

½ teaspoon baking powder

¼ teaspoon salt

2 cups (1 pound) tightly packed light brown sugar

3 large eggs

½ cup sour cream

2 teaspoons pure vanilla extract

1 cup semisweet chocolate chips

GOLDEN SUGAR

2 cups granulated sugar

1 teaspoon fresh lemon juice

CARAMEL

2½ cups granulated sugar

1 teaspoon fresh lemon juice

1 cup heavy cream

CARAMEL BUTTERCREAM

1¼ pounds (5 sticks) unsalted butter, cut into ½-ounce pieces

½ cup granulated sugar

¼ cup light corn syrup

3 large egg yolks

baking sheet with sides and place in the freezer to harden, about 10 minutes. (If you are short on room in your freezer, you may harden the sugar in the refrigerator, about 20 minutes; the sugar will also harden in an air-conditioned room, about 30 minutes.)

Use the top edge of the blade of a cook's knife to strike and break the hardened caramelized sugar into smaller pieces. Pulse the pieces of golden sugar in a food processor fitted with a metal blade for about 45 seconds, until it is finely chopped. Sift the sugar in a medium-gauge strainer. Remove the chopped sugar from the strainer, and store it in a tightly sealed plastic container until ready to use for decorating the cake. (Save the finely sifted golden sugar to sweeten your coffee.)

Prepare the Caramel

Place 2½ cups sugar and 1 teaspoon fresh lemon juice in a large saucepan. Stir with a whisk to combine.

Caramelize the sugar for about 12 minutes over medium-high heat, stirring constantly with a whisk to break up any lumps. Remove the saucepan from the heat. Slowly add 1 cup heavy cream to the bubbling hot sugar, whisking vigorously until smooth. (Adding the cream to the sugar creates very hot steam, so be careful to avoid a steam burn on your whisking hand.) Transfer the caramel to a medium bowl and set aside at room temperature.

Make the Caramel Buttercream

Place 1¼ pounds butter in the bowl of an electric mixer fitted with a paddle. Mix on low speed for 1 minute, then beat on medium for 2 minutes. Scrape down the sides of the bowl and the paddle. Beat on medium-high for 4 minutes until pale yellow in color and almost double in volume. Transfer the whipped butter to a medium bowl and set aside until needed.

Heat ¼ cup of the sugar and ¼ cup light corn syrup in a small saucepan over medium heat. Stir to combine and bring to a boil. Meanwhile place 3 egg yolks and remaining ¼ cup sugar in the bowl of an electric mixer fitted with a balloon whip. Whisk on high until pale yellow in color and slightly thickened, about 3 minutes. At this point the sugar syrup should be boiling and clear. Slowly drizzle the boiling syrup into the egg yolks while whisking on medium. Once the mixture is combined, increase the speed to high, and whisk for 5 minutes until thoroughly mixed. Scrape down the sides of the bowl. Add 1 cup of the caramel from the bowl and whisk on high for 5 more minutes. Add about half the amount of whipped butter and whisk on medium for 30 seconds, then add the remaining butter and whisk on medium for another 15 seconds. Scrape down the sides of the bowl. Now whisk on high for 5 minutes until the caramel buttercream is light and fluffy. Set aside at room temperature until ready to assemble the cake. (Cover the remaining caramel with plastic wrap and set it aside at room temperature as well.)

Assemble the Cake

Transfer 1 cup of caramel buttercream to a pastry bag fitted with a medium star tip. Set aside.

Use a cake spatula to spread 1½ cups caramel buttercream evenly and smoothly over the top and sides of one of the inverted cake layers. Turn the second cake layer right side up, place it on top of the iced cake layer, and press down gently but firmly to level the layers. Smoothly spread the remaining caramel buttercream (excluding the buttercream in the pastry bag) over the top and sides of the cake. Pipe out a circle of stars (about 1 inch high and 1 inch wide), each one touching the next, along the outside edge of the top of the cake. Press the finely chopped golden sugar into the sides of the cake, coating evenly. Finally, pour the remaining caramel onto the top of the cake. (The caramel should spread over the top to the inside edges of the buttercream stars.)

Refrigerate for several hours before serving.

To Serve

Heat the blade of a serrated slicer under hot running water and wipe the blade dry before cutting each slice. Place each slice onto a serving plate and keep at room temperature for about 30 minutes before serving. (This will allow the caramel to flow attractively and deliciously over the sides.)

THE CHEF'S TOUCH

When my wife, Connie, told her parents that she and her four brothers and sisters were planning a fiftieth anniversary party for them, her parents said they did not want a party. The young-at-heart couple felt they weren't old enough to celebrate a fiftieth anniversary. Visions of a swarm of septuagenarians toasting the good old days was not their idea of fun. The siblings fell into their traditional childish roles, and disobeyed their parents by throwing an "Anti-versary" party. To appease, they promised the couple that they would be the oldest ones there, and pledged a night of celebratory decadence. Decadent indeed—especially the Chocolate Chip Brownie Cake that The Trellis's pastry chef, Kelly Bailey, created for the occasion. (P.S. The children were forgiven.)

Is caramel really burnt sugar? Not unless it is burnt caramel. Although caramel is easy enough to prepare, it's also fairly easy to burn if you don't give it your undivided attention.

If the caramel for the top of the cake becomes too stiff to pour, place the bowl of caramel in a container of hot water to warm until the caramel is free-flowing but not hot; otherwise, it will melt the buttercream.

The caramel on top of the cake must be very firm before the cake can be cut into perfect slices; otherwise, the caramel will drool down the sides of the piece of cake (an appealingly sexy alternative presentation). For a perfectly clean cut, refrigerate the cake for 24 hours before slicing.

The cooled Brownie Cake layers may be frozen for an extended period (up to 3 to 4 weeks). Be certain to thoroughly wrap the cakes in plastic wrap to prevent dehydration and to protect them from freezer odors. The Golden Sugar may also be stored in an airtight plastic container in the freezer for an indefinite period of time.

This cake may be prepared over 3 days. DAY 1: Bake the Brownie Cake layers. Once cooled, cover each layer with plastic wrap and refrigerate until assembling the whole cake.

Prepare the Golden Sugar, then store in an airtight plastic container in the freezer until needed. DAY 2: Prepare the Caramel and the Caramel Buttercream, then assemble the cake and refrigerate until the next day. DAY 3: Slice and serve the cake as directed.

Of course, a Golden Anniversary celebration would not be complete without champagne. To complement the rich textures and unrestrained sweetness of this cake, I would select a very dry but lively (lots of persistent bubbles) 1990 Perrier Jouët Fleur de Champagne.

UNCLE SAM'S *in the* BLACK CAKE

SERVES 12 TO 16

Prepare the Very Dark Chocolate Cake

Preheat the oven to 325°F. Assemble a 10 × 2¾-inch nonstick springform pan with the bottom insert turned over (the lip of the insert facing down). Lightly coat the inside of the springform pan with the 1 teaspoon of melted butter. Set aside.

Melt the remaining 1 pound of butter and 1 pound chopped semisweet chocolate in the top half of a double boiler or in a microwave oven (see pages 197–98 for details).

While the chocolate and butter are melting, put 1 cup hot coffee and 1 cup sugar in the bowl of an electric mixer fitted with a paddle, and mix on low speed until the sugar is dissolved. Add the melted chocolate mixture to the coffee and combine on low speed for 30 seconds. Add all 6 egg yolks to the chocolate at once, and combine on medium speed for 1 minute until incorporated. Scrape down the sides of the bowl. Add the 6 whole eggs, one at a time, mixing on medium speed and waiting until each egg is incorporated into the mixture before adding the next. Remove the bowl from the mixer and use a rubber spatula to scrape down the sides of the bowl and finish mixing the batter until smooth and thoroughly combined.

Transfer the batter to the prepared springform pan; spread it evenly using a rubber spatula. Place the pan onto a baking sheet with sides on the center rack in the preheated oven. Bake for 1 hour, until the internal temperature of the cake reaches 170°F. (The cake may still appear to be moist, especially toward the center, but the internal temperature of the cake is the key.) Remove the cake from the oven and let it cool in the pan at room temperature for 15 minutes. Refrigerate the cake (in the pan) for 1 hour.

Make the Toasted Oatmeal Raisin Topping

Preheat the oven to 325°F. Toast 2 cups oats on a baking sheet in the preheated oven for 18 to 20 minutes until lightly golden. (The toasting does much to enhance the flavor of the oats.) Set aside. Place 12 ounces chopped semisweet chocolate in a medium bowl. Heat 1 cup heavy cream in a small saucepan over medium-high heat. Bring to a boil. Pour the boiling cream over the chopped chocolate. Set aside for 5 minutes before stirring with a whisk until smooth. Add the oats and the raisins to the chocolate and cream mixture and use a rubber spatula to stir until thoroughly combined. Set aside for a few minutes.

Prepare the White Chocolate Glaze

Heat ½ pound chopped white chocolate and ¼ cup heavy cream together in the top half of a double boiler over medium-low heat. Use a

VERY DARK CHOCOLATE CAKE

1 pound (4 sticks) unsalted butter, cut into ½-ounce pieces; plus 1 teaspoon (melted)

1 pound semisweet baking chocolate, coarsely chopped

1 cup brewed full-strength coffee, hot

1 cup granulated sugar

6 large egg yolks

6 large eggs

TOASTED OATMEAL RAISIN TOPPING

2 cups Old-Fashioned Quaker Oats

12 ounces semisweet baking chocolate, coarsely chopped

1 cup heavy cream

1½ cups raisins

WHITE CHOCOLATE GLAZE

½ pound white chocolate, coarsely chopped

¼ cup heavy cream

rubber spatula to stir the chocolate and cream until completely melted and smooth, 6 to 6½ minutes. Remove from the heat and set aside until needed.

Assemble the Cake

Remove the cake from the refrigerator. Transfer the Toasted Oatmeal Raisin Topping to the top of the cake inside the pan, and use a rubber spatula to spread the topping evenly over the surface of the cake. Pour the White Chocolate Glaze over the topping, and use a cake spatula to spread the glaze evenly over the surface of the topping. Refrigerate the cake in the pan for several hours before slicing and serving.

To Serve

Remove the cake from the refrigerator. Using a thin-bladed paring knife, cut around the inside edges of the pan, then release the cake from the sides of the springform pan. (Leave the cake on the bottom of the pan.) Heat the blade of a serrated slicer under hot running water and wipe the blade dry before cutting each slice. Keep the slices at room temperature for 20 to 30 minutes before serving.

THE CHEF'S TOUCH

Uncle Sam's in the Black Cake won't guarantee a refund on your taxes, but it may make it easier to face the tax man, armed with this tantalizingly dark, rich, and chewy cake. The White Chocolate Glaze could be a metaphor for the light at the end of the tunnel.

Turning over the bottom insert of the springform pan (the lip of the bottom insert facing down) before assembling the pan will make it easier to remove the cake slices from the bottom insert.

Batter may seep from the bottom of the springform pan, so it's wise to bake the cake on a baking sheet with sides. If you have a dented or misshapen springform pan, consider wrapping the sides and bottom of the pan with a single sheet of aluminum foil.

For variety, try dried fruits other than raisins for the topping, such as dried tart red cherries or cranberries. Adding more than one fruit won't increase your deductions, but it will leave a more pleasant taste in your mouth than that tax bill will!

Refrigerate the cake for several hours so that it is firm enough to be cut into perfect slices. Overnight refrigeration would ensure an easily sliced cake.

CRISPY COCONUT COCOA CREAM CROCUS CAKE

SERVES 8

Make the Crocus Cake

Preheat the oven to 325°F. Place 2 to 3 pinches saffron threads in a cup-size container. Pour ⅓ cup boiling water over the saffron and steep for 15 minutes. Stir occasionally to help the dissipation of the saffron.

Lightly coat the insides of two 9 × 1½-inch nonstick cake pans with some of the 2 teaspoons of melted butter. Line the bottoms of the pans with parchment paper (or wax paper); then lightly coat the paper with more melted butter. Set aside.

In a sifter combine 2 cups cake flour, 1½ teaspoons baking powder, and ½ teaspoon salt. Sift onto a large piece of parchment paper (or wax paper). Set aside.

Place ¾ cup of the sugar and 5 ounces butter in the bowl of an electric mixer fitted with a paddle. Mix on low speed for 1 minute, then beat on medium-high for 3 minutes. Use a rubber spatula to scrape down the sides of the bowl, then beat on medium-high for an additional 2 minutes until soft. Scrape down the sides of the bowl. Operate the mixer on low while gradually adding half the sifted dry ingredients; mix for 30 seconds. Gradually add the water and saffron mixture, and mix on low to incorporate, about 20 seconds. While continuing to operate the mixer on low, gradually add the remaining sifted dry ingredients, and mix for 30 seconds. Scrape down the sides of the bowl. Add ⅔ cup milk, 1 teaspoon vanilla extract, and 3 to 4 drops yellow food coloring and mix on low for 20 seconds; then beat on medium for 30 seconds. Remove the bowl from the mixer and use a rubber spatula to finish mixing the ingredients until thoroughly combined. Set aside while whisking the egg whites.

Place 4 egg whites in the (very clean and very dry) bowl of an electric mixer fitted with a balloon whip. Whisk on high speed until soft peaks form, about 1 minute. Add the remaining ¼ cup of granulated sugar and whisk on high until stiff, but not dry, about 1 minute. Remove the bowl from the mixer. Using a rubber spatula, quickly fold about half the whisked egg whites into the saffron-colored mixture, then fold in the remaining whisked egg whites until thoroughly combined.

Immediately divide the batter into the prepared pans, spreading it evenly. Bake on the center rack in the preheated oven until a toothpick inserted into the center of each cake layer comes out clean, about 25 minutes. Remove the layers from the oven and cool in the pans at room temperature for 15 minutes. Invert the cake layers onto cake circles (or onto cake plates) covered with parchment paper (or wax paper). Carefully peel the paper away

CROCUS CAKE

2 to 3 pinches saffron threads (0.8 gram)

⅓ cup boiling water

5 ounces unsalted butter, cut into ½-ounce pieces; plus 2 teaspoons (melted)

2 cups cake flour

1½ teaspoons baking powder

½ teaspoon salt

1 cup granulated sugar

⅔ cup whole milk

1 teaspoon pure vanilla extract

3 to 4 drops yellow food coloring

4 large egg whites

COCOA CREAM

2 cups heavy cream

½ cup confectioners' sugar

¼ cup unsweetened cocoa powder

1 tablespoon pure vanilla extract

GARNISH

4 ounces dried coconut flakes

1 red peanut M&M

from the bottoms of the cake layers. Refrigerate until needed.

Make the Cocoa Cream

Place 2 cups heavy cream and ½ cup confectioners' sugar in the bowl of an electric mixer fitted with a balloon whip. Mix on low speed for 15 seconds, then increase speed to medium-high, and whisk for 1 minute until soft peaks form. Add ¼ cup cocoa powder and mix on low for 15 seconds, then increase speed to high and whisk until stiff peaks form, 20 to 25 seconds. Add 1 tablespoon vanilla extract and whisk on medium for 10 seconds. Refrigerate until needed.

To Assemble the Cake

Preheat the oven to 325°F. Toast 4 ounces dried coconut on a baking sheet in the preheated oven until golden and crispy, 5 to 6 minutes. Remove the coconut from the oven and set aside at room temperature until needed.

Remove the cake layers from the refrigerator. Turn one of the inverted cakes over and back onto the cake circle (or cake plate), baked top facing up. Use a cake spatula to evenly and smoothly spread 1½ cups of the Cocoa Cream over the top and to the edges of the cake layer. Place the peanut M&M (oh, sweet morsel, your destiny awaits) into the Cocoa Cream. Invert the second cake layer onto the Cocoa Cream–coated cake layer and gently press into place. Spread the remaining Cocoa Cream evenly and smoothly over the top and sides of the cake. Refrigerate the cake for 30 minutes. Press the Crispy Coconut onto the top and into the sides of the cake. Refrigerate for 1 hour before serving.

To Serve

Heat the blade of a serrated slicer under hot running water and wipe the blade dry before making each slice. Place each slice onto a serving plate and keep at room temperature for 10 to 15 minutes before serving. (The cake is also good directly from the refrigerator, but it really blossoms in flavor after a few minutes out of the fridge.)

THE CHEF'S TOUCH

It's a mystery . . . a mystery. Who will get the slice of Crocus Cake with the concealed red M&M? How will saffron taste in a cake? But why quibble; this unusual combination of flavors may sound inscrutable, but it's elementally delicious.

We purchased saffron threads at the supermarket, packaged 0.4 gram in a glass jar, which, at the time, set us back $8.99 each.

If you don't have a second mixing bowl for your table-model mixer (you will find that having a second or third bowl is a great convenience for many recipes), whisk the egg whites by hand, using a wire whisk or a handheld mixer, in an impeccably clean and dry stainless steel or copper bowl.

Dried coconut flakes can be located in the bulk-foods section of most supermarkets, probably near the dried fruits or nuts. Other types of packaged coconut or fresh coconut will not work for this recipe because they won't get crispy.

After assembly, you may keep the Crispy Coconut Cocoa Cream Crocus Cake in the refrigerator for a day or two before serving. However, if the cake is not to be served within 2 to 3 hours after final assembly, wait until just before serving to apply the crispy coconut to the top and sides of the cake; otherwise, the coconut will lose its crispiness. To avoid permeating the cake with refrigerator odors, place the cake in a large, tightly sealed plastic container.

This cake may be prepared over 3 days. DAY 1: Bake the Crocus Cake layers. Once cooled, cover each layer with plastic wrap and refrigerate until the next day. DAY 2: Make the Cocoa Cream, then ice the cake (don't forget to hide the red peanut M&M), and refrigerate in a sealed plastic container until the next day. DAY 3: Two to 3 hours before serving, toast the coconut garnish and assemble the cake. Slice and serve the cake.

The tongue may struggle to pronounce Trockenbeerenausle, but the honey and apricot essence of this German Riesling will lull it back into place. Matched with the Crocus Cake, an indulgent harmony will occur (any bacchanalian results are not the responsibility of the author).

MRS. D'S CHOCOLATE BIRTHDAY EXTRAVAGANZA CAKE

SERVES 12 TO 24

Make Her Favorite Chocolate Cake

Preheat the oven to 325°F. Lightly coat the insides of four 9 × 1½-inch nonstick cake pans using some of the 1 tablespoon of melted butter. Line the bottoms of the pans with parchment paper (or wax paper), and then lightly coat the paper with more melted butter. Set aside.

In a sifter combine 1½ cups flour, 2 teaspoons baking powder, and 1 teaspoon salt. Sift onto a large piece of parchment paper (or wax paper) and set aside until needed.

Melt together 6 ounces chopped semisweet chocolate, 3 ounces chopped unsweetened chocolate, and ¼ pound butter in the top half of a double boiler, or in a microwave oven. (See pages 197–98 for more details.)

Place 7 eggs and 1½ cups sugar in the bowl of an electric mixer fitted with a paddle. Beat on medium-high speed for 2 minutes until slightly thickened. Add the melted chocolate and butter mixture and beat on medium speed for 30 seconds until combined. Operate the mixer on low while gradually adding the sifted dry ingredients; mix until incorporated, about 30 seconds. Use a rubber spatula to scrape down the sides of the bowl. Add ½ cup sour cream and 1 tablespoon vanilla extract and mix on medium to combine, about 30 seconds.

Remove the bowl from the mixer and use a rubber spatula to finish mixing the ingredients until thoroughly combined. The batter certainly looks "lickable," but don't do it— raw egg consumption is a no-no. Immediately divide the cake batter into the prepared pans (a bit more than 1½ cups of batter in each pan), spreading it evenly. Bake on the top and center racks in the preheated oven until a toothpick inserted in the center of each cake layer comes out clean, about 22 minutes. (Rotate the pans from top to center halfway through the baking time.) Remove the cake layers from the oven and cool in the pans for 10 minutes at room temperature. Invert the cake layers onto cake circles (or cake plates) that have been wrapped with plastic wrap or lined with parchment paper or wax paper. Carefully peel the paper away from the bottoms of the cake layers. Refrigerate the layers for at least 30 minutes before assembling.

Prepare the Quintessential Chocolate Ganache

While the cake layers are baking, prepare the ganache. Place 12 ounces semisweet chocolate and 4 ounces unsweetened chocolate in a large bowl.

HER FAVORITE CHOCOLATE CAKE

¼ pound (1 stick) unsalted butter, cut into ½-ounce pieces; plus 1 tablespoon (melted)

1½ cups cake flour

2 teaspoons baking powder

1 teaspoon salt

6 ounces semisweet baking chocolate, coarsely chopped

3 ounces unsweetened chocolate, coarsely chopped

7 large eggs

1½ cups granulated sugar

½ cup sour cream

1 tablespoon pure vanilla extract

QUINTESSENTIAL CHOCOLATE GANACHE

12 ounces semisweet baking chocolate, coarsely chopped

4 ounces unsweetened baking chocolate, coarsely chopped

2 cups heavy cream

2 tablespoons granulated sugar

CHOCOLATE CASHEW MOUSSE

2 cups heavy cream

¾ cup granulated sugar

4 ounces unsweetened baking chocolate, coarsely chopped and melted (pages 197–98)

1 cup whole unsalted cashews, toasted (page 199) and coarsely chopped

MINI-MORSEL EXTRAVAGANZA

12 ounces semisweet chocolate mini-morsels

Heat 2 cups heavy cream and 2 table-spoons sugar in a small saucepan over medium-high heat. When hot, stir to dissolve the sugar. Bring to a boil. Pour the boiling cream over the chopped chocolate. Set aside for 5 minutes before stirring with a whisk until smooth. Pour the ganache onto a baking sheet with sides, spreading it evenly. Set the ganache aside at room temperature until needed.

Begin the Cake Assembly

Remove the cake layers from the refrigerator. Use a cake spatula to evenly and smoothly spread 1 cup of the ganache over the top and to the edges of each of 3 of the inverted cake layers. Stack the ganache-coated cake layers (use a utility turner to remove them from the cake circles); then top with the last inverted cake layer, bottom facing up. Refrigerate the cake for 2 hours, until the ganache layers are firm, before making the mousse.

Make the Chocolate Cashew Mousse

Place 2 cups heavy cream and ¾ cup sugar in the bowl of an electric mixer fitted with a balloon whip. Whisk on medium-high for 1½ minutes until firm, but not stiff, peaks form. Add 1 cup of the whipped cream to 4 ounces melted unsweetened chocolate, and use a rubber spatula to fold together until thoroughly combined. Add the combined whipped cream and chocolate to the remaining whipped cream, and use a rubber spatula to fold together until smooth and thoroughly combined. Add 1 cup chopped cashews to the mousse, and use a rubber spatula to quickly fold the nuts into the mousse. Refrigerate until needed.

Finish Assembling the Cake and Garnish with Mini-morsels

Remove the cake from the refrigerator. With a smooth cake spatula, smooth the ganache that has flowed over to the sides of the cake layers. Use a cake spatula to evenly spread the Chocolate Cashew Mousse onto the top and sides of the cake. Refrigerate the cake for 30 minutes.

Press 12 ounces semisweet chocolate mini-morsels into the sides of the cake, coating evenly. Refrigerate the cake for 2 hours before cutting and serving.

THE CHEF'S TOUCH

Mrs. D (my mom) celebrated her eightieth birthday with a surprise extravaganza at my sister Paulette's home in Warwick, Rhode Island. Besides all of Mrs. D's kids (there are six of us) and their spouses, joining us were a handful of grandchildren, a gaggle of cousins, and a horde of friends, bringing the crowd to one hundred or so. Although we hired a caterer to feed the enthusiastic throng, the birthday cake was, of course, my responsibility.

I informed Kelly Bailey, Trellis pastry chef, of Mrs. D's favorite ingredients—lots of chocolate, vanilla, heavy cream, and cashews. Her creation was a sensual, tongue-massaging confection of such delight that everyone wondered about the fuss over Viagra.

After I was emboldened by a sufficient quantity of fermented grape juice, I kiddingly asked Mrs. D if she could spell "octogenarian." Her tart reply was "I can, and now I'm working on 'centenarian.'" I have marked my calendar for November 8, 2018, for quite a party.

This cake can easily serve up to 24 people (at The Trellis, we usually cut ours into 10 pieces). A downside to the smaller pieces is not only less chocolate pleasure but the thinner slices would need to be placed cut side down on the plate rather than standing tall.

This cake may be prepared over 3 days. DAY 1: Bake Her Favorite Chocolate Cake layers. Once cooled, refrigerate the layers for at least 30 minutes. While the cake layers are baking, make the Quintessential Chocolate Ganache. Coat each cake layer with ganache. Stack the layers, then refrigerate in a large, tightly sealed plastic container. DAY 2: Make and then cover the cake with the Chocolate Cashew Mousse. Decorate with the mini-morsels, then refrigerate the cake in a large, tightly sealed plastic container. DAY 3: Slice and serve the cake as directed.

When my wife, Connie, and I headed north from Williamsburg toward Warwick with cakes in tow, we also brought the beverage to fit the occasion: bubbly as a starry night, pinkish in color, smooth and creamy in flavor, and possessing taste characteristics of fresh plums. I'm afraid the pedigree of the liquid will stay secret until the statute of limitations is no longer in force for interstate transport of what you have already surmised. Let's just say it was perfect with the cake.

JULIA'S EIGHTY-FIFTH BIRTHDAY CAKE

SERVES 12 TO 24

Make the Chocolate Almond Cake

Preheat the oven to 325°F. Lightly coat the insides of four 9 × 1½-inch nonstick cake pans with some of the 1 tablespoon of melted butter. Line the bottoms of the pans with parchment paper (or wax paper), then lightly coat the paper with more melted butter. Set aside.

In a sifter combine 2½ cups flour, 1 teaspoon baking powder, 1 teaspoon baking soda, and 1 teaspoon salt. Sift onto a large piece of parchment paper (or wax paper) and set aside until needed.

Place ½ pound butter and 1 cup sugar in the bowl of an electric mixer fitted with a paddle. Mix on low speed for 1 minute, then beat on medium-high for 3 minutes until soft. Use a rubber spatula to scrape down the sides of the bowl and the paddle, then beat on medium-high for an additional minute. Scrape down the sides of the bowl. Add 2 eggs, one at a time, beating on medium for 20 seconds after each addition, and scraping down the sides of the bowl once both eggs have been incorporated. Operate the mixer on low while gradually adding half the sifted dry ingredients; mix until incorporated, about 30 seconds. Add ½ cup sour cream and 2 teaspoons almond extract and mix on medium to combine, about 15 seconds. Gradually add the remaining dry ingredients while

mixing on low speed until combined, about 20 seconds. Add ½ cup amaretto in a slow, steady stream and mix on low to combine, about 30 seconds. Remove the bowl from the mixer, add ¾ cup sliced toasted almonds and the grated chocolate, and use a rubber spatula to finish mixing the ingredients until thoroughly combined. Immediately divide the cake batter into the prepared pans (about 1½ cups of batter in each pan), spreading it evenly. Bake on the top and center racks in the preheated oven until a toothpick inserted in the center of each cake layer comes out clean, about 20 minutes. (Rotate the pans from top to center halfway through the baking time.) Remove the cakes from the oven and cool in the pans for 15 minutes at room temperature. Invert the layers onto cake circles (or directly onto cake plates). Carefully peel the paper away from the bottoms of the cake layers. Refrigerate the cake layers until needed.

Prepare the Chocolate Red Raspberry Mousse

Place 2¼ cups heavy cream, ½ cup sugar, and 1 tablespoon instant espresso powder in the bowl of an electric mixer fitted with a balloon whip. Whisk on medium-high for 2 minutes until firm, but not stiff, peaks form. Add 1½

CHOCOLATE ALMOND CAKE

½ pound (2 sticks) unsalted butter, cut into ½-ounce pieces; plus 1 tablespoon (melted)

2½ cups all-purpose flour

1 teaspoon baking powder

1 teaspoon baking soda

1 teaspoon salt

1 cup granulated sugar

2 large eggs

½ cup sour cream

2 teaspoons almond extract

½ cup amaretto

¾ cup sliced almonds, toasted (page 199)

3 ounces semisweet baking chocolate, finely grated

CHOCOLATE RED RASPBERRY MOUSSE

2¼ cups heavy cream

½ cup granulated sugar

1 tablespoon instant espresso powder

6 ounces unsweetened baking chocolate, coarsely chopped and melted (pages 197–98)

1 pint fresh red raspberries

QUINTESSENTIAL CHOCOLATE GANACHE

12 ounces semisweet baking chocolate, coarsely chopped

4 ounces unsweetened baking chocolate, coarsely chopped

2 cups heavy cream

2 tablespoons granulated sugar

THE FINISHING TOUCH

1 cup sliced almonds

1 ounce milk chocolate,
coarsely chopped

1 ounce semisweet baking
chocolate, coarsely chopped

cups of the whipped cream to 6 ounces melted unsweetened chocolate, and use a rubber spatula to fold together until thoroughly combined. Add the combined whipped cream and chocolate to the remaining whipped cream and use a rubber spatula to fold together until smooth and thoroughly combined. Now use the rubber spatula to fold in 1 pint red raspberries.

Begin the Cake Assembly

Remove the cake layers from the refrigerator. Use a cake spatula to evenly and smoothly spread about 1¾ cups of Chocolate Red Raspberry Mousse over the top and to the edges of each of 3 of the inverted cake layers. Stack the mousse-coated cake layers (use a utility turner to remove the layers from the cake circles); then top with the last inverted cake layer, bottom facing up. Refrigerate the cake for 1 hour, until the mousse layers have firmed, before making the ganache.

Make the Quintessential Chocolate Ganache and Coat the Cake

Place 12 ounces chopped semisweet chocolate and 4 ounces chopped unsweetened chocolate in a large bowl.

Heat 2 cups heavy cream and 2 tablespoons sugar in a small saucepan over medium-high heat. When hot, stir to dissolve the sugar. Bring to a boil. Pour the boiling cream over the chopped chocolate. Set aside for 5 minutes before stirring with a whisk until smooth.

Remove the cake from the refrigerator. Smooth the mousse on the sides of the cake with a cake spatula. Use a utility turner to remove the whole cake from the cake circle. Place the cake onto a baking sheet with sides. Ladle three 4-ounce ladles of the ganache over the top of the cake. Use a cake spatula to spread a smooth coating of ganache over the top and sides of the cake. (This looks like an ocean of ganache, but it is the correct amount; of course, too much ganache is always perfect.) Refrigerate the cake for 20 minutes to set the ganache.

Remove the cake from the refrigerator and pour the remaining ganache over the top of the cake; then use a cake spatula to spread the ganache smoothly and evenly over the top and sides of the cake. Use a utility turner to transfer the cake onto a clean cardboard cake circle. Refrigerate the cake for 20 minutes to set the ganache.

Prepare and Apply the Finishing Touches

Preheat the oven to 325°F. Toast 1 cup sliced almonds on a baking sheet in the preheated oven for 10 minutes, until light golden brown. Remove the almonds from the oven and cool at room temperature for 10 minutes. Holding about ½ cup of the cooled sliced almonds at a time in the palms of your hands, crush them into irregular-size pieces (this is the best method to break almonds into irregular-size pieces without creating fine particles of almonds). Set aside.

Melt 1 ounce chopped milk chocolate in the top half of a double boiler over medium-low heat. Use a rubber spatula to stir the chocolate until completely melted and smooth, 2 to 2½ minutes. Remove from the heat, then transfer the chocolate to another small Ziploc bag.

(The milk chocolate may also be melted in a small Ziploc bag in a microwave oven set at medium power for 1 minute. After removing the chocolate from the microwave, the chocolate will be completely melted and ready to use.)

Now melt 1 ounce chopped semisweet chocolate in the top half of a double boiler over medium-low heat. Use a rubber spatula to stir the chocolate until completely melted and smooth, about 2 to 2½ minutes. Remove from the heat, then transfer the chocolate to another small Ziploc bag.

(As with the milk chocolate, the semisweet chocolate may also be melted in a small Ziploc bag in a microwave oven set at medium power for 1 minute. After removing the chocolate from the microwave, the chocolate will be completely melted and ready to use.)

Snip the tip from a bottom corner of the Ziploc bag containing the melted milk chocolate. Pipe the entire amount of chocolate in the Ziploc bag across the top of the cake, going from left to right in a zigzag pattern. Snip the tip from a bottom corner of the Ziploc bag containing the semisweet chocolate. Turn the cake 90 degrees. Pipe the entire amount of chocolate in the bag across the sur-face of the milk-chocolate-topped cake, again moving from left to right in a zigzag pattern to create a free-form lattice of piped chocolate. Refrigerate the cake for 10 to 15 minutes to set the chocolate lattice.

Press the crushed almonds into the sides of the cake, coating it evenly. Refrigerate for 2 hours before serving.

To Serve

Heat the blade of a serrated slicer under hot running water and wipe the blade dry before making each slice. Serve immediately.

THE CHEF'S TOUCH

I had the good fortune of being invited to prepare dessert for Julia Child's eightieth birthday celebration sponsored by a PBS television station in Boston in 1992, and once again for her eighty-fifth birthday bash in Washington, D.C., in 1997. The party for her eighty-fifth was a special tribute to Julia organized by the American Institute of Wine and Food. (Julia is a cofounder of this organization.)

Of course, it is an honor to receive such an invitation, and a lot of pressure as well. I asked Trellis pastry chef Kelly Bailey to come up with a concept for a cake that would embody many of Julia's favorite confectionery synergies, such as chocolate, almonds, raspberries, and liqueurs. Julia praised Kelly personally that evening, and I stood in the background, relieved that the eggs were in the cake and not on our faces.

The standard packaging for raspberries is a ½ pint unit, which yields about 5½ ounces of berries. (You will need to purchase 2 individual ½ pint units for this recipe.) Most of the berries we have purchased at the supermarket are packed in a lidded plastic container. Before purchasing, take a good look at the berries to make certain that the majority are not moldy and/or blemished. (Open up the lid to get a good look.) Changes in humidity can diminish the quality of berries overnight, so it's a good idea to purchase this delicate fruit the day you need it.

If your kitchen is on the cool side, and the melted chocolate in the Ziploc bags begins to firm, place the bags on a heating pad set on medium for a few minutes, or place the Ziploc bags in a microwave oven set on medium for a few seconds, until the chocolate is flowing again.

MARCEL'S FIRST BIRTHDAY CHOCOLATE HIGH *and* FLUFFY-ON-TOP CAKE

SERVES 12 TO 48—ENOUGH TO CALL IT A PARTY

Make the Chocolate Mmm! Mmm! Good Cake

Preheat the oven to 350°F. Lightly coat the inside of a 9 × 13 × 2-inch nonstick pan with some of the 2 teaspoons of melted butter. Line the bottom of the pan with parchment paper (or wax paper); then lightly coat the paper with more melted butter. Set aside.

In a sifter combine 2½ cups flour, ½ cup cocoa powder, 1 teaspoon baking powder, 1 teaspoon baking soda, and 1 teaspoon salt. Sift onto a large piece of parchment paper (or wax paper). Set aside.

Place 1½ cups granulated sugar and 5 ounces butter in the bowl of an electric mixer fitted with a paddle. Mix on low speed for 1 minute; then beat on medium for 3 minutes until soft. Use a rubber spatula to scrape down the sides of the bowl and the paddle, and then beat on medium for an additional 2 minutes until very soft. Scrape down the sides of the bowl. Add 3 eggs, one at a time, beating on medium for 10 seconds after each addition, and scraping down the sides of the bowl once all the eggs have been incorporated. (For the best cake texture, the mixing time when adding the eggs is relatively short; consequently, the mixture will appear curdled at this point, but it will eventually come together.)

Add the melted chocolate and mix on medium for 15 seconds. Operate the mixer on low while gradually adding half the sifted dry ingredients; mix until incorporated, about 30 seconds. Gradually add ½ cup of the milk and mix on low to incorporate, about 15 seconds. While continuing to operate the mixer on low, gradually add the remaining sifted dry ingredients and mix for 30 seconds. Gradually add the remaining ½ cup of milk and mix on low for 15 seconds.

Slowly add ½ cup hot water and mix on low to combine, about 30 seconds. Scrape down the sides of the bowl. Add 1 teaspoon vanilla extract and mix on medium for 15 seconds. Remove the bowl from the mixer and use a rubber spatula to finish mixing the ingredients until thoroughly combined. Transfer the cake batter to the prepared pan, using a rubber spatula to spread it evenly.

Bake on the center rack in the preheated oven until a toothpick inserted in the center of each cake comes out clean, about 40 minutes. Remove the cake from the oven and cool in the pan for 15 minutes at room temperature. Invert the cake onto a baking sheet (or onto a large rectangular platter). Carefully peel the paper away from the bottom of the cake. Refrigerate the cake until needed.

CHOCOLATE MMM! MMM! GOOD CAKE

- 5 ounces unsalted butter, cut into ½-ounce pieces; plus 2 teaspoons (melted)
- 2½ cups all-purpose flour
- ½ cup unsweetened cocoa powder
- 1 teaspoon baking powder
- 1 teaspoon baking soda
- 1 teaspoon salt
- 1½ cups granulated sugar
- 3 large eggs
- 3 ounces unsweetened baking chocolate, coarsely chopped and melted (pages 197–98)
- 1 cup whole milk
- ½ cup hot water
- 1 teaspoon pure vanilla extract

VERY FLUFFY VANILLA FROSTING

- 4 cups (1 pound) confectioners' sugar
- ½ pound (2 sticks) unsalted butter, cut into ½-ounce pieces
- 3 tablespoons whole milk
- 1 tablespoon pure vanilla extract

Prepare the Very Fluffy Vanilla Frosting

Sift 4 cups confectioners' sugar onto a large piece of parchment paper (or wax paper). Set aside.

Place ½ pound butter in the bowl of an electric mixer fitted with a paddle. Mix on low speed for 1 minute, then increase the speed to medium-high and beat for 2 minutes until soft. Scrape down the sides of the bowl and the paddle. Beat on medium for 2 more minutes until softer. Add the sifted confectioners' sugar and mix on the lowest speed to combine, about 1 minute. Add 3 tablespoons milk and 1 tablespoon vanilla extract and mix on low speed for 15 seconds, until the mixture appears moist. Now beat the mixture on medium-high for 2 minutes. Scrape down the sides of the bowl. Beat the frosting on medium-high for 2 additional minutes until a state of "high fluffiness" is achieved.

Assemble and Serve

Remove the cake from the refrigerator. Gently turn the cooled cake out onto a cutting board, baked top facing up. (You may want to use a utility turner or large wide spatula to facilitate this step.) Use a cake spatula to spread the frosting evenly over the top of the cake.

Use a serrated slicer to cut the cake into as many portions as necessary (from 12 to 48).

For a clean cut, heat the blade of the slicer under hot running water and wipe the blade dry before making each cut. Serve as soon as the celebrant has blown the candle out.

THE CHEF'S TOUCH

My Uncle Gerry, who gave me my first cooking lesson (how to prepare catfish) when I was ten years old, was by trade a baker. He and my Aunt Minnie (my mother's sister) lived upstairs with their four children, and my mother and her six kids lived downstairs in the two-story tenement house that my mother owned. As a young single parent, my mom was happy having caring relatives nearby. That was especially true when any of the kids had a birthday. Uncle Gerry always came through with one of his sheet cakes topped by a fluffy white cloud of frosting. For my first taste of that cake, my mother tells me that I was particularly enamored of dragging my fingers through the frosting.

Although my mom tried to persuade me to say "mmm! mmm! good," like the Campbell Soup kids, I would only utter a long-drawn-out "m-m-m-m-mmmmm!"

I guarantee that whatever exclamation emanates from the birthday kid-of-any-age, it certainly will be a joyful sound.

CHOCOLATE TENDER PASSION

SERVES 2

Prepare the Passion Fruit Nucleus

Heat 1 inch of water in a medium saucepan over medium heat. When the water begins to simmer, place 2 egg yolks, 3 tablespoons passion fruit juice, and 2 tablespoons sugar in a medium stainless steel bowl. Set the bowl into the saucepan (the bottom of the bowl should not be touching the water). Using a handheld whisk, gently and constantly whisk the mixture until thickened, but not dry and lifeless, 2½ to 3 minutes. (The mixture should reach a temperature of 160°F on an instant-read test thermometer.)

Remove the saucepan with the bowl from the heat. (Leave the bowl in place in the saucepan.) Whisk 2 ounces butter into the egg mixture, ½ ounce at a time, until incorporated. Remove the bowl from the saucepan and cool in an ice-water bath until the nucleus is cold to the touch. Cover the bowl with plastic wrap and refrigerate until needed.

Make the Chocolate Ruby Cake

Preheat the oven to 350°F. Lightly coat the insides of two 6 × 2-inch heart-shaped cake pans with the 2 teaspoons of melted butter. Flour the insides of both pans using the 2 teaspoons of flour. Shake any excess flour out of the pans. Set aside until needed.

Melt together 1 ounce butter and 1 ounce chopped semisweet chocolate in the top half of a double boiler, or in a microwave oven. (See pages 197–98 for details.)

In a sifter combine the remaining ¼ cup of flour and ⅛ teaspoon baking soda. Sift onto a large piece of parchment paper (or wax paper) and set aside until needed.

Place 1 egg and 3 tablespoons sugar in the bowl of an electric mixer fitted with a paddle. Beat on high speed for 3 minutes until slightly thickened and light in color. Use a rubber spatula to scrape down the sides of the bowl; then beat on high for an additional 2 minutes until a little thicker and pale in color. Add the melted butter and chocolate and mix on medium to combine, about 10 seconds. Operate the mixer on low while gradually adding the sifted dry ingredients; mix until incorporated, about 30 seconds. Add 2 teaspoons buttermilk, ½ teaspoon red food coloring, and ¼ teaspoon vanilla extract and mix on medium to combine, about 15 seconds.

Remove the bowl from the mixer and use a rubber spatula to finish mixing the ingredients until thoroughly combined. Immediately divide the cake batter into the prepared pans (about 6 tablespoons [3 ounces] of batter in each pan), spreading it very evenly. Bake on the center rack in the preheated oven until a toothpick inserted in the center of each cake layer comes out clean, 9 to 10 minutes. Remove the cake layers from the oven and

PASSION FRUIT NUCLEUS

2 large egg yolks

3 tablespoons fresh passion fruit juice

2 tablespoons granulated sugar

2 ounces (½ stick) unsalted butter, cut into ½-ounce pieces

CHOCOLATE RUBY CAKE

1 ounce unsalted butter, cut into ½-ounce pieces; plus 2 teaspoons (melted)

¼ cup plus 2 teaspoons all-purpose flour

1 ounce semisweet baking chocolate, coarsely chopped

⅛ teaspoon baking soda

1 large egg

3 tablespoons granulated sugar

2 teaspoons buttermilk

½ teaspoon red food coloring

¼ teaspoon pure vanilla extract

RED RASPBERRY RHAPSODY SAUCE

One 10-ounce package frozen whole red raspberries, thawed

¼ cup granulated sugar

6 tablespoons Alizé

COCOA DUSTING

2 tablespoons unsweetened cocoa powder

cool in the pans for 10 minutes at room temperature. Invert the cake layers onto cake circles (or onto cake plates). Refrigerate the cake layers for 20 minutes until cold.

Assemble the Chocolate Tender Passion

Remove the cake layers from the refrigerator. Turn the cakes baked tops facing up. Transfer ⅓ cup of the Passion Fruit Nucleus to one of the cake layers, and use a small spatula to spread it evenly over the top of the cake. Place the remaining cake layer, baked top facing up, on top of the nucleus, pressing the cake gently into place. Evenly spread a light coating of the remaining nucleus on the top and sides of the cake, and refrigerate until needed.

Prepare the Red Raspberry Rhapsody Sauce

Heat the 10-ounce package of thawed raspberries, ¼ cup sugar, and 4 tablespoons of the Alizé in a medium saucepan over medium-high heat. When hot, stir to dissolve the sugar. Bring to a boil, then adjust the heat and simmer the mixture for 15 minutes, stirring occasionally, until thick and syrupy. Remove from the heat and strain the syrup through a medium-gauge strainer into a small, noncorrosive bowl. Discard the raspberry seeds. Add the remaining 2 tablespoons of Alizé to the strained syrup and stir to combine. Cool in an ice-water bath until cold to the touch. Cover the bowl with plastic wrap and refrigerate until needed.

Apply the Cocoa Dusting and Serve

Remove the cake from the refrigerator. Use a sifter to dust the top and sides of the cake with 2 tablespoons cocoa powder. Flood the base of a large serving plate with the Red Raspberry Rhapsody Sauce. Place the Chocolate Ruby Cake in the center. Use one fork and begin the intimate ritual.

THE CHEF'S TOUCH

Prepared as a token of affection, this dessert for two is certain to arouse the rapture associated with Valentine's Day, but entirely appropriate for any day you want to feel romantic and indulgent.

Passion fruit is surprisingly unattractive. Its quirky, egg-shaped visage, which resembles a purple Ping-Pong ball after a Chinese masters tournament, belies its succulent interior. Cut it open to reveal the yellow pulp studded with tiny seeds. The seeds are edible, although we do not use them for this recipe. You can find passion fruit throughout most of the year, but it is most plentiful during summer and fall. Two to three whole fresh passion fruits (each weighing 1½ to 2 ounces) are needed to yield the 3 tablespoons of fresh passion fruit juice for the Passion Fruit Nucleus. To harvest fresh passion fruit juice, cut the passion fruit in half lengthwise with a serrated knife, then use a teaspoon to scoop the pulp and seeds into a medium-gauge strainer placed over a bowl. With a rubber spatula, press the pulp through the strainer into the bowl. (Discard the seeds, but not without snacking on a few.) Once strained, the pulp turns to liquid.

Aluminum heart-shaped cake pans are available from Wilton Enterprises. Check them out online at www.wilton.com. Alizé, available at the liquor store, is a blend of passion fruit juices and French Cognac.

You'll need a delicate touch to successfully dust the cake with cocoa powder. If you're especially coordinated, try removing the cake from the cake circle (or cake plate), and hold the cake in the palm of one hand while sifting the powdered cocoa over the top and sides of the cake with the other hand (tilting the cake as needed to get the cocoa powder on the sides). Or you can dust the cake on a cooling rack placed over a larger sheet pan (so that the pan catches the excess powder), elevating the pan slightly on one side as you dust the sides of the cake.

CHOCOLATE PEANUT ROOT BEER RUMBLE

SERVES 10

Make the Chocolate Root Beer Cake

Preheat the oven to 350°F. Lightly coat the insides of two 9 × 1½-inch nonstick cake pans using some of the 2 teaspoons of melted butter. Line the bottoms of the pans with parchment paper (or wax paper), then lightly coat the paper with more melted butter. Set aside.

In a sifter, combine 1½ cups flour, 2 tablespoons cocoa powder, 1 teaspoon baking soda, ½ teaspoon baking powder, and ½ teaspoon salt. Sift onto a large piece of parchment paper and set aside until needed.

Place ¾ cup sugar and 2 large eggs in the bowl of an electric mixer fitted with a paddle. Beat on medium-high speed for 2 minutes until slightly thickened. Operate the mixer on medium while slowly adding ⅔ cup vegetable oil in a steady stream. Mix until incorporated, about 1 minute. Use a rubber spatula to scrape down the sides of the bowl. Add 3 ounces melted semisweet baking chocolate and beat on medium speed until combined, about 20 seconds. Operate the mixer on low while slowly adding the sifted dry ingredients; mix until incorporated, about 1 minute. Scrape down the sides of the bowl. Add ½ cup sour cream, ¼ cup root beer concentrate, and 1 teaspoon vanilla extract, and mix on low for 30 seconds until combined. Remove the bowl from the mixer and use a rubber spatula to mix the batter until thoroughly combined. Immediately divide the cake batter into the prepared pans (about 1¾ cups of batter in each pan), spreading it evenly.

Bake on the center rack in the preheated oven until a toothpick inserted in the center of each cake layer comes out clean, about 20 minutes. Remove the cake layers from the oven and cool in the pans for 15 minutes at room temperature. Invert the cake layers onto cake circles (or directly onto cake plates). Carefully peel the paper away from the bottoms of the cake layers. Set aside at room temperature.

Heat ½ cup Concord grape jelly in a small nonstick pan over medium heat, stirring occasionally with a rubber spatula until melted and smooth, about 2 minutes. Remove the hot jelly from the heat and use a pastry brush to evenly apply about half of the jelly over the entire top of each cake layer. Refrigerate the cake layers while preparing the frosting.

Make the Peanut-Butter Cream-Cheese Frosting

Place 8 ounces cream cheese and ½ cup sugar in the bowl of an electric mixer fitted with a paddle. Mix on low for 30 seconds, then beat on medium-high for 2 minutes until soft and combined. Use a rubber spatula to scrape down the sides of the bowl and the paddle. Add 1 cup creamy peanut butter. Beat on medium for 30 seconds until thoroughly combined. Transfer the mixture to a large bowl. Set aside.

Place ⅔ cup heavy cream in the bowl of

CHOCOLATE ROOT BEER CAKE

2 teaspoons unsalted butter, melted
1½ cups all-purpose flour
2 tablespoons unsweetened cocoa powder
1 teaspoon baking soda
½ teaspoon baking powder
½ teaspoon salt
¾ cup granulated sugar
2 large eggs
⅔ cup vegetable oil
3 ounces semisweet baking chocolate, coarsely chopped and melted (pages 197–98)
½ cup sour cream
¼ cup root beer concentrate
1 teaspoon pure vanilla extract
½ cup Concord grape jelly

PEANUT-BUTTER CREAM-CHEESE FROSTING

8 ounces cream cheese, cut into 1-ounce pieces
½ cup granulated sugar
1 cup creamy peanut butter
⅔ cup heavy cream
¼ cup semisweet chocolate mini-morsels

RUMBLE GARNISH

1½ cups unsalted dry roasted peanuts
10 candy root beer barrels

an electric mixer fitted with a balloon whip. Whisk on medium-high for 1 minute and 45 seconds until soft peaks form. Add the whipped cream to the cream-cheese and peanut-butter mixture, and use a rubber spatula to fold the ingredients together until thoroughly combined. Transfer 1 cup of the Peanut-Butter Cream-Cheese Frosting to a small bowl, then add ¼ cup semisweet chocolate mini-morsels and use a rubber spatula to fold them into the frosting.

Assemble the Cake

Remove the cake layers from the refrigerator. Use a cake spatula to evenly spread the mini-morsel-laden frosting over the top and to the edges of one of the inverted cake layers. Place the second cake layer, jelly-coated side facing up, onto the frosting-coated cake layer. (The jelly-coated, inverted tops of the cake layers are very sticky, so do not touch them or press the top layer into place; it will settle onto the frosting-coated bottom layer when the frosting is applied to the top layer.) Evenly and smoothly spread the remaining 2¼ cups frosting onto the top and sides of the cake.

Press 1½ cups of the dry roasted peanuts into the sides of the cake, coating them evenly. Refrigerate for 2 hours before slicing and serving.

To Serve

Heat the blade of a slicer under hot running water and wipe the blade dry before cutting each slice. Keep the slices at room temperature for 20 to 30 minutes before serving. Prior to serving, decorate the top of each slice of cake with a root beer barrel.

THE CHEF'S TOUCH

This cake may be prepared over 2 days. DAY 1: Bake the Chocolate Root Beer Cake layers. Do not brush with jelly. Once cooled, cover each layer with plastic wrap and refrigerate until the next day. DAY 2: Remove the cake layers from the refrigerator. Heat the jelly, then brush the cake layers with the jelly as described in the recipe. Refrigerate the jelly-coated cake layers while preparing the frosting. Prepare the Peanut-Butter Cream-Cheese Frosting, then frost the cake. Garnish the sides of the cake with the dry roasted peanuts and the top with the candy root beer barrels. Refrigerate the cake for 2 hours before slicing and serve as directed in the recipe.

Root beer concentrate can be found near the extracts in the baking supplies section.

As I mentioned in the recipe, the jelly-coated cake layers are very sticky. If touched with a finger or other object, a portion of cake proportionate to what touched the cake will be removed when the finger or object is pulled away from it, so cake snatchers beware.

OUT-OF-STATE CAKES

CROSS-COUNTRY MEANDERINGS ON THE ROAD TO CHOCOLATE NIRVANA

CHOCOLATE "MAI TAI"

SERVES 12

Make the Pineapple Almond Cake

Preheat the oven to 325°F. Lightly coat the insides of two 9 × 1½-inch nonstick cake pans with some of the 2 teaspoons of melted butter. Line the bottoms of the pans with parchment paper (or wax paper); then lightly coat the paper with more melted butter. Set aside.

In a sifter combine 2 cups flour, 1 teaspoon baking powder, 1 teaspoon baking soda, and ½ teaspoon salt. Sift onto a large piece of parchment paper (or wax paper). Set aside.

Heat the diced dried pineapple pieces and ¾ cup of water in a small saucepan over medium heat. Bring to a simmer; then remove from heat and set aside until needed.

Place ½ pound butter and 1 cup sugar in the bowl of an electric mixer fitted with a paddle. Mix on low speed for 1 minute, and then beat on medium-high until soft, about 2 minutes. Scrape down the sides of the bowl and the paddle. Beat on medium-high for an additional 3 minutes until very soft. Scrape down the sides of the bowl. Add 2 eggs, one at a time, beating on medium for 30 seconds after each addition, and scraping down the sides of the bowl once both eggs have been incorporated. Now beat on medium-high for 1 minute until fluffy. Operate the mixer on low while gradually adding the sifted dry ingredients; mix until incorporated, about 1 minute. Add the pineapple and residual cooking water and mix on the lowest speed to combine, 30 to 40 seconds. Add ½ cup sour cream and 1 teaspoon almond extract and mix on low to combine, about 15 seconds.

Remove the bowl from the mixer, and add the toasted almonds; then use a rubber spatula to finish mixing the ingredients until thoroughly combined. (The cake batter will appear to be alluringly delicious, but resist the temptation to taste it—and do believe the FDA warnings regarding the consumption of raw eggs.) Immediately divide the cake batter into the prepared pans (about 2½ cups of batter in each pan), spreading it evenly.

Bake on the center rack in the preheated oven until a toothpick inserted in the center of each cake layer comes out clean, 28 to 30 minutes. Remove the cake layers from the oven and cool in the pans for 15 minutes at room temperature. Invert the cake layers onto cake circles wrapped with plastic wrap or lined with parchment paper or wax paper (or onto cake plates). Carefully peel the paper away from the bottoms of the cake layers. Refrigerate the cake layers until needed.

Prepare the Out-of-This-World Orange Buttercream

Place ½ pound butter in the bowl of an electric mixer fitted with a paddle. Mix on low

PINEAPPLE ALMOND CAKE

½ pound (2 sticks) unsalted butter, cut into ½-ounce pieces; plus 2 teaspoons (melted)

2 cups all-purpose flour

1 teaspoon baking powder

1 teaspoon baking soda

½ teaspoon salt

½ pound dried pineapple rings, cut into ¼-inch pieces

¾ cup water

1 cup granulated sugar

2 large eggs

½ cup sour cream

1 teaspoon almond extract

¾ cup sliced almonds, toasted (page 199)

OUT-OF-THIS-WORLD ORANGE BUTTERCREAM

½ pound (2 sticks) unsalted butter, cut into ½-ounce pieces

1 tablespoon minced orange zest

1 tablespoon orange liqueur

½ cup granulated sugar

2 large egg whites

DARK RUM CHOCOLATE MOUSSE

¾ cup heavy cream

2 tablespoons dark rum

¼ cup granulated sugar

2 ounces unsweetened baking chocolate, coarsely chopped and melted (pages 197–98)

QUINTESSENTIAL CHOCOLATE GANACHE

12 ounces semisweet baking chocolate, coarsely chopped

4 ounces unsweetened baking chocolate, coarsely chopped

2 cups heavy cream

2 tablespoons granulated sugar

CHOCOLATE ALMOND PINEAPPLE GARNISH

2 cups sliced almonds, toasted (page 199)

6 dried pineapple rings, cut in half

4 ounces semisweet baking chocolate, coarsely chopped and melted (pages 197–98)

speed for 1 minute; then increase the speed to medium-high and beat for 2 minutes until soft.

Scrape down the sides of the bowl and the paddle. Beat on medium for 2 more minutes until very soft. Add 1 tablespoon orange zest and 1 tablespoon orange liqueur and beat on medium for an additional 4 minutes until even softer. Transfer the orange-enhanced butter to a medium bowl and set aside at room temperature until needed.

Heat 1 inch of water in a large saucepan over medium heat. When the water begins to simmer, place ½ cup sugar and 2 egg whites in a large bowl. Set the bowl into the saucepan (the bottom of the bowl should not touch the water). Using a hand-held whisk, gently whisk the sugar and egg whites until the mixture reaches a temperature of 140°F, 3 to 4 minutes.

Transfer the heated egg white mixture to the bowl of an electric mixer fitted with a balloon whip. (Make certain that the bowl and whip are meticulously clean and dry, otherwise the egg white mixture will not whisk properly.) Whisk on high until very shiny and fluffy (looks like Fluff), about 2 minutes. Add half of the orange-enhanced whipped butter to the egg whites and whisk on high for 30 seconds. Add the remaining whipped butter to the mixing bowl and whisk on high for 30 seconds. Scrape down the sides of the bowl. Transfer the orange buttercream to a medium bowl, cover the bowl with plastic wrap, and set aside at room temperature until needed.

Make the Dark Rum Chocolate Mousse

Place ¾ cup heavy cream, 2 tablespoons dark rum, and ¼ cup sugar in the bowl of an electric mixer fitted with a balloon whip. Whisk on medium-high speed until stiff, 2 to 2½ minutes.

Using a handheld whisk, vigorously whisk about half of the whipped cream into 2 ounces melted unsweetened chocolate until incorporated. Add the combined whipped cream and chocolate to the whipped cream in the mixer bowl, and whisk by hand until smooth and completely combined. Refrigerate until needed.

Prepare the Quintessential Chocolate Ganache

Place 12 ounces chopped semisweet chocolate and 4 ounces chopped unsweetened chocolate in a large bowl.

Heat 2 cups heavy cream and 2 tablespoons sugar in a small saucepan over medium-high heat. When hot, stir to dissolve the sugar. Bring to a boil. Pour the boiling cream over the chopped chocolate. Set aside for 5 minutes; then stir with a whisk until smooth. Set aside at room temperature until needed.

Make the Chocolate Almond Pineapple Garnish

Crush the toasted and cooled almonds in the palm of your hand to break them into irregular pieces. Set aside until needed.

Line a baking sheet with parchment paper (or wax paper). Transfer ⅔ cup of the almond pieces to a small bowl. (The remaining almonds will be used to decorate the sides of the cake.) One at a time, hand dip three-quarters of a dried pineapple half ring into the melted chocolate. Allow the excess chocolate to drip into the bowl of melted chocolate; then dip the chocolate-coated portion of the pineapple into the bowl of almond pieces to coat the chocolate with almonds. Place the coated pineapple half ring onto the baking sheet. Repeat this procedure with the remaining pineapple half rings and refrigerate until needed.

Assemble the Cake

Remove the cake layers and the mousse from the refrigerator. Transfer the mousse to the top of one of the inverted cake layers. Use a cake spatula to spread the mousse evenly and smoothly over the top of the cake to the edges. Turn the second inverted cake layer with the baked top facing up, place it onto the mousse-covered cake layer, and firmly press it into place. Use a cake spatula to smooth the mousse around the outside edges in between the cake layers. Refrigerate the cake for 30 minutes.

Remove the cake from the refrigerator. Reserve ½ cup of the orange buttercream to decorate the top of the cake. Spread the remaining buttercream evenly and smoothly over the sides of the cake, but not the top. Pour the ganache onto the top of the cake and use a cake spatula to spread an even layer of ganache to the edges of the top, being careful not to spread ganache over the sides and onto the buttercream. Refrigerate the cake for 5 minutes (not any longer, or the buttercream will become too firm to hold the toasted almonds).

Remove the cake from the refrigerator. Press the remaining crushed almonds into the sides of the cake, coating them evenly.

Fill a pastry bag fitted with a medium star tip with the remaining buttercream. Pipe a circle of 12 evenly spaced buttercream stars along the edge of the top of the cake. Decorate each star with a chocolate-and-almond-coated pineapple half ring. Refrigerate the cake for 3 to 4 hours (long enough to firm the mousse layer) before cutting and serving.

To Serve

Heat the blade of a serrated slicer under hot running water and wipe the blade dry before making each slice. Allow the cake slices to stand at room temperature for 15 to 20 minutes before serving.

THE CHEF'S TOUCH

Several years ago, I agreed to present a cooking class as the first prize of a national contest sponsored by Baker's Chocolate. The prize was awarded to the high school home economics class that submitted the best humorous essay on chocolate. I anticipated that my luck would place me in a North Dakota classroom during a blizzard, or in a rural Kansas schoolhouse during a drought. To my delight, the winning essay was submitted by a class from Ka'u High School on the island of Hawaii.

On our first evening on the Big Island, my wife, Connie, and I attended a luau at the King Kamehameha Hotel on the Kona coast. Of course mai tais were served, and although I have not had the lush drink since our visit in 1990, the rich flavors linger in my memory. When Brett Bailey suggested creating a mai tai cake for this book, I was an eager accomplice.

Because these cake layers are very moist and sticky, be sure you invert them onto cardboard cake circles that have been wrapped with plastic wrap or lined with parchment paper or wax paper. Otherwise the cake layers may stubbornly stick to the surface of the cardboard.

The orange liqueur most frequently mentioned as a component in a mai tai is çuracao. Other clear and colorless orange-flavored spirits such as triple sec or Cointreau are also superb substitutes.

The West Indies produces the most estimable rum on the planet. Of the many dark rums, one stands out not only for its quaffability but for its affinity with confections, Myers's rum from Jamaica. Aged like fine wine, Jamaica's best deserves a spot in your liquor cabinet and kitchen cupboard.

This cake may be prepared over 3 days. DAY 1: Bake the Pineapple Almond Cake layers. Remove from the oven, cool to room temperature, then refrigerate. Make the Dark Rum Chocolate Mousse. Transfer the mousse to one of the inverted cake layers and spread over the top to the edges. Top the mousse with the second inverted cake layer. Cover with plastic wrap and refrigerate until the next day. DAY 2: Prepare the Out-of-This-World Orange Buttercream, the Quintessential Chocolate Ganache, and the Chocolate Almond Pineapple Garnish. Finish assembling the cake as directed in the recipe. Refrigerate in a sealed plastic container until the next day. DAY 3: Slice and serve the cake.

MOCHA MUD CAKE *with* ESPRESSO CHOCOLATE CHUNK MUD SLIDE

SERVES 12

Make the Mocha Mud Cake

Preheat the oven to 275°F. Assemble a 9 × 2¾-inch nonstick springform pan with the bottom insert turned over (the lip of the insert facing down). Lightly coat the inside of the springform pan with some of the 1 teaspoon of melted butter. Line the bottom of the pan with parchment paper (or wax paper), then lightly coat the paper with more melted butter. Set aside.

In a sifter combine 2 cups flour, 1 teaspoon baking soda, and ¼ teaspoon salt. Sift onto a large piece of parchment paper (or wax paper). Set aside until needed.

Place 1¾ cups hot coffee, ½ pound butter, 5 ounces chopped unsweetened chocolate, and ¼ cup rum in the top half of a double boiler over medium-low heat. Use a rubber spatula to stir the mixture until the butter and chocolate are completely melted and combined with the coffee and rum, 2½ to 3 minutes.

The chocolate and butter may also be melted with the coffee and rum in a medium glass bowl in a microwave oven set at medium power for 2 minutes. After removing the mixture from the microwave oven, use a rubber spatula to stir until smooth and combined.

Transfer the melted butter and chocolate mixture to the bowl of an electric mixer fitted with a paddle. Add 2 cups sugar and mix on low speed for 1 minute. Operate the mixer on low while gradually adding the sifted dry ingredients. Once they have been incorporated, about 1 minute, add 2 eggs and 1 tablespoon vanilla extract and mix on medium speed for 1 minute. Remove the bowl from the mixer and use a rubber spatula to finish mixing the ingredients until thoroughly combined. Pour the batter into the prepared springform pan. Place the pan on a baking sheet with sides on the center rack in the preheated oven.

Bake until a toothpick inserted in the center of the cake comes out clean, about 2 hours. Remove the cake from the oven and cool in the pan for 30 minutes. Release the cake from the springform pan and invert it onto a cake circle (or plate). Remove the bottom insert, then carefully peel the parchment paper away from the cake bottom. Turn the cake over, onto another cake circle (or plate) and set aside at room temperature while preparing the Mud Slide.

Prepare the Espresso Chocolate Chunk Mud Slide

Place 1½ cups heavy cream, 6 tablespoons sugar, and 2 teaspoons espresso powder in the bowl of an electric mixer fitted with a balloon whip. Whisk on high for 1 minute until soft peaks form. Remove the bowl from the mixer

MOCHA MUD CAKE

½ pound (2 sticks) unsalted butter, cut into ½-ounce pieces; plus 1 teaspoon (melted)

2 cups all-purpose flour

1 teaspoon baking soda

¼ teaspoon salt

1¾ cups brewed full-strength coffee, hot

5 ounces unsweetened baking chocolate, coarsely chopped

¼ cup dark rum

2 cups granulated sugar

2 large eggs

1 tablespoon pure vanilla extract

ESPRESSO CHOCOLATE CHUNK MUD SLIDE

1½ cups heavy cream

6 tablespoons granulated sugar

2 teaspoons instant espresso powder

4 ounces semisweet baking chocolate, coarsely chopped

and use a rubber spatula to fold in 4 ounces semisweet chocolate.

To Serve

Heat the blade of a serrated slicer under hot running water and wipe the blade dry before cutting each slice. Spoon 2 to 3 heaping table-spoons of the Mud Slide over each piece of the cake and serve.

THE CHEF'S TOUCH

Whether the origins of this American dessert are north or south of the Mason-Dixon Line, its popularity has certainly spread. My daughter Danielle returned from an Australian vacation a few years ago with a photo of a cafe in Perth; its blackboard, out front, boasted Death by Chocolate, featuring Mississippi Mud Pie. The global village, indeed.

Turning over the bottom insert of the springform pan (the lip of the bottom insert facing down) before assembling the pan will make it easier to separate the insert from the baked cake.

The seemingly insignificant amount of rum in the cake infuses it with a bold flavor. If you prefer, you can eliminate the rum and increase the amount of brewed full-strength coffee to 2 cups, rather than 1¾ cups.

Due to its dense texture, the cake stays warm for at least an hour after being removed from the oven. And "warm" is the way to eat this dessert, with just-whipped Espresso Chocolate Chunk Mud Slide cascading down the sides. Let's see our Aussie friends abscond with this one.

As suggested, the cake is extraordinary served warm, but it can also be deliciously enjoyed at room temperature. Once cooled, the cake may be kept, covered with plastic wrap, at room temperature for up to 24 hours. You may also refrigerate the cake for 3 to 4 days. To avoid permeating the cake with refrigerator odors, place the cake in a large, tightly sealed plastic container. If refrigerated, keep the slices at room temperature for 30 minutes before serving. A tall *café latte* would be the perfect beverage to accompany this Mississippi madness.

This cake may be prepared over 2 days. DAY 1: Bake the Mocha Mud Cake. Once cooled, cover with plastic wrap and keep at room temperature for up to 24 hours. DAY 2: Prepare the Espresso Chocolate Chunk Mud Slide. Slice and serve the cake as directed in the recipe.

THE KING'S CHOCOLATE PEANUT BUTTER BANANA BOURBON CAKE

SERVES 12

Make the Banana Cake

Preheat the oven to 325°F. Lightly coat the insides of three 9 × 1½-inch nonstick cake pans with some of the 1 tablespoon of melted butter. Line the bottoms of the pans with parchment paper (or wax paper); then lightly coat the paper with more melted butter. Set aside.

In a sifter combine 2 cups flour, 1 teaspoon baking powder, 1 teaspoon baking soda, and ½ teaspoon salt. Sift onto a large piece of parchment paper (or wax paper), and set aside until needed.

Peel the bananas, and cut each one into 1-inch pieces.

Place ½ pound butter and 1 cup sugar in the bowl of an electric mixer fitted with a paddle. Mix on low speed for 1 minute; then beat on medium-high until soft and thoroughly combined, about 3 minutes. Scrape down the sides of the bowl and the paddle. Add 2 eggs, one at a time, beating on medium for 1 minute after each addition. Scrape down the sides of the bowl once both eggs have been incorporated. Add the banana pieces and mix on medium speed to combine, about 20 seconds. Operate the mixer on low while gradually adding the sifted dry ingredients; mix until incorporated, about 1 minute.

Add ½ cup boiling water in a slow, steady stream and mix on the lowest speed (stir) to combine, about 15 seconds. Add ½ cup banana liqueur and mix on low to combine, about 15 seconds. Scrape down the sides of the bowl, and then resume mixing at medium speed for 2 additional minutes. Remove the bowl from the mixer and use a rubber spatula to finish mixing the ingredients until thoroughly combined.

Immediately divide the cake batter into the prepared pans (about 1¾ cups of batter in each pan), spreading it evenly. Bake on the top and center racks in the preheated oven until a toothpick inserted in the center of each cake layer comes out clean, 28 to 30 minutes. (Rotate the pans from top to center halfway through the baking time.) Remove the cake layers from the oven and cool in the pans for 30 minutes at room temperature.

Invert the cake layers onto cake circles that have been wrapped with plastic wrap or lined with parchment paper or wax paper (or invert onto cake plates). Carefully peel the paper away from the bottoms of the cake layers. Using a clean pastry brush, brush the layers with 2 tablespoons bourbon. Refrigerate the cake layers while preparing the icing.

BANANA CAKE

½ pound (2 sticks) unsalted butter, cut into ½-ounce pieces; plus 1 tablespoon (melted)

2 cups all-purpose flour

1 teaspoon baking powder

1 teaspoon baking soda

½ teaspoon salt

1¾ pounds medium ripe bananas, unpeeled

1 cup granulated sugar

2 large eggs

½ cup boiling water

½ cup banana liqueur

2 tablespoons bourbon

SWEET CHOCOLATE PEANUT BUTTER ICING

1¾ cups creamy peanut butter (one 18-ounce jar)

½ cup confectioners' sugar

4 ounces Baker's German's Sweet Chocolate, coarsely chopped and melted (pages 197–98)

QUINTESSENTIAL CHOCOLATE GANACHE

12 ounces semisweet baking chocolate, coarsely chopped

4 ounces unsweetened baking chocolate, coarsely chopped

2 cups heavy cream

2 tablespoons granulated sugar

PEANUT AND BANANA GARNISH

1 cup unsalted dry roasted peanuts

1 medium ripe banana, unpeeled

Prepare the Sweet Chocolate Peanut Butter Icing

Place 1¾ cups peanut butter and ½ cup confectioners' sugar in the bowl of an electric mixer fitted with a paddle. Mix on low speed for 15 seconds. Increase the mixer speed to high and beat until the peanut butter mixture is very smooth, about 4 minutes. Add the melted chocolate and beat on medium-high speed for 1 minute. Remove the bowl from the mixer; then scrape down the sides of the bowl, and set aside at room temperature until needed.

Begin Assembling the Cake

Transfer ¾ cup of the icing to a pastry bag fitted with a medium straight tip, and set it aside at room temperature until needed.

Remove the cake layers from the refrigerator. Use a cake spatula to spread ½ cup of icing evenly and smoothly over the top and to the edges of one of the inverted cake layers. Place a second cake layer, bottom facing up, onto the iced cake layer and gently press it into place. Spread ½ cup of icing evenly over the top and to the edges of the second cake layer; then top the icing with the third cake layer, bottom facing up, and gently press the cake into place. Spread the remaining icing evenly and smoothly on the top and sides of the cake. Refrigerate the cake for several hours, until the icing is firm to the touch, before making the ganache.

Prepare the Quintessential Chocolate Ganache

Place 12 ounces chopped semisweet chocolate and 4 ounces chopped unsweetened chocolate in a large bowl.

Heat 2 cups heavy cream and 2 tablespoons sugar in a small saucepan over medium-high heat. When hot, stir to dissolve the sugar. Bring to a boil. Pour the boiling cream over the chopped chocolate. Set aside for 5 minutes; then stir with a whisk until smooth.

Finish Assembling and Garnish the Cake

Remove the cake from the refrigerator. Smooth the icing on the top and sides of the cake with a cake spatula. Use a utility turner to remove the whole cake from the cake circle. Place the cake onto a baking sheet with sides. Ladle the ganache over the top of the iced cake. Use a cake spatula to spread a smooth coating of ganache over the top and sides of the cake. Refrigerate the cake for 15 to 20 minutes, until the ganache is firm.

While the cake is in the refrigerator, reserve 12 whole peanuts from the 1 cup for garnish, and place the remaining peanuts in a food processor fitted with a metal blade. Pulse the peanuts for 15 seconds until coarsely chopped (or chop the nuts by hand using a cook's knife). Set aside for a few moments.

Peel the banana and cut it into twelve ¼- to ½-inch-thick slices.

Remove the cake from the refrigerator. Use a utility turner to transfer it to a clean cardboard cake circle. Place a large piece of parchment paper (or wax paper) onto the work surface. Holding the bottom of the cake circle in the palm of one hand, use your free hand to press the chopped peanuts into the ganache on the sides of the cake, coating them evenly. Do this over the paper and allow the peanuts that do not adhere to the sides of the cake to fall onto the paper; then scoop them up and reapply. Pipe a ring of 12 evenly spaced swirls of the reserved icing in the pastry bag along the outside edge of the top of the cake. Top each swirl with a banana slice and a whole peanut. Refrigerate the cake for 15 to 20 minutes before serving.

To Serve

Heat the blade of a serrated slicer under hot running water and wipe the blade dry before cutting each slice. Serve immediately.

THE CHEF'S TOUCH

In May 1998 I traveled to Memphis, Tennessee, for "A Celebration of Southern Chefs" at the venerable Peabody Hotel. The occasion was a fund-raiser for "Share Our Strength" to feed the homeless.

As part of such fund-raising events, local eateries often host the guest chefs when they are not on duty. For lunch, we found ourselves at Elvis Presley's Memphis, at 126 Beale Street. This pulsating memorial to the King fused the bebop '50s of Elvis's heyday with modern technology. Stainless steel tables had red leatherette seating; waitresses with beepers and multiple earrings took our order. Whenever slick renditions of Elvis's music by contemporary artists ceased playing (such as U2's "Don't Be Cruel"), drop-down screens displayed vintage clips of familiar scenes from the Memphis native's life. Just like Elvis himself, kitsch collided with rock 'n' roll.

Even the food was paradoxical, but hardly unpleasant. For appetizers, the house favorite (and mine, too) was a grilled peanut butter and banana sandwich, which was accompanied by fried pickle chips. Grilled in butter, the sandwich was warm enough to melt the peanut butter but left a delightful chill on the bananas. I mentioned to my wife, Connie, that the sandwich could be covered in ganache and served for dessert. Brett and Kelly Bailey were with us at that luncheon, and they took me at my word by creating this swinging cake.

The required 1¼ pounds of unpeeled bananas will yield about 1 pound of peeled fruit. For best results, avoid using over- or under-ripe bananas for this recipe. Shop for bananas that are predominantly yellow with few if any green or brown spots.

Because this cake is very moist and sticky (Elvis would have loved it), invert the layers onto cardboard cake circles that have been wrapped with plastic wrap or lined with parchment paper or wax paper. Otherwise, the cake may stick to the surface of the cardboard.

The icing takes several hours to become firm enough to be covered with ganache. You may speed up this process by placing the cake in the freezer. In any event, the exact amount of time will depend on how cold your refrigerator or freezer is, and how much air circulation is present. (The less free space, the longer it will take.)

The sliced banana garnish will discolor at room temperature after 60 minutes; plan accordingly.

After assembly, you can keep The King's Chocolate Peanut Butter Banana Bourbon Cake in the refrigerator for 2 days before serving. (If you plan on refrigerating the cake, hold off on the banana garnish until you're ready to serve.) To avoid permeating the cake with refrigerator odors, place the cake in a large, tightly sealed plastic container.

This cake may be prepared over 3 days. DAY 1: Bake the Banana Cake layers. Prepare the Sweet Chocolate Peanut Butter Icing. Ice the cake. Refrigerate overnight. DAY 2: Prepare the Quintessential Chocolate Ganache. Cover the cake with ganache and refrigerate for 20 minutes. Pipe the remaining icing in swirls onto the top of the cake. Place the cake in a large, tightly sealed plastic container and refrigerate. DAY 3: Garnish the cake with banana slices and peanuts. Slice and serve as directed.

COCOA SKILLET CAKE *with* TEQUILA SUNSHINE SALSA

SERVES 6

Make the Tequila Sunshine Salsa

Combine the orange sections, grapefruit sections, diced lime, 1 teaspoon julienne of lime zest, 2 tablespoons sugar, and 2 tablespoons tequila in a medium noncorrosive bowl. Cover the bowl with plastic wrap and refrigerate until needed.

Make the Cocoa Skillet Cake

Preheat the oven to 350°F. Place an 8-inch seasoned cast-iron skillet in the preheated oven for 15 minutes. Remove the skillet from the oven. (Handle with care. The skillet will be very hot.) Lightly brush the bottom and sides of the skillet with the 1 teaspoon vegetable oil. Sprinkle the bottom and sides with the 1 tablespoon of *masa harina*. Set aside at room temperature while preparing the cake batter.

In a sifter combine ¾ cup *masa harina*, ½ cup all-purpose flour, ¼ cup cocoa powder, ½ teaspoon baking powder, ½ teaspoon baking soda, and ½ teaspoon salt. Sift onto a large piece of parchment paper (or wax paper) and set aside until needed.

Place ¼ pound butter and ½ cup light brown sugar in the bowl of an electric mixer fitted with a paddle. Mix on low speed for 1 minute; then beat on medium for 3 minutes until soft. Scrape down the sides of the bowl and the paddle. Add 2 eggs, one at a time, beating on medium for 1 minute after each addition, and scraping down the sides of the bowl once both eggs have been incorporated. (Don't be put off because the mixture looks like watery scrambled eggs at this point—that's just the way it is.) Operate the mixer on low while gradually adding the sifted dry ingredients. Once they have been incorporated, about 30 seconds, add ¼ cup sour cream and mix on low for 30 seconds. Now add ¼ cup hot water and mix on low for another 30 seconds. Finally, add 1 tablespoon orange zest and 1 teaspoon vanilla extract and mix on low for 10 seconds. Remove the bowl from the mixer and use a rubber spatula to finish mixing the ingredients until thoroughly combined.

Transfer the batter to the skillet, spreading it evenly. Sprinkle 2 tablespoons turbinado sugar evenly over the batter. Bake on the center rack of the preheated oven until a toothpick inserted in the center of the cake comes out clean, about 45 minutes.

Remove the cake from the oven and set aside at room temperature for 15 minutes before serving. The cake is at its best eaten

TEQUILA SUNSHINE SALSA

4 large navel oranges (about 8 ounces each), peeled and sectioned

2 medium pink grapefruit (about 14 ounces each), peeled and sectioned

1 lime, peeled, sectioned, and diced

1 teaspoon thin julienne of lime zest

2 tablespoons granulated sugar

2 tablespoons tequila

COCOA SKILLET CAKE

1 teaspoon vegetable oil

¾ cup plus 1 tablespoon *masa harina* (corn flour)

½ cup all-purpose flour

¼ cup unsweetened cocoa powder

½ teaspoon baking powder

½ teaspoon baking soda

½ teaspoon salt

¼ pound (1 stick) unsalted butter, cut into ½-ounce pieces

½ cup (4 ounces) tightly packed light brown sugar

2 large eggs

¼ cup sour cream

¼ cup hot water

1 tablespoon thin julienne of orange zest

1 teaspoon pure vanilla extract

2 tablespoons turbinado sugar

warm, rather than piping hot, directly out of the oven. For planning purposes you may like to know that the cake will stay deliciously warm for 1 hour or more if kept in the skillet after being removed from the oven.

To Serve

Use a serrated knife with a rounded tip to cut the warm cake into 6 slices. For a clean cut, heat the blade under hot running water and wipe the blade dry before making each cut. Spoon an equal amount of salsa onto each plate, then place a piece of cake on top and serve immediately.

THE CHEF'S TOUCH

Our Cocoa Skillet Cake evokes images of cowboys, campfire gatherings, and the kind of comfort food that is easily associated with Mexican hospitality. Bringing the cake to the table, or fireside, in the cast-iron skillet would seal this pastoral vision of friendship and eating pleasure.

I know folks who are so fond of their cast-iron skillets that they speak about them in reverential terms more commonly associated with discussing an old friend. As a matter of fact, a well-cared-for piece of cast-iron cookware will probably outlive most friendships.

A newly purchased cast-iron skillet must be "seasoned" before using it: First, wash the skillet with warm, soapy water. Never—now or later—scour the pan with an abrasive pad. Dry the skillet thoroughly.

Lightly brush the inside bottom and sides with vegetable oil. Place the skillet in a preheated 350°F oven for 1 hour. Remove the seasoned skillet from the oven and cool to room temperature before storing. Although a seasoned skillet is not entirely nonstick, it should be fairly easy to clean after using it. I usually wipe the insides clean with paper towels, then brush the pan with a very thin coating of oil, to prevent rusting, before storing it. Contrary to popular opinion, you can wash the skillet, if necessary, with a mild detergent.

Consider spicing up the salsa with the addition of ⅛ teaspoon cayenne pepper and ¼ teaspoon cracked black pepper.

You should be able to locate *masa harina* at most supermarkets. Cornmeal is not a suitable substitute for *masa harina* in this recipe. Turbinado sugar is commonly available at most supermarkets under the brand name Sugar in the Raw. Refined to eliminate contaminants but to retain the molasses, Sugar in the Raw has a rich sweetness and an attractive blond color.

The Cocoa Skillet Cake should be served warm. As previously mentioned, the cake will stay warm in the skillet for up to 1 hour after being removed from the oven. For the sake of convenience, the cake can be removed from the skillet, cooled to room temperature, and then refrigerated, covered with plastic wrap, for up to 2 days. To serve, warm the cake slices in the microwave oven for 30 seconds at high power.

CHOCOLATE WALNUT COFFEE CAKE
with MAPLE WALNUT BUTTER

SERVES 16

Make the Chocolate Walnut Coffee Cake

Preheat the oven to 325°F. Assemble a 9 × 2¾-inch nonstick springform pan with the bottom insert turned over (the lip of the insert facing down). Lightly coat the inside of the springform pan with some of the 1 teaspoon of melted butter. Line the bottom of the pan with parchment paper (or wax paper); then lightly coat the paper with more melted butter. Set aside.

In a sifter combine 1½ cups flour, 6 tablespoons cocoa powder, 1 teaspoon baking soda, and ¼ teaspoon salt. Sift onto a large piece of parchment paper (or wax paper). Set aside until needed.

Place ½ pound butter and 1 cup sugar in the bowl of an electric mixer fitted with a paddle. Mix on low speed for 1 minute; then beat on medium-high for 4 minutes until very soft. Scrape down the sides of the bowl and the paddle. Add 2 eggs, one at a time, beating on medium for 30 seconds after each addition. Add the melted chocolate and mix on medium for 15 seconds to combine. Operate the mixer on low speed while gradually adding the sifted dry ingredients. Once they have been incorporated, about 50 seconds, gradually add ½ cup milk and ½ cup walnut liqueur and mix on low for 1 minute. Remove the bowl from the mixer and use a rubber spatula to finish mixing the ingredients until thoroughly combined.

Transfer the batter to the prepared springform pan, spreading it evenly. Sprinkle ¾ cup of the chopped walnut halves evenly over the batter in the springform pan; then do the same with ½ cup of the chocolate chips. Repeat the process with the remaining ¾ cup walnuts and ½ cup chocolate chips. Place the springform pan on a baking sheet with sides on the center rack of the preheated oven.

Bake until a toothpick inserted into the center of the cake comes out clean (this may get a little tricky with all of those chocolate chips), about 1 hour and 15 minutes. Remove the cake from the oven and cool in the pan for 20 minutes at room temperature. Release the cake from the springform pan and gently invert it onto a cake circle (or cake plate). Remove the bottom insert; then carefully peel the paper away from the inverted cake. Turn the cake over onto a cake circle (or plate) and set aside at room temperature for 30 minutes before slicing and serving. (If the cake is difficult to slice, refrigerate it for 10 minutes or so until firm enough to cut.)

Prepare the Maple Walnut Butter

Place ¾ pound butter in the bowl of an electric mixer fitted with a paddle. Mix on low

---

CHOCOLATE WALNUT COFFEE CAKE

½ pound (2 sticks) unsalted butter, cut into ½-ounce pieces; plus 1 teaspoon (melted)

1½ cups all-purpose flour

6 tablespoons unsweetened cocoa powder

1 teaspoon baking soda

¼ teaspoon salt

1 cup granulated sugar

2 large eggs

2 ounces unsweetened baking chocolate, coarsely chopped and melted (pages 197–98)

½ cup whole milk

½ cup walnut liqueur

1½ cups walnut halves, coarsely chopped

1 cup semisweet chocolate chips

MAPLE WALNUT BUTTER

¾ pound (3 sticks) unsalted butter, cut into ½-ounce pieces

½ cup grade A Vermont maple syrup

¼ cup walnut liqueur

speed for 1 minute to soften the butter, then beat on medium-high for 3 minutes. Scrape down the sides of the bowl and the paddle. Beat for 2 more minutes on medium-high until the butter is very soft. Scrape down the sides of the bowl. Operate the mixer on medium speed while gradually adding first ½ cup maple syrup then ¼ cup walnut liqueur; continue mixing until incorporated, about 45 seconds. Finally, beat on medium for 2 minutes. (To avoid splattering the Maple Walnut Butter, use a pouring shield attachment, or place a towel or plastic wrap over the top of the mixer and down the sides to the bowl.) Set aside at room temperature until needed.

To Serve

Heat the blade of a serrated slicer under hot running water and wipe the blade dry before cutting each slice. Serve each slice accompanied by 1 to 2 tablespoons of Maple Walnut Butter.

THE CHEF'S TOUCH

Guilty as charged for serving chocolate even at breakfast. When The Trellis announced a limited breakfast menu in the spring of 1998, pastry chef Kelly Bailey immediately proclaimed that her Chocolate Walnut Coffee Cake would have the masses standing in line at whatever time we chose to open the doors. Understand that some restraint in what would be offered was necessary, because

Kelly and her crew would have to start their magic at 2:00 A.M. every morning. Soon The Trellis cafe started buzzing with coffee and chocolate addicts at 8:30 A.M. every day of the week. Other choices are offered, of course, besides Kelly's extraordinary chocolate coffee cake—for example, chocolate muffins, chocolate bread . . . There are also some nonchocolate, slightly more bridled selections, such as breakfast pizza and sticky buns (the latter, Connie's Sticky Buns, from *Desserts to Die For*).

Turning over the bottom insert of the springform pan (the lip of the bottom insert facing down) before assembling the pan will make it easier to remove the insert from the baked cake.

The highly refined, almost nutty flavor of grade A Vermont Maple Syrup makes it my first choice for this recipe. If you buy an alternative, be certain that you select a syrup labeled "pure maple syrup." A lot of unfortunate syrup is sold as pancake and/or breakfast syrup that does not have as its source the sweet sap harvested from sugar maple trees.

At Ganache Hill we used Nocello, a walnut liqueur from Italy, to prepare the Maple Walnut Butter. If you fail to locate this special liqueur, I suggest substituting the commonly available Frangelico, a hazelnut-flavored liqueur. In fact, you could certainly substitute hazelnuts for the walnuts in this recipe. (The combination of chocolate and hazelnuts is renowned.)

After baking and cooling it, you may keep the Chocolate Walnut Coffee Cake, covered with plastic wrap, at room temperature for up to 24 hours. The cake can also be refrigerated for 2 to 3 days. To avoid permeating the cake with refrigerator odors, place the cake in a large, tightly sealed plastic container. If refrigerated, slice the cake when cold, then hold the slices at room temperature for 10 to 15 minutes before serving. Personally, I love the coffee cake warm—about 30 seconds in a microwave oven set on medium power will achieve the appropriate results.

Sarah Gunn, owner-operator of The Toymaker of Williamsburg, located adjacent to The Trellis, is a purveyor of puerile treats. But when it comes to her early morning habits, Sarah exercises her adult prerogatives in The Trellis cafe with a cup of coffee that she prefers "black and hot like hell" and a chocolate treat that melts the stress of retailing, Chocolate Walnut Coffee Cake!

WHITE and DARK CHOCOLATE BLACKBERRY JAM CAKE

SERVES 4 TO 6

Make the White and Dark Chocolate Chunk Cake

Preheat the oven to 350°F. Lightly coat the inside of a 9 × 9 × 1½-inch nonstick square cake pan with the 1 teaspoon of melted butter. Set aside until needed.

In a sifter combine 1¼ cups flour, 1 teaspoon baking powder, and ½ teaspoon salt. Sift onto a large piece of parchment paper (or wax paper). Set aside until needed.

Place ¾ cup sugar and ¼ pound butter in the bowl of an electric mixer fitted with a paddle. Mix on low speed for 1 minute; then beat on medium for 2 minutes until soft. Scrape down the sides of the bowl, then beat on medium for 2 additional minutes until a little softer. Scrape down the sides of the bowl. Add 2 eggs, one at a time, beating on medium for 30 seconds after each addition, and scraping down the sides of the bowl once both eggs have been combined. (At this point the mixture appears curdled, but it will pull together once the flour and buttermilk are added.)

Operate the mixer on low while gradually adding half of the sifted dry ingredients followed by ⅓ cup buttermilk; continue mixing about 1 minute. Gradually add the remaining sifted dry ingredients, and mix on low until blended, about 20 seconds. Remove the bowl from the mixer, add 3 ounces chopped semisweet chocolate chunks and 3 ounces chopped white chocolate chunks, and use a rubber spatula to finish mixing the batter until thoroughly combined.

Transfer the batter to the prepared cake pan, spreading it evenly. Bake on the center rack in the preheated oven until a toothpick inserted in the center of the cake comes out clean, about 40 minutes. Remove the cake from the oven and cool in the pan for 15 minutes at room temperature. Invert the cake onto a cake circle, then turn the cake baked top facing up. Refrigerate the cake until needed.

Prepare the Berry Creamy Berry Jam Icing

Place 8 ounces cream cheese, 3 tablespoons blackberry jam, and ¼ cup confectioners' sugar in the bowl of an electric mixer fitted with a paddle. Mix on low speed for 1 minute; then beat on medium-high for 2 minutes. Scrape down the sides of the bowl and the paddle. Beat on high for 2 minutes. Scrape down the sides of the bowl, and then beat on high for 1 additional minute until very creamy, smooth, and delectable. Transfer the

WHITE AND DARK CHOCOLATE CHUNK CAKE

- ¼ pound (1 stick) unsalted butter, cut into ½-ounce pieces; plus 1 teaspoon (melted)
- 1¼ cups all-purpose flour
- 1 teaspoon baking powder
- ½ teaspoon salt
- ¾ cup granulated sugar
- 2 large eggs
- ⅓ cup buttermilk
- 3 ounces semisweet baking chocolate, chopped into ½-inch chunks
- 3 ounces white chocolate, chopped into ½-inch chunks

BERRY CREAMY BERRY JAM ICING

- 8 ounces cream cheese cut into 2-ounce pieces
- 3 tablespoons blackberry jam
- ¼ cup confectioners' sugar, sifted

BLACKBERRY GARNISH

- 1½ pints fresh blackberries

icing to a small bowl, cover with plastic wrap, and set aside at room temperature until needed.

Ice and Garnish the Cake

Remove the cake from the refrigerator. Use a cake spatula to spread the icing over the top of the cake evenly and smoothly. Neatly arrange the whole blackberries, stem ends down, on top of the icing, gently pressing them into place.

Refrigerate the cake for 45 to 50 minutes to firm the icing before cutting and serving.

To Serve

Heat the blade of a serrated slicer under hot running water and wipe the blade dry before cutting the cake into the desired number of portions.

THE CHEF'S TOUCH

Picking blackberries in the backyard of my godfather André Desaulniers's home in Succasunna, New Jersey, was a thorny affair. On the positive side, I never suffered through poison ivy, like I did when I picked my favorite berry—the blueberry—back home in Rhode Island. So when it came time for André's wife, Pauline, to turn my harvest into her chocolate blackberry cake, any nostalgia I may have felt for my favorite berry was assuaged by the delightful flavor without the itch.

When selecting blackberries, make certain that the drupelets (the individual juicy bumps of flesh) are free of mold and blemishes. Like most berries, blackberries are susceptible to changes in temperature, so I recommend using them within 2 to 3 days.

Strawberries would make an attractive alternative to blackberries in this recipe. If you prefer to top the cake with fresh strawberries, replace the blackberry jam in the icing with an equal amount of strawberry jam.

After assembly, you may keep the White and Dark Chocolate Blackberry Jam Cake in the refrigerator for 2 days before serving. To avoid permeating the cake with refrigerator odors, place the cake in a large, tightly sealed plastic container.

This cake may be prepared over 2 days. DAY 1: Bake the White and Dark Chocolate Chunk Cake. Once cooled, cover with plastic wrap and refrigerate. DAY 2: Prepare the Berry Creamy Berry Jam Icing. Ice and garnish the cake as directed in the recipe. Refrigerate for about 45 minutes to firm the icing before cutting and serving.

You will garner smiles and adulation no matter where you serve this cake, but I can assure you that it would be a welcome confection on your next picnic. And it would be nicely accompanied by the chilled pinot noir you were contemplating for a gorgeous summer afternoon.

MILK CHOCOLATE PEACH PECAN UPSIDE-DOWN CAKE *with* PEACH *and* BOURBON ICE CREAM

SERVES 6

Prepare the Peach and Bourbon Ice Cream

Heat ¾ cup bourbon and ¼ cup of the sugar in a medium saucepan over medium-high heat. When the mixture is hot, stir to dissolve the sugar. Bring to a boil; then add the peach pieces. Adjust the heat to simmer, and cook the peaches for 3 minutes. Remove from the heat. Drain the peaches, reserving the liquid. Place the peaches on a dinner plate and refrigerate to cool. Return the reserved liquid to the saucepan and bring to a simmer. Continue simmering until the liquid is very syrupy and reduced to ¼ cup, about 10 minutes. Pour the syrup over the peaches to coat, and keep in the refrigerator until needed.

Heat 1½ cups heavy cream, 1½ cups half-and-half cream and ¼ cup of the sugar in a medium saucepan over medium-high heat. When hot, stir to dissolve the sugar. Bring to a boil.

While the cream mixture is heating, place 4 egg yolks and the remaining ¼ cup sugar in the bowl of an electric mixer fitted with a paddle. Beat on high speed for 2 minutes until thoroughly combined; then use a rubber spatula to scrape down the sides of the bowl. Beat on high for an additional 2 minutes until slightly thickened and pale yellow. If at this point the cream mixture has not yet started to boil, adjust the mixer speed to low, and continue to mix until it does boil; otherwise, undesirable lumps may form when the boiling cream mixture is added.

Gradually pour the boiling cream mixture into the beaten egg yolks and sugar, and mix on medium to combine, about 1 minute. (To avoid splattering the boiling cream mixture, use a pouring shield attachment, or place a towel or plastic wrap over the top of the mixer and down the sides to the bowl.)

Return the combined mixture to the saucepan, using a rubber spatula to facilitate transferring all of the mixture; then heat over medium heat, stirring constantly. Bring to a temperature of 185°F, about 3 minutes. Remove from the heat and transfer to a large stainless steel bowl. Cool in an ice-water bath to a temperature of 40° to 45°F.

When the mixture is cold, freeze in an ice cream freezer following the manufacturer's instructions. Transfer the semifrozen ice cream to a 2-quart plastic container. Add the chilled, syrup-coated peach pieces to the ice cream and use a rubber spatula to fold until well combined. Securely cover the container; then place in the freezer for several hours before serving.

PEACH AND BOURBON ICE CREAM

¾ cup bourbon

¾ cup granulated sugar

2 medium ripe peaches, washed, dried, unpeeled, pitted, and chopped into ½-inch pieces (about 1¾ cups)

1½ cups heavy cream

1½ cups half-and-half cream

4 large egg yolks

MILK CHOCOLATE PEACH PECAN UPSIDE-DOWN CAKE

¼ pound (1 stick) unsalted butter, cut into ½-ounce pieces; plus 1 teaspoon (melted)

¾ cup all-purpose flour

½ teaspoon baking powder

½ teaspoon salt

1 medium ripe peach, washed, dried, unpeeled, pitted, and cut into 16 slices

1 cup pecan halves, toasted (page 199) and coarsely chopped

¾ cup granulated sugar

1 large egg

2 large egg yolks

¼ cup sour cream

2 tablespoons whole milk

1 teaspoon pure vanilla extract

4 ounces milk chocolate, chopped into ¼-inch chunks

MILK CHOCOLATE DRIZZLE

1 ounce milk chocolate, coarsely chopped and melted (pages 197–98)

Make the Milk Chocolate Peach Pecan Upside-Down Cake

Preheat the oven to 325°F. Lightly coat the inside of a 9 × 2¾-inch nonstick cake pan using some of the 1 teaspoon of melted butter. Line the bottom of the pan with parchment paper (or wax paper); then lightly coat the paper with more melted butter. Set aside.

In a sifter combine ¾ cup flour, ½ teaspoon baking powder, and ½ teaspoon salt. Sift onto a large piece of parchment paper (or wax paper), and set aside until needed.

Arrange 14 of the peach slices, each cut side down (each inside cut edge touching or close to the next unpeeled edge, but not overlapping), in a circle on the buttered paper inside the cake pan. Place the 2 remaining peach slices in the center with rounded edges facing away from each other. Sprinkle 5 tablespoons of the chopped pecans over the peaches (making an effort to get as many chopped pecans as possible into the gaps between the peach slices).

Place ¾ cup sugar and ¼ pound butter in the bowl of an electric mixer fitted with a paddle. Mix on low speed for 1 minute; then beat on medium for 2 minutes. Scrape down the sides of the bowl and the paddle. Beat for 1 more minute on medium until soft. Scrape down the sides of the bowl. Add 1 egg and beat on medium for 1 minute. Add 2 egg yolks, one at a time, beating on medium for 30 seconds after each addition, and scraping down the sides of the bowl once the egg and the egg yolks have been incorporated. Oper-ate the mixer on low while gradually adding the sifted dry ingredients; mix until incorporated, about 30 seconds. Add ¼ cup sour cream and mix on low to combine, about 20 seconds. Add 2 tablespoons milk and 1 teaspoon vanilla extract and mix on low to combine, about 10 seconds. The batter may be lumpy at this point; if so, scrape down the sides of the bowl, then resume the mixing at medium speed for just 10 to 15 seconds. (You should now have smooth batter.) Remove the bowl from the mixer, add 4 ounces of milk chocolate chunks and the remaining chopped pecans, and use a rubber spatula to finish mixing the ingredients until thoroughly combined.

Transfer the cake batter to the prepared pan, spreading it gently and evenly over the peach slices. Bake on the center rack in the preheated oven until a toothpick inserted in the center of the cake comes out clean, about 55 minutes.

Remove the cake from the oven and cool in the pan for only 5 minutes at room temperature. Invert the cake onto a cardboard cake circle (or onto a cake plate). Lift the cake pan from the cake. (Use dry towels to hold the edges of the pan, since it will probably still be hot after only 5 minutes out of the oven.) Carefully peel the paper away from the bottom of the cake.

Apply the Milk Chocolate Drizzle

Use a soup spoon to drizzle the melted milk chocolate onto the peaches and over the entire top of the cake.

To Serve

Heat the blade of a slicer under hot running water and wipe it dry before cutting each slice. Serve each slice of warm cake with a scoop or two of the Peach and Bourbon Ice Cream.

THE CHEF'S TOUCH

As the soft and succulent flesh of a ripe peach yields to your gentle bite, you probably are wondering why Georgia is called the Peach State. But before the sweet juiciness tingles each taste bud to distraction, please note that the state of Virginia preceded the state of Georgia in the commercial planting of peaches in the nineteenth century. As the sweet perfume enlivens your senses, you should know that, for some time, Georgia has eclipsed Virginia by many millions of pounds a year in the production of peaches; yet California surpasses even Georgia in production. Now let the luscious piece of fruit pass your lips, and focus your wonder on the peach itself.

No matter what state produces the peaches that you use for this ambrosial confection, be certain to avoid bruised fruit with soft spots. Peaches will continue to ripen at room temperature. Store ripe peaches in the refrigerator, and conversely, store underripe fruit at room temperature for a couple of days (this works particularly well if you place the peaches in a brown paper bag), until the flesh yields gently to your touch.

Once cut, peaches will oxidize and turn brown; so don't cut the fruit until a few minutes before utilizing. The standard manner to prevent fruit from oxidizing is to dip it in acidulated water (water with lemon juice). I prefer not to do this with peaches, as the lemon permeates the flesh and takes away from the true flavor of the fruit.

The cake is most enjoyable when served warm (or at room temperature). So if it is refrigerated, heat the individual slices in the microwave oven for 35 seconds on defrost power before serving (or keep at room temperature for 30 to 40 minutes).

Rather than using a spoon to apply the Milk Chocolate Drizzle to the top of the cake, try using a small Ziploc bag. Put the chopped milk chocolate in the Ziploc bag and place it in a microwave oven set at medium power for 1½ minutes. After removing the chocolate from the microwave (the chocolate will be completely melted), simply snip the tip from a bottom corner of the bag. Pipe the entire amount of chocolate from the bag across the top of the cake.

ROSE LEVY BERANBAUM'S MARBLE EMPIRE CAKE *with* APPLE CRUMBLE ICE CREAM

SERVES 10

Prepare the Apple Crumble Ice Cream

Heat 1½ cups apple juice in a medium saucepan over medium-high heat. Bring to a boil; then reduce the heat to maintain a simmer for 25 minutes, until the apple juice has reduced to about ¼ cup. Remove from the heat. Transfer the reduced apple juice to a small bowl.

Wash and dry the unpeeled Granny Smith apple. Core, quarter, and then dice the apple into ¼-inch pieces. Immediately place the diced apples into the warm apple juice. Stir to thoroughly coat each piece of apple with the reduced juice. (Thoroughly coating the apple pieces with the juice will prevent them from discoloring.) Place the bowl, uncovered, in the refrigerator to cool until needed.

Heat 1½ cups heavy cream, ½ cup half and-half cream, ¼ cup light brown sugar, ⅛ teaspoon cinnamon, ⅛ teaspoon nutmeg, small pinch allspice, and a small pinch cloves in a medium saucepan over medium-high heat. When hot, stir to dissolve the sugar. Bring to a boil.

While the cream mixture is heating, place ¼ cup granulated sugar and 3 egg yolks in the bowl of an electric mixer fitted with a paddle. Beat on high speed for 2 minutes until thoroughly combined, then use a rubber spatula to scrape down the sides of the bowl. Beat on high for an additional 2 minutes until slightly thickened and pale yellow. If at this point the cream mixture has not yet started to boil, adjust the mixer speed to low and continue to mix until it does boil; otherwise, undesirable lumps may form when the boiling cream mixture is added.

Gradually pour the boiling cream mixture into the beaten sugar and egg yolks and mix on medium to combine, about 1 minute. (To avoid splattering the boiling cream mixture, use a pouring shield attachment, or place a towel or plastic wrap over the top of the mixer and down the sides to the bowl.)

Return the combined mixture to the saucepan (use a rubber spatula to facilitate transferring all of the mixture); then heat over medium heat, stirring constantly. Bring to a temperature of 185°F, about 3 minutes. Remove from the heat and transfer to a large stainless steel bowl. Cool in an ice-water bath to a temperature of 40° to 45°F.

When the mixture is cold, freeze in an ice cream freezer following the manufacturer's instructions. Transfer the semifrozen ice cream to a 2-quart plastic container. Add the diced apple and reduced apple juice mixture; then use a rubber spatula to fold the apples into the ice cream. Add the graham cracker pieces, and fold to combine. Cover the container, then place in the freezer for several hours before serving.

APPLE CRUMBLE ICE CREAM

- 1½ cups 100 percent pure apple juice
- 1 Granny Smith apple
- 1½ cups heavy cream
- ½ cup half-and-half cream
- ¼ cup (2 ounces) tightly packed light brown sugar
- ⅛ teaspoon ground cinnamon
- ⅛ teaspoon freshly grated nutmeg
- Small pinch ground allspice
- Small pinch ground cloves
- ¼ cup granulated sugar
- 3 large egg yolks
- 4 double graham crackers (2 ounces total) broken into approximately ½-inch pieces

MARBLE EMPIRE CAKE

- 6 ounces (1½ sticks) unsalted butter, cut into ½-ounce pieces (softened); plus 2 teaspoons (melted)
- 2 cups cake flour
- ½ teaspoon baking powder
- ½ teaspoon baking soda
- ¼ teaspoon salt
- 1 ounce semisweet baking chocolate, coarsely chopped and melted (pages 197–98)
- ½ ounce unsweetened baking chocolate, coarsely chopped and melted (pages 197–98)
- 4 large egg yolks
- ⅔ cup sour cream
- 1½ teaspoons pure vanilla extract
- 1 cup superfine sugar

Make the Marble Empire Cake

Preheat the oven to 350°F. Lightly coat the inside of a 9½ × 3¼-inch nonstick fluted tube pan using the 2 teaspoons of melted butter. Set aside.

In a sifter combine 2 cups cake flour, ½ teaspoon baking powder, ½ teaspoon baking soda, and ¼ teaspoon salt. Sift onto a large piece of parchment paper (or wax paper) and set aside until needed.

In a medium bowl, combine the melted 1 ounce semisweet baking chocolate and ½ ounce unsweetened baking chocolate. Set aside.

In a small bowl, lightly combine 4 egg yolks with ⅓ cup of the sour cream and 1½ teaspoons vanilla extract. Set aside.

Place the sifted dry ingredients and 1 cup superfine sugar in the bowl of an electric mixer fitted with a paddle. Mix on low speed to combine, about 30 seconds. Add 6 ounces softened butter and the remaining ⅓ cup sour cream and mix on low speed for 1 minute until the ingredients are combined and resemble a moist dough. Beat the mixture on medium speed for 1½ minutes until slightly fluffy.

Use a rubber spatula to scrape down the sides of the bowl. Add the egg yolk mixture, about one-third of the mixture at a time, mixing on low for 20 seconds after each addition, and scraping down the sides of the bowl once all of the egg yolk mixture has been added. Finally, beat the batter on medium for 10 seconds. Remove the bowl from the mixer and use a rubber spatula to finish mixing the ingredients until thoroughly combined. Transfer 1 cup of batter to the bowl of melted chocolate and use a rubber spatula to stir until uniform in color. Transfer 1 cup of the remaining plain batter to the prepared pan, using a rubber spatula to spread it evenly.

Portion 6 individual heaping tablespoons of the chocolate batter, evenly spaced, onto the layer of plain batter in the pan. Use a rubber spatula to gently, but evenly, spread the chocolate batter over the entire surface of the plain batter. Transfer 1 more cup of plain batter onto the layer of chocolate batter and spread evenly. Portion the remaining 6 to 7 heaping tablespoons of chocolate batter, evenly spaced, onto the layer of plain batter in the pan and spread evenly. Top the layer of chocolate batter with the remaining 1 cup or so of plain batter, and spread it evenly. Marbleize the cake by dipping the flat blade of a dinner knife into the batter, without touching the bottom, and then lifting the blade of the knife out of the batter in a folding motion, like the roll of a wave; repeat about 12 times, working around the entire pan. Smooth the surface of the batter with a rubber spatula.

Bake on the center rack in the preheated oven until a toothpick inserted in the center of the cake comes out clean and the cake springs back when pressed lightly in the center, about 40 minutes. Remove the cake from the oven and cool in the pan for 10 minutes at room temperature. Invert the cake onto a cake circle (or onto a cake plate).

To Serve

Heat the blade of a serrated slicer under hot running water and wipe the blade dry before cutting each slice. Serve each portion of cake while still warm or at room temperature with a #20 scoop of Apple Crumble Ice Cream.

THE CHEF'S TOUCH

"Marcel, someone on the phone is writing a story for the *New York Times,* and she wants to know if we forage for food served at The Trellis. Do you want to talk to her?"

"Yes, indeed," I replied one spring day in 1986. The delicate voice on the other end didn't sound like it belonged to an investigative reporter. Nevertheless, I wasted no time in venting my ire over a question that seemed to imply that in Virginia, the acquisition of food was as antiquated as the buildings on Duke of Gloucester Street. Laughing at my sensitivity, the scribe—Rose Levy Beranbaum—explained that the story she was writing focused on folks who forage for scarce comestibles and sell these foods to chefs who enjoy cooking the unusual.

I didn't realize at the time that I would become friends with Rose as a result of our mutual interest in writing dessert recipes. (Rose is the author of the award-winning *Cake Bible* cookbook, plus others.) Our friendship has included occasionally contributing a recipe or an inspiration to each other's books. The Marble Empire Cake, created by Rose, exemplifies her keen knowledge of the science of baking and the artistry of dessert making.

Ganache Hill test kitchen chef Brett Bailey, like Rose, grew up in New York State.

Brett was eager to develop an ice cream accompaniment for Rose's dessert. He was inspired by old-fashioned fruit desserts, such as cobblers, and also by the bounty of apples in his home state, to devise the exceptional Apple Crumble Ice Cream.

The ice cream recipe calls for a Granny Smith apple, but other firmly textured and tart-flavored apples can be used. Brett favors the Empire apple from the Finger Lakes region, where he grew up.

The 6 ounces of butter needed for the Marble Empire Cake may be softened in a microwave oven. Place the butter in a small glass bowl in a microwave set at medium-low for 30 seconds. Remove the bowl from the microwave and stir the butter with a rubber spatula. Return the butter to the microwave for 30 more seconds on medium-low. Remove the bowl from the microwave and stir the butter until softened and smooth.

Spooning warm Quintessential Chocolate Ganache (page 157) over the cake and ice cream will bring this cake to the level of indulgence only tolerable to those not troubled by conscience. And if you are of that ilk, I additionally recommend a snifter of a fine Cognac to further please the palate and the soul.

This dessert may be prepared over 2 days. DAY 1: Prepare and freeze the Apple Crumble Ice Cream. DAY 2: Make the Marble Empire Cake. Slice and serve the cake with the ice cream.

SKY-HIGH CAKES

DANGEROUSLY TOWERING CHOCOLATE DELECTABLES

CHOCOLATE ROCKY ROAD

SERVES 12

Make the Chocolate Bypass Cake

Preheat the oven to 325°F. Lightly coat the insides of three 9 × 1½-inch nonstick cake pans using some of the 1 tablespoon melted butter. Line the bottoms of the pans with parchment paper (or wax paper): then lightly coat the paper with more melted butter. Set aside.

In a sifter combine ½ cup all-purpose flour, ½ cup cake flour, 2 teaspoons baking powder, and ¼ teaspoon baking soda. Sift onto a large piece of parchment paper (or wax paper) and set aside until needed.

Place ½ pound butter and 1 cup sugar in the bowl of an electric mixer fitted with a paddle. Mix on low speed for 1 minute, then beat on medium for 2 minutes until soft. Use a rubber spatula to scrape down the sides of the bowl and the paddle. Beat on medium for an additional 2 minutes until very soft. Scrape down the sides of the bowl. Add 2 eggs and 2 egg whites, one at a time, beating on medium for 30 seconds after each addition, and scraping down the sides of the bowl once all the eggs have been incorporated. (The batter looks like cottage cheese at this point; it will look more appetizing once the melted chocolate is added. Doesn't everything look better with melted chocolate?)

Add the melted semisweet and unsweetened chocolate and beat on medium for 15 seconds until combined. Scrape down the sides of the bowl. Operate the mixer on low while gradually adding the sifted dry ingredients; mix until incorporated, about 45 seconds. Add 1 cup sour cream and mix on low to combine, about 20 seconds. Remove the bowl from the mixer. Add 1 cup chocolate mini-morsels and the coarsely chopped pecans. Use a rubber spatula to finish mixing the batter until thoroughly combined.

Immediately divide the cake batter into the prepared pans (about 2½ cups of batter in each pan), spreading it evenly. Bake on the top and center racks in the preheated oven until a toothpick inserted in the center of each cake layer comes out clean, about 32 minutes. (Rotate the pans from top to center halfway through the baking time.) Remove the cake layers from the oven and cool in the pans for 15 minutes at room temperature. Invert the cake layers onto cake circles (or onto cake plates). Carefully peel the paper away from the bottoms of the cake layers. Refrigerate the cake layers until needed.

Prepare the Cocoa Kit and Caboodle Icing

In a sifter combine 3 cups of the confectioners' sugar and ½ cup of the cocoa powder. Sift onto a large piece of parchment paper (or wax paper). Combine the 3 remaining cups of con-

CHOCOLATE BYPASS CAKE

½ pound (2 sticks) unsalted butter, cut into ½-ounce pieces; plus 1 tablespoon (melted)

½ cup all-purpose flour

½ cup cake flour

2 teaspoons baking powder

¼ teaspoon baking soda

1 cup granulated sugar

2 large eggs

2 large egg whites

8 ounces semisweet baking chocolate, coarsely chopped and melted (pages 197–98)

2 ounces unsweetened baking chocolate, coarsely chopped and melted (pages 197–98)

1 cup sour cream

1 cup semisweet chocolate mini-morsels

1 cup pecan halves, toasted (page 199) and coarsely chopped

COCOA KIT AND CABOODLE ICING

6 cups confectioners' sugar

1 cup unsweetened cocoa powder

8 ounces cream cheese, cut into 1-ounce pieces

½ pound (2 sticks) unsalted butter, cut into ½-ounce pieces

6 tablespoons granulated sugar

¼ cup whole milk

2 teaspoons pure vanilla extract

1½ cups miniature marshmallows

½ cup semisweet chocolate mini-morsels

½ cup pecan halves, toasted (page 199) and coarsely chopped

ROCKY ROAD GARNISH

1 cup pecan halves, toasted (page 199) and coarsely chopped

3 ounces semisweet baking chocolate, coarsely chopped

1 cup miniature marshmallows, coarsely chopped

fectioners' sugar and remaining ½ cup of cocoa in a sifter, and sift onto another large piece of parchment paper (or wax paper). Set both aside until needed.

Place 8 ounces cream cheese, ½ pound butter, and 6 tablespoons granulated sugar in the bowl of an electric mixer fitted with a paddle. Mix on low speed for 1 minute, then beat on medium-high for 2 minutes until soft. Scrape down the sides of the bowl and the paddle. Beat on medium for 2 more minutes until very soft. Add the combined sifted 3 cups confectioners' sugar and ½ cup cocoa powder from one of the sheets of parchment paper and mix on the lowest speed to combine, about 1 minute. Add ¼ cup milk and 2 teaspoons vanilla extract and mix on low for 15 seconds. Add the remaining combined sifted 3 cups confectioners' sugar and ½ cup cocoa powder and mix on low for 15 seconds; then beat on medium for 15 seconds. Remove the bowl from the mixer and use a rubber spatula to finish mixing the ingredients until thoroughly combined.

Transfer 3 cups of the icing to a medium bowl and set aside. (This plain icing, minus "the whole kit and caboodle"—the pecans, chocolate mini-morsels, and miniature marshmallows—will ice the top and sides of the assembled cake layers.) Add 1½ cups miniature marshmallows, ½ cup semisweet chocolate mini-morsels, and ½ cup chopped pecans to the mixing bowl with the remaining icing, and use a rubber spatula to finish mixing the ingredients until thoroughly combined. Set aside.

Prepare the Rocky Road Garnish

Thoroughly combine 1 cup chopped pecans, 3 ounces chopped semisweet chocolate, and 1 cup chopped miniature marshmallows in a medium bowl. (Your hands are the preferred tools for this task.) Set aside.

Construct the Rocky Road Cake

Remove the cake layers from the refrigerator. Use a cake spatula to evenly and smoothly spread 2 cups of the Cocoa Kit and Caboodle Icing (that's the icing with the chopped pecans, mini-morsels, and marshmallows) over the top and to the edges on each of two of the inverted cake layers. (Given the texture of Cocoa Kit and Caboodle Icing, "evenly and smoothly" are relative terms.) Stack the two layers, then top with the last inverted cake layer, bottom facing up. (Use a utility turner to remove the cake layers from the cardboard cake circles.) Gently press the layers into place. Spread the remaining 3 cups of plain icing evenly and smoothly over the top and sides of the cake. Refrigerate the cake for 15 minutes.

Remove the cake from the refrigerator. Set aside ¾ cup of the Rocky Road Garnish. Press the remaining amount into the sides of the cake, coating it evenly. (Do this over a baking sheet with sides to contain the construction debris.) Now sprinkle the reserved amount evenly over the entire top of the cake. Refrigerate for 12 hours before serving.

To Serve

Heat the blade of a serrated slicer under hot running water and wipe the blade dry before making each slice. Serve immediately.

THE CHEF'S TOUCH

Back in the '70s, when my wife, Connie, and I ran marathons, we had an insatiable addiction to rocky road ice cream. We could knock off a half-gallon container in two seatings. Going into the twenty-first century, it seems that our metabolisms have changed, and we must be more circumspect about our daily confectionery experience, especially now that our running mileage is more moderate. But don't worry about my nostalgic musings; I'll never be a bully pulpit for chocolate moderation. Rather, I am going to let you in on a little secret: Chocolate Rocky Road is even more outrageously phenomenal than rocky road ice cream. Does that mean we must start running marathons again?

As much as I admire the food processor, there are some chopping tasks that must be done by hand. Case in point: marshmallows. We tried coarsely chopping miniature marsh-

mallows in a food processor, and all we garnered were rutty marshmallow balls. (Now that's a rocky road.)

After assembly, you may keep the Chocolate Rocky Road in the refrigerator for a day or two. To avoid permeating the cake with refrigerator odors, place the cake in a large, tightly sealed plastic container.

This cake may be prepared over 3 days. DAY 1: Bake the Chocolate Bypass Cake layers. Once cooled, cover each layer with plastic wrap and refrigerate until the next day. DAY 2: Prepare the Cocoa Kit and Caboodle Icing. Ice the cake as directed in the recipe, then refrigerate it in a sealed plastic container until the next day. DAY 3: Two to 3 hours before serving, make the Rocky Road Garnish and assemble the cake. Slice and serve the cake.

One aspect of the diet regimen that Connie and I adapted in our marathon days, and one to which we subscribe today, is our breakfast meal of a big bowl of cereal with lots of fruit and fat-free milk. However, with Chocolate Rocky Road, go for high-test—pour whole milk and enjoy.

CHOCOLATE NUT *and* HONEY CAKE *with* GRANNY'S HARD APPLESAUCE

SERVES 12

Make the Nutty Applejack Cake

Preheat the oven to 325°F. Combine 1 cup cashews, 1 cup pecan halves, and 1 cup walnut halves together in a medium bowl. Set aside. Lightly coat the insides of three 9 × 1½-inch nonstick cake pans using some of the 1 tablespoon of melted butter. Line the bottoms of the pans with parchment paper (or wax paper), then lightly coat the paper with more melted butter. Set aside.

In a sifter combine 2 cups flour, 1 teaspoon baking powder, 1 teaspoon baking soda, 1 teaspoon ground cinnamon, and ½ teaspoon salt. Sift onto a large piece of parchment paper (or wax paper) and set aside until needed.

Place ½ pound butter and 1 cup sugar in the bowl of an electric mixer fitted with a paddle. Mix on low speed for 1 minute, then beat on medium-high until soft, about 2 minutes. Scrape down the sides of the bowl and the paddle. Beat on medium-high for an additional 2 minutes until very soft. Add 2 eggs, one at a time, beating on medium for 30 seconds after each addition, and scraping down the sides of the bowl once both eggs have been incorporated. Now beat on medium-high for 1 minute until fluffy. Operate the mixer on low while gradually adding the sifted dry ingredients; mix until incorporated, about 1 minute. Add ½ cup sour cream

and 1 cup of the chopped nuts (the remaining chopped nuts will be used to garnish the sides of the cake), and mix on low to combine, about 20 seconds. Add ½ cup apple juice and ½ cup apple brandy and mix on low speed for 20 seconds. Remove the bowl from the mixer and use a rubber spatula to finish mixing the ingredients until thoroughly combined.

Immediately divide the cake batter into the prepared pans (about 2 cups of batter in each pan), spreading it evenly. Bake on the top and center racks in the preheated oven until a toothpick inserted in the center of each cake layer comes out clean, 28 to 30 minutes. (Rotate the pans from top to center halfway through the baking time.) Remove the cake layers from the oven and cool in the pans for 15 minutes at room temperature. Invert the cake layers onto cake circles (or onto cake plates). Carefully peel the paper away from the bottoms of the cake layers. Refrigerate the cake layers until needed.

Prepare the Chocolate Honey Buttercream

Place 1 pound butter in the bowl of an electric mixer fitted with a paddle. Mix on low speed for 1 minute; then increase the speed to medium-high and beat for 2 minutes until soft. Scrape down the sides of the bowl and the paddle. Beat on medium for 2 minutes

NUTTY APPLEJACK CAKE

1 cup cashews, toasted (page 199) and chopped

1 cup pecan halves, toasted (page 199) and chopped

1 cup walnut halves, toasted (page 199) and chopped

½ pound (2 sticks) unsalted butter, cut into ½-ounce pieces; plus 1 tablespoon (melted)

2 cups all-purpose flour

1 teaspoon baking powder

1 teaspoon baking soda

1 teaspoon ground cinnamon

½ teaspoon salt

1 cup granulated sugar

2 large eggs

½ cup sour cream

½ cup apple juice

½ cup apple brandy

CHOCOLATE HONEY BUTTERCREAM

1 pound (4 sticks) unsalted butter, cut into ½-ounce pieces

4 ounces unsweetened baking chocolate, coarsely chopped and melted (pages 197–98)

½ teaspoon ground cinnamon

½ cup mild-flavored honey

½ cup granulated sugar

2 large egg whites

GRANNY'S HARD APPLESAUCE

1 teaspoon fresh lemon juice

2 quarts of cold water

6 Granny Smith apples

½ cup apple juice

¼ cup granulated sugar

¼ teaspoon ground cinnamon

¼ teaspoon freshly grated nutmeg

1 cup apple brandy

more until very soft. Add the melted unsweetened chocolate and ½ teaspoon ground cinnamon and beat on medium until combined, about 1 minute. Scrape down the sides of the bowl. Gradually add ½ cup honey while beating on medium for 2 minutes until fluffy. Transfer the chocolate-and-honey-enhanced butter to a medium bowl and set aside at room temperature until needed.

Heat 1 inch of water in a large saucepan over medium heat. When the water begins to simmer, place ½ cup sugar and 2 egg whites in a large bowl. Set the bowl into the saucepan. (The bottom of the bowl should not be touching the water.) Using a hand-held whisk, gently whisk the sugar and egg whites until the mixture reaches a temperature of 140°F, 3 to 4 minutes.

Transfer the heated egg white mixture to the bowl of an electric mixer fitted with a balloon whip. (Make certain that the bowl and whip are meticulously clean and dry; otherwise the egg white mixture will not whisk properly.) Whisk on high until very shiny and gooey (looks like marshmallow topping from the grocery store), about 2 minutes. Add half of the chocolate-and-honey-enhanced butter to the egg whites and whisk on high for 30 seconds. Add the remaining butter mixture to the mixing bowl and whisk on high for 30 seconds. Scrape down the sides of the bowl. Transfer the Chocolate Honey Buttercream to a medium bowl, cover the bowl with plastic wrap, and set aside at room temperature until needed.

Assemble the Nutty Applejack Cake

Remove the cake layers from the refrigerator. Use a cake spatula to evenly and smoothly spread 1½ cups of buttercream over the top and to the edges of one of the cake layers. Place a second cake layer onto the buttercream-coated cake layer and gently press it into place. Spread 1½ cups of buttercream evenly over the top and to the edges of the second cake layer; then top with the third cake layer, gently pressing it into place. Spread the remaining buttercream onto the top and sides of the cake; refrigerate the cake for 15 minutes.

Remove the cake from the refrigerator. Press the remaining chopped nuts into the sides of the cake, coating them evenly. Refrigerate for 2 hours before serving.

Make Granny's Hard Applesauce

In a medium bowl, combine 1 teaspoon lemon juice and 2 quarts of cold water. One at a time, core and quarter 4 of the apples. Cut the quarters in half lengthwise; then immediately place the apple sections in the acidulated water to prevent them from discoloring. Drain the apple sections in a colander, rinse under cold water, and shake dry.

Heat the apple sections, ½ cup apple juice, ¼ cup sugar, ¼ teaspoon ground cinnamon, and ¼ teaspoon grated nutmeg in a medium saucepan, covered, over medium heat. Bring to a boil; then lower the heat and simmer for 20 minutes until the apples are tender. Remove the lid, and simmer for an additional 2 minutes. Remove from the heat.

Process the mixture in a food processor fitted with a metal blade for 30 seconds until completely pureed. Transfer the apple puree to a medium bowl. Add 1 cup apple brandy and stir to combine.

Wash and dry the remaining 2 apples. Peel, core, quarter, and then cut the apples into ¼-inch dice. Immediately place the diced apples into the warm applesauce. Stir to combine. The applesauce can be served right away or cooled to room temperature and then refrigerated in a covered noncorrosive container for several days before serving.

To Serve

Heat the blade of a serrated slicer under hot running water and wipe the blade dry before cutting each slice. Place each slice onto a dessert plate and keep at room temperature for about 30 minutes before serving. When ready to serve, ladle ¼ cup of Granny's Hard Applesauce around the cake on each plate.

THE CHEF'S TOUCH

In New England, where I grew up, "applejack" was what we called apple cider that was fortified with brandy. The combination, I like to believe, reflects my French Canadian ancestors' link to their Normandy roots. Needless to say, I have been fond of applejack for a number of years. And besides being a palatable component of this recipe, the joining together of apple brandy and apple cider is a most agreeable marriage.

A virtual panoply of honey varieties can be found at the supermarket. Some are quite exotic, but for this recipe you should select a mild, all-purpose honey, such as clover honey.

Served warm or cold, Granny's Hard Applesauce will give you a nice glow. If it is too boozy for your taste, consider adding an additional ¼ cup of sugar to soften the alcoholic flavor, or cut back the quantity to ½ cup of apple brandy. Not feeling bibulous? Then replace the brandy with additional apple juice or apple cider.

Cider brandy has been distilled for centuries in Europe. Calvados, the most famous and arguably the best of these is an eau-de-vie (a colorless spirit) produced in Normandy. You may select a Calvados for this recipe, or do as we did and choose a more economical American regional apple brandy like Captain Apple Jack apple brandy, which is distilled in North Garden, Virginia.

CHOCOLATE PORTO ENCHANTMENT CAKE

SERVES 12

Make the Cocoa Pine Nut Cake

Preheat over to 350°F. Lightly coat the insides of four 9 × 1½-inch nonstick cake pans using some of the 1 tablespoon of melted butter. Line the bottoms of the pans with parchment paper (or wax paper), then lightly coat the paper with more melted butter. Set aside.

In a sifter combine 2 cups flour, 2 tablespoons cocoa powder, and 1 teaspoon baking soda. Sift onto a large piece of parchment paper (or wax paper) and set aside until needed.

Place 1 cup light brown sugar and ¼ pound butter in the bowl of an electric mixer fitted with a paddle. Mix on low speed for 1 minute; then beat on medium for 2 minutes until soft. Use a rubber spatula to scrape down the sides of the bowl. Add 1 egg and beat on medium for 1 minute until incorporated. Scrape down the sides of the bowl.

Operate the mixer on low while gradually adding half of the sifted dry ingredients; mix until incorporated, about 30 seconds. Gradually add ½ cup of the buttermilk and mix on low to incorporate, about 20 seconds. While continuing to operate the mixer on low, gradually add the remaining sifted dry ingredients and mix for 20 seconds. Gradually add the remaining ½ cup of buttermilk and mix on low for 20 seconds. Add 1 teaspoon vanilla extract and mix on medium for 10 seconds. Remove the bowl from the mixer, add the ¼-inch pieces of pine nuts, and use a rubber spatula to finish mixing the ingredients until thoroughly combined.

Immediately divide the cake batter into the prepared pans (about 1 cup of batter in each pan), spreading it evenly. Bake on the top and center racks in the preheated oven until a toothpick inserted in the center of each cake layer comes out clean, about 12 minutes. (Although the cakes bake rather quickly, for best results, rotate the pans from top to center halfway through the baking time.) Remove the cake layers from the oven and cool in the pans for 10 minutes at room temperature. Invert the layers onto cake circles (or onto cake plates). Carefully peel the paper away from the bottoms of the layers. Using a very clean pastry brush, brush each cake layer with 1 tablespoon port wine. Refrigerate the cake layers until needed.

Make the Chocolate Porto–Fig Buttercream

Heat 1 cup of port wine and the fig pieces in a medium saucepan over medium-high heat. Bring to a boil; then reduce the heat to maintain a simmer for 20 to 22 minutes, until the port has almost completely evaporated and

COCOA PINE NUT CAKE

¼ pound (1 stick) unsalted butter, cut into ½-ounce pieces; plus 1 tablespoon (melted)

2 cups all-purpose flour

2 tablespoons unsweetened cocoa powder

1 teaspoon baking soda

1 cup (8 ounces) tightly packed light brown sugar

1 large egg

1 cup buttermilk

1 teaspoon pure vanilla extract

¾ cup pine nuts, toasted (page 199) and chopped by hand into ¼-inch pieces

¼ cup port wine

CHOCOLATE PORTO–FIG BUTTERCREAM

1 cup port wine

8 dried figs (about 5 ounces), stemmed and cut into ⅛-inch pieces

½ pound (2 sticks) unsalted butter, cut into ½-ounce pieces

½ cup granulated sugar

2 large egg whites

6 ounces semisweet baking chocolate, coarsely chopped and melted (pages 197–98)

CHOCOLATE PINE NUT BUTTERCREAM

¾ **pound (3 sticks) unsalted butter, cut into ½-ounce pieces**

½ **cup granulated sugar**

3 large egg whites

½ **cup pine nuts, toasted (page 199) and coarsely chopped**

2 ounces semisweet baking chocolate, coarsely chopped and melted (pages 197–98)

infused the figs with a juicy berrylike flavor. Transfer the port-steeped figs to a dinner plate, spread them evenly, and place, uncovered, in the refrigerator to cool.

Place ½ pound butter in the bowl of an electric mixer fitted with a paddle. Mix on low speed for 1 minute, then increase the speed to medium-high and beat for 2 minutes until soft. Scrape down the sides of the bowl and the paddle. Beat on medium for 2 more minutes until very soft. Transfer the butter to a small bowl and set aside at room temperature until needed.

Heat 1 inch of water in a large saucepan over medium heat. When the water begins to simmer, place ½ cup sugar and 2 egg whites in a large bowl. Set the bowl into the saucepan (the bottom of the bowl should not be touching the water). Using a handheld whisk, gently whisk the sugar and egg whites until the mixture reaches a temperature of 140°F, 3 to 4 minutes.

Transfer the heated egg white mixture to the bowl of an electric mixer fitted with a balloon whip. (Make certain that the bowl and whip are meticulously clean and dry; otherwise, the egg white mixture will not whisk properly.) Whisk on high until shiny and very viscous (looks like a commercial marshmallow topping), about 2 minutes. Add half of the whipped butter to the egg whites and whisk on high for 30 seconds. Scrape down the sides of the bowl. Add the remaining butter, the port-steeped figs, and 6 ounces melted semisweet chocolate to the mixing bowl and whisk on high for 30 seconds. Scrape down

the sides of the bowl. Reserve 1 cup of buttercream in a small bowl; then transfer the remaining buttercream to a pastry bag fitted with a medium straight tip, and set aside at room temperature until needed.

Make the Chocolate Pine Nut Buttercream

Place ¾ pound butter in the bowl of an electric mixer fitted with a paddle. Mix on low speed for 1 minute; then increase the speed to medium-high and beat for 2 minutes until soft. Scrape down the sides of the bowl and the paddle. Beat on medium for 2 more minutes until very soft. Transfer the butter to a small bowl and set aside at room temperature until needed.

Heat 1 inch of water in a large saucepan over medium heat. When the water begins to simmer, place ½ cup sugar and 3 egg whites in a large bowl. Set the bowl into the saucepan (the bottom of the bowl should not be touching the water). Using a handheld whisk, gently whisk the sugar and egg whites until the mixture reaches a temperature of 140°F, 3 to 4 minutes. Transfer the heated egg white mixture to the bowl of an electric mixer fitted with a balloon whip. (Make certain that the bowl and whip are meticulously clean and dry; otherwise, the egg white mixture will not whisk properly.)

Whisk on high until slightly shiny and thick (this 3-egg-white mixture has a less lustrous look than the 2-egg-white mixture in the Chocolate Porto-Fig Buttercream), about 2 minutes. Add half of the whipped butter to the egg whites and whisk on high for 30 seconds. Add the remaining butter, coarsely chopped pine nuts, and 2 ounces melted semisweet chocolate to the mixing bowl and whisk on high for 30 seconds. Scrape down the sides of the bowl. Reserve 1¾ cups of buttercream in a small bowl, then transfer the remaining buttercream to a pastry bag fitted with a medium straight tip. Set aside at room temperature until needed.

Assemble the Cake

Remove the cake layers from the refrigerator. Pipe a ¾-inch-wide and ½-inch-high ring of the Chocolate Porto-Fig Buttercream along the outside edge of a port-wine-brushed cake layer.

Pipe a similar ring of the Chocolate Pine Nut Buttercream alongside the Porto-Fig Buttercream, on the inside. Continue to pipe alternating rings of the two buttercreams until the surface of the cake layer is covered.

Place a second cake layer, port-wine-brushed side up, onto the rings of buttercream and gently press down on the cake to set it into place; repeat the procedure of piping alternating rings of buttercream until the second cake layer is covered. Repeat this procedure with the third cake layer; then top the third layer of buttercream rings with the last cake layer, once again with port-wine-brushed side up. Press down gently on the last layer to set it into place.

Use a cake spatula to evenly spread 1¾ cups of Chocolate Pine Nut Buttercream over the top of the cake, to the edges.

Transfer the remaining Chocolate Porto-Fig Buttercream to a pastry bag fitted with a large straight tip. Pipe a ring of 12 evenly spaced "kiss"-like portions of buttercream (envision a large chocolate candy "kiss") along the outside edge of the top of the cake. Refrigerate the cake for 2 hours before serving.

To Serve

Heat the blade of a serrated slicer under hot running water and wipe the blade dry before cutting each slice. Serve immediately.

THE CHEF'S TOUCH

Those who have been enchanted by Porto through the centuries are legion. Words like "peculiar," "complex," and "persevering" flow easily from the palate of those who drink it. After all, what other wine is produced from so many grape varieties? Most quality ports are produced from six or seven varietals, which are grown in such hardscrabble earth that the rocky soil must be dynamited before the vines can be planted. The ambrosial sweetness of this wine makes for confectionery synergy; and what a symphony of pleasure awaits in our Chocolate Porto Enchantment Cake, with chocolate, figs, pine nuts, and port playing out one delightful mouthful after the other.

Pick prime dried figs at your specialty grocer or health food store. Calimyrna figs, from California, and their ancestor the Smyrna fig, from Turkey, possess a unique nutty flavor that is enhanced by steeping the figs in port: yet the figs retain a pleasing texture.

After assembly, you may keep the Chocolate Porto Enchantment Cake in the refrigerator for 2 to 3 days before serving. To avoid permeating the cake with refrigerator odors, place the cake in a large, tightly sealed plastic container.

This cake may be prepared over 3 days. DAY 1: Bake the Cocoa Pine Nut Cake layers; once cooled, cover with plastic wrap and refrigerate overnight. DAY 2: Prepare the Chocolate Porto-Fig Buttercream and the Chocolate Pine Nut Buttercream. Assemble the cake as directed. Place the cake in a large, tightly sealed plastic container and refrigerate. DAY 3: Slice and serve the cake.

Although a first-rate ruby port from California would work for this recipe, why not seek the higher ground and select a port from its ancestral geography—Portugal? At Ganache Hill, we used a Taylor Fladgate First Estate Reserve for this recipe. Although this premium ruby-style porto is nonvintage, it delivers an opulence of fruit suitable for sipping as well as baking.

PEANUT BUTTER CHOCOLATE CHIP ICE CREAM CAKE

SERVES 12

Make the Chocolate Goober Ice Cream

Heat ¾ cup of the heavy cream, 4 ounces chopped semisweet chocolate, and 1 ounce chopped unsweetened chocolate in the top half of a double boiler, or in a microwave oven (see pages 197–98 for more details), and stir until smooth. Set aside until needed.

Heat the remaining 1¼ cups heavy cream, 1½ cups half-and-half cream, and ¾ cup of the sugar in a medium saucepan over medium-high heat. When hot, stir to dissolve the sugar. Bring to a boil.

While the cream mixture is heating, place 4 egg yolks and the remaining ¾ cup sugar in the bowl of an electric mixer fitted with a paddle. Beat on high speed for 2 minutes until thoroughly combined; then use a rubber spatula to scrape down the sides of the bowl. Beat on high for an additional 2 minutes until slightly thickened and pale yellow. If at this point the cream mixture has not yet started to boil, adjust the mixer speed to low and continue to mix until it does boil; otherwise, undesirable lumps may form when the boiling cream mixture is added.

Gradually pour the boiling cream mixture into the beaten egg yolks and sugar and mix on low to combine, about 1 minute. (To avoid splattering the boiling cream mixture, use a pouring shield attachment, or place a towel or plastic wrap over the top of the mixer and down the sides to the bowl.) Return the combined mixture to the saucepan, using a rubber spatula to facilitate transferring all of the mixture from the bowl. Heat over medium heat, stirring constantly. Bring to a temperature of 185°F, about 2 minutes. Remove from the heat and transfer to a large stainless steel bowl. Add the melted chocolate and heavy cream mixture and stir to incorporate. Cool in an ice-water bath to a temperature of 40° to 45°F. When the mixture is cold, freeze in an ice cream freezer following the manufacturer's instructions. Transfer the semifrozen ice cream to a 2-quart plastic container. Add 1 cup unsalted peanuts, and use a rubber spatula to fold the peanuts into the ice cream. Cover the container securely, then place in the freezer for 2 to 3 hours before assembling the ice cream cake.

Make the Peanut Butter Chocolate Chip Cake

Preheat the oven to 325°F. Lightly coat the insides of three 9 × 1½-inch nonstick baking pans using some of the 1 tablespoon of melted butter. Line the bottoms of the pans with parchment paper (or wax paper); then lightly coat the paper with more melted butter. Set aside.

In a sifter combine 1 cup flour, ¼ teaspoon baking powder, ¼ teaspoon baking

CHOCOLATE GOOBER ICE CREAM

2 cups heavy cream

4 ounces semisweet baking chocolate, coarsely chopped

1 ounce unsweetened baking chocolate, coarsely chopped

1½ cups half-and-half cream

1½ cups granulated sugar

4 large egg yolks

1 cup unsalted dry roasted peanuts

PEANUT BUTTER CHOCOLATE CHIP CAKE

2 ounces (½ stick) unsalted butter, cut into ½-ounce pieces; plus 1 tablespoon (melted)

1 cup all-purpose flour

¼ teaspoon baking powder

¼ teaspoon baking soda

¼ teaspoon salt

½ cup (4 ounces) tightly packed light brown sugar

3 ounces creamy peanut butter

1 large egg

1 large egg yolk

¼ cup sour cream

¼ cup hot water

½ teaspoon pure vanilla extract

½ cup semisweet chocolate chips

CHOCOLATE PEANUT ICING

10 ounces semisweet baking chocolate, coarsely chopped

1 cup heavy cream

¼ cup granulated sugar

3 tablespoons creamy peanut butter

2 tablespoons unsalted butter

soda, and ¼ teaspoon salt. Sift onto a large piece of parchment paper (or wax paper) and set aside until needed.

Place ½ cup light brown sugar, 3 ounces peanut butter, and 2 ounces butter in the bowl of an electric mixer fitted with a paddle. Mix on low speed for 1 minute, then beat on medium-high for 2 minutes until slightly fluffy. Use a rubber spatula to scrape down the sides of the bowl and the paddle, then beat on medium-high for an additional 2 minutes until very fluffy. Scrape down the sides of the bowl. Add 1 egg and 1 egg yolk and beat on medium for 30 seconds to combine. Scrape down the sides of the bowl. Operate the mixer on low while gradually adding half of the sifted dry ingredients; mix until incorporated, about 20 seconds. Add ¼ cup sour cream and mix on medium to combine, about 20 seconds. Gradually add the remaining sifted dry ingredients while mixing on low to combine, about 20 seconds. Add ¼ cup hot water in a slow, steady stream and mix on low to combine, about 30 seconds. Add ½ teaspoon vanilla extract and mix on medium for 10 seconds. Remove the bowl from the mixer, add ½ cup chocolate chips, and use a rubber spatula to finish mixing the ingredients until thoroughly combined.

Immediately divide the cake batter into the prepared pans (slightly more than 1 cup of batter in each pan), spreading it evenly. Bake on the top and center racks in the preheated oven until a toothpick inserted in the center of each cake layer comes out clean, about 22 minutes. (Rotate the pans from top to center halfway through the baking time.) Remove the cake layers from the oven and cool in the pans for 10 minutes at room temperature. Invert the cake layers onto cake circles (or cake plates). Carefully peel the paper away from the bottoms of the layers. Refrigerate the cake layers for 10 to 15 minutes, until chilled, before assembling the cake.

Begin the Assembly

Remove the cake layers from the refrigerator and the ice cream from the freezer. Turn one of the inverted cake layers baked top facing up, and place into a clean and dry 9 × 1½-inch nonstick cake pan. Portion about half of the ice cream on top of the cake layer. Use a rubber spatula to spread the ice cream evenly over the cake. Turn another inverted cake layer over, and gently press into place onto the layer of ice cream in the cake pan. Cover the top of the pan with plastic wrap and place in the freezer. Turn the last inverted cake layer over and into another clean and dry 9 × 1½-inch nonstick cake pan. Portion the remaining ice cream over the cake and spread it evenly to the edges. Cover the pan with plastic wrap and place in the freezer with the other pan for at least 12 hours, until the ice cream is solid to the touch.

Continue the Assembly

After the cake and ice cream sections have been in the freezer for 12 hours, remove them from the freezer. Remove and discard the plastic wrap. Use a paring knife to cut all around the frozen cake and ice cream in each of the two pans, running the blade between the outside edges of the cake and the inside edges of the cake pan. Invert both frozen cake and ice cream sections onto cake circles (or cake plates). Take the section that has only 1 cake layer and invert again, onto another cake circle, so that the ice-cream layer is facing up. Place the other portion of the cake on top of the first section. Use a cake spatula to smooth the ice cream that has oozed out onto the sides of the cake, spreading it evenly around the entire cake. Place the cake in the freezer while preparing the icing.

Prepare the Chocolate Peanut Icing

Place 10 ounces chopped semisweet chocolate in a large bowl.

Heat 1 cup heavy cream, ¼ cup sugar, 3 tablespoons peanut butter, and 2 tablespoons butter in a medium saucepan over medium-high heat. When hot, stir to dissolve the peanut butter and sugar. Bring to a boil. Pour the boiling cream mixture over the chopped chocolate. Set aside for 5 minutes before stirring with a whisk until smooth. Now pour the chocolate mixture onto a baking sheet with sides and spread it evenly toward the edges of the baking sheet. Place the baking sheet in the refrigerator until the chocolate mixture is firm to the touch, about 45 minutes.

Transfer the chilled chocolate mixture to the bowl of an electric mixer fitted with a paddle. Beat on medium speed for 2 minutes. Scrape down the sides of the bowl. Beat on medium-high for 1 more minute until fluffy.

Ice the Cake and Serve

Remove the ice cream cake from the freezer. Use a cake spatula to spread the icing evenly over the top and sides of the cake. Return the cake to the freezer for 1 hour before cutting and serving it.

To Serve

Heat the blade of a serrated slicer under hot running water and wipe the blade dry before cutting each slice. Serve immediately.

THE CHEF'S TOUCH

The chocolate mixture for the Chocolate Peanut Icing must be thoroughly chilled before it is transferred to the electric mixer; otherwise, it will separate during the beating process.

If the Chocolate Goober Ice Cream is too hard to be spread evenly onto the cake layers, soften it in the refrigerator for about 45 minutes or so.

After removing the ice-cream-topped cake layers from the freezer, you may find them frozen stubbornly to the pans. If the paring knife used to cut around the edges of the pan isn't sufficient to release the cakes, place the pans on a heating pad or a large hot towel for a few moments to facilitate their release.

After assembly, you may keep the Peanut Butter Chocolate Chip Ice Cream Cake in the freezer for several days. To avoid permeating the cake with freezer odors, place the cake in a large, tightly sealed plastic container.

This cake may be prepared over 3 days. DAY 1: Make and freeze the Chocolate Goober Ice Cream. Bake the Peanut Butter Chocolate Chip Cake layers. Once cooled, cover each layer with plastic wrap and refrigerate until the next day. DAY 2: Remove the cake layers from the refrigerator and the ice cream from the freezer. Spread the ice cream onto the cake layers as directed in the recipe. If the ice cream is too hard to spread, soften (but don't thaw) the ice cream in the refrigerator for 45 to 60 minutes before spreading. Freeze the cake and ice cream layers until final assembly. DAY 3: Stack the frozen cake and ice cream layers, and place in the freezer. Prepare the Chocolate Peanut Icing. Ice the cake and return to the freezer for 1 hour before cutting and serving.

EXCESSIVELY EXPRESSIVE ESPRESSO ECSTASY

SERVES 12

Make the Chocolate Espresso Cake

Preheat the oven to 350°F. Lightly coat the insides of four 9 × 1½-inch nonstick cake pans with some of the 1 tablespoon of melted butter. Line the bottoms of the pans with parchment paper (or wax paper), then lightly coat the paper with more melted butter. Set aside.

In a sifter combine 1¼ cups flour, 1 teaspoon baking powder, and ½ teaspoon salt. Sift onto a large piece of parchment paper (or wax paper) and set aside until needed.

Melt 6 ounces chopped semisweet chocolate, 5 ounces butter, and 3 ounces chopped unsweetened chocolate in the top half of a double boiler, or in a microwave oven (see pages 197–98 for more details), and stir until smooth.

Place 1½ cups sugar, 5 eggs, and ¼ cup espresso powder in the bowl of an electric mixer fitted with a paddle. Beat on medium-high speed for 2 minutes until thick. Use a rubber spatula to scrape down the sides of the bowl. Add the melted chocolate mixture and mix on medium to combine, about 20 seconds. Operate the mixer on low while gradually adding the sifted dry ingredients; mix until incorporated, about 30 seconds. Add ½ cup sour cream and 2 tablespoons vanilla extract and mix on low to combine, about 15

seconds. Remove the bowl from the mixer and use a rubber spatula to finish mixing the ingredients until thoroughly combined.

Immediately divide the cake batter into the prepared pans (about 1⅔ cups of batter in each pan), spreading it evenly. Bake on the top and center racks in the preheated oven until a toothpick inserted in the center of each cake layer comes out clean, about 22 minutes. (Rotate the pans from top to center halfway through the baking time.) Remove the cake layers from the oven and cool in the pans for 15 minutes at room temperature. Invert the cake layers onto cake circles (or onto cake plates). Carefully peel the paper away from the bottoms of the layers. Refrigerate the cake layers until needed.

Prepare the Quintessential Chocolate Ganache

Place 12 ounces chopped semisweet chocolate and 4 ounces chopped unsweetened chocolate in a large bowl.

Heat 2 cups heavy cream and 2 tablespoons sugar in a small saucepan over medium-high heat. When hot, stir to dissolve the sugar. Bring to a boil. Pour the boiling cream over the chopped chocolate. Set aside for 5 minutes; then stir with a whisk until smooth.

CHOCOLATE ESPRESSO CAKE
- 5 ounces unsalted butter cut into ½-ounce pieces; plus
- 1 tablespoon (melted)
- 1¼ cups all-purpose flour
- 1 teaspoon baking powder
- ½ teaspoon salt
- 6 ounces semisweet baking chocolate, coarsely chopped
- 3 ounces unsweetened baking chocolate, coarsely chopped
- 1½ cups granulated sugar
- 5 large eggs
- ¼ cup instant espresso powder
- ½ cup sour cream
- 2 tablespoons pure vanilla extract

QUINTESSENTIAL CHOCOLATE GANACHE
- 12 ounces semisweet baking chocolate, coarsely chopped
- 4 ounces unsweetened baking chocolate, coarsely chopped
- 2 cups heavy cream
- 2 tablespoons granulated sugar

ESPRESSO MOUSSE
- 2 cups heavy cream
- ¾ cup granulated sugar
- ¼ cup instant espresso powder
- 4 ounces unsweetened baking chocolate, coarsely chopped and melted (pages 197–98)

THE EXPRESSION
- ¼ cup espresso beans
- ¾ cups sliced almonds, toasted (page 199) and crushed with your hands
- 12 chocolate-covered espresso beans

Transfer 1½ cups of the ganache to a baking sheet with sides, spreading it evenly. Set aside at room temperature the remaining ganache and the ganache on the baking sheet until needed.

Make the Espresso Mousse

Place 2 cups heavy cream, ¾ cup sugar, and ¼ cup instant espresso powder in the bowl of an electric mixer fitted with a balloon whip. Whisk on medium-high for 2 minutes until firm, but not stiff, peaks form. Add 1½ cups of the whipped cream to 4 ounces melted unsweetened chocolate, and use a rubber spatula to fold them together until thoroughly combined. Add the combined whipped cream and chocolate to the remaining whipped cream and use a rubber spatula to fold them together until smooth and thoroughly combined.

Begin Assembling the Cake

Remove the cake layers from the refrigerator. Use a cake spatula to spread about 1½ cups of Espresso Mousse evenly and smoothly over the top and to the edges of each of 2 of the inverted cake layers. Transfer the 1½ cups of ganache from the baking sheet to the top of another inverted cake layer, and use a cake spatula to spread the ganache evenly over the top and to the edges. Refrigerate the remaining amount of mousse (about 1 cup) until needed to complete the assembly of the cake. Use a utility turner to remove the ganache-coated cake layer from the cake circle; then

stack that cake layer onto one of the mousse-coated layers. Top with the other mousse-coated layer. Place the remaining inverted cake layer onto the top of the preceding mousse layer and gently press it into place. Refrigerate the cake for 1 hour, until the mousse layers have firmed, before completing the assembly.

Make the Expression and Complete the Cake Assembly

Place ¼ cup espresso beans in the bowl of a food processor fitted with a metal blade. Pulse the espresso beans for 45 seconds until coarsely chopped. Combine the almonds and espresso beans on a baking sheet with sides. Set aside.

Transfer the remaining ganache to the top of the cake. Use a cake spatula to spread a smooth coating of ganache over the top and sides. Refrigerate the cake for 30 minutes. Use a utility turner to transfer the cake onto a clean cardboard cake circle.

Press the chopped almond and espresso bean mixture into the sides of the cake, coating it evenly. (Do this over the baking sheet to prevent a mess.) Fill a pastry bag fitted with a large star tip with the remaining cup of mousse. Pipe a circle of 12 evenly spaced mousse stars along the outside edge of the top of the cake. (Depending on the size of the stars, you may end up with a wee bit of mousse left over. Mmm!) Top each star with a chocolate-covered espresso bean. Refrigerate for 1 hour before slicing and serving.

To Serve

Heat the blade of a serrated slicer under hot running water and wipe the blade dry before cutting each slice. Serve immediately.

THE CHEF'S TOUCH

No hyperbole is needed for this confection, but it may need an explanation. A few years ago, I was champing at the bit (not the chocolate one) to appear on an extremely popular daytime talk show. The host, known for her outrageous antics, was just the kind of person to get turned on by excessive chocolate desserts. I knew, however, that it's the producer who gets you air time. So I confabulated with pastry chef Kelly Bailey, who devised this sybaritic showcase for chocolate and espresso. The cake was overnighted to the producer in New York, and the "fix" worked: an invitation for a coveted spot on the program was secured. Perhaps you saw the show? It was the one where the host drank warm ganache straight from the mixing bowl. Now that's excessive!

For long-term storage, keep whole espresso beans in a tightly sealed container in your freezer. Chocolate-covered espresso beans are usually found at specialty grocery stores or at your local coffee/espresso bar. Beware of consuming too many of these little jewels, or you'll surely be on a caffeine high.

This cake may be prepared over 3 days. DAY 1: Bake the Chocolate Espresso Cake layers; once cooled, cover with plastic wrap and refrigerate overnight. DAY 2: Prepare the Quintessential Chocolate Ganache and make the Espresso Mousse. Spread the cake layers with mousse and ganache as directed in the recipe. Refrigerate the cake in a large, tightly sealed plastic container. DAY 3: Prepare the almond-espresso bean combination, and cover the sides of the cake with the mixture. Decorate with mousse stars and chocolate-covered espresso beans. Refrigerate for 1 hour. Slice and serve as directed in the recipe.

After assembly, you may keep the Excessively Expressive Espresso Ecstasy in the refrigerator for 2 days before serving. To avoid permeating the cake with refrigerator odors, place the cake in a large, tightly sealed plastic container.

MIMI MONTANO'S CHOCOLATE ZUCCHINI CAKE

SERVES 18

Preheat the oven to 325°F. Liberally coat the inside of a 9½ × 4-inch nonstick angel food cake pan with the 1 tablespoon melted butter. Set aside.

In a sifter combine 3 cups flour, 2 teaspoons ground cinnamon, 1½ teaspoons baking powder, 1 teaspoon baking soda, and 1 teaspoon salt. Sift onto a large piece of parchment paper (or wax paper) and set aside until needed.

Grate 1 large zucchini in a food processor fitted with a medium grating disk (or use a box grater). Set aside.

Place 1½ cups sugar and 4 eggs in the bowl of an electric mixer fitted with a paddle. Beat on medium-high speed for 2 minutes until light in color and thickened; then use a rubber spatula to scrape down the sides of the bowl. Operate the mixer on medium while slowly adding 1½ cups vegetable oil in a steady stream (it's a good idea to use a pouring shield attachment or to cover the top of the mixer and sides of the bowl with a towel or plastic wrap to avoid splattering oil outside of the mixing bowl). Continue to mix until the batter is yellow in color and thick, about 1½ minutes. Scrape down the sides of the bowl. Add the melted chocolate and mix for 30 seconds on medium speed. Continue to operate the mixer on medium speed and slowly add the sifted dry ingredients. Mix until incorporated, about 1 minute. Add the grated zucchini and mix on low for 15 seconds. Add 2 cups chocolate chips and mix on low for another 15 seconds. Remove the bowl from the mixer and use a rubber spatula to finish mixing the batter until thoroughly combined. Transfer the batter to the prepared angel food cake pan, using a rubber spatula and spreading it evenly.

Place the pan onto a baking sheet with sides on the center rack in the preheated oven. Bake until a wooden skewer inserted into the center of the cake comes out clean, about 1 hour and 50 minutes. Remove the cake from the oven and cool in the pan for 30 minutes at room temperature. Unmold the cake from the pan. Place the cake, baked top facing up, on a cake circle (or onto a cake plate) and cool at room temperature for 1 additional hour before slicing.

To Serve

Heat the blade of a serrated slicer under hot running water and wipe the blade dry before cutting each slice. Serve immediately, or wrap in plastic wrap and take a piece or two of cake along for the ride.

---

1 tablespoon unsalted butter, melted

3 cups all-purpose flour

2 teaspoons ground cinnamon

1½ teaspoons baking powder

1 teaspoon baking soda

1 teaspoon salt

1 large zucchini (about ¾ pound), washed, and stem removed

1½ cups granulated sugar

4 large eggs

1½ cups vegetable oil

3 ounces unsweetened baking chocolate, coarsely chopped and melted (pages 197–98)

2 cups semisweet chocolate chips (one 12-ounce package)

THE CHEF'S TOUCH

When I asked assistant pastry chef Michele Montano if her mom had a recipe suitable for this book, she lost no time telling one tale out of school after another about baking disasters at the Montano home over the years. As I shook my head with disappointment over an upbringing that provided so few confectionery pleasures, Michele added, "But don't feel sorry for us. Aunt Mimi Montano redeemed the family with her incredible chocolate zucchini cake."

Not only did Mimi's cake bring joy to the side of the Montano family that suffered dearly from a lack of baking skills; Mimi also encouraged young Michele to attend the Culinary Institute of America and study baking. Seems like Mimi's legacy will be as grand as her cake.

The irony of zucchini is its position near the end of the dictionary, and its low status because of its pervasiveness on menus. But why be an "ini"-meanie and snub such a bountiful and intriguing vegetable? In this chocolate scenario, zucchini supplies subtle flavor and lends texture and moisture. Do you think more curious vegetables, say okra or Brussels sprouts, would do the same?

After baking and cooling it, you may keep the Chocolate Zucchini Cake covered with plastic wrap at room temperature for up to 24 hours. You may also refrigerate the cake for 7 to 10 days. To avoid permeating the cake with refrigerator odors, place the cake in a large, tightly sealed plastic container. If refrigerated, slice the cake when cold; then keep the slices at room temperature for 10 minutes before serving.

I took Michele's word for it on this one: She insisted that Aunt Mimi likes to savor a slice of zucchini cake with a miniglass of grappa. Sure enough, Mimi is my kind of gal.

CHOCOLATE STRAWBERRY TEARDROP CAKE

SERVES 10

Make the Strawberry Cinnamon Cake

Preheat the oven to 350°F. Lightly coat the insides of two 9 × 1½-inch nonstick cake pans with some of the 2 teaspoons of melted butter. Line the bottom of the pans with parchment paper (or wax paper); then lightly coat the paper with more melted butter. Set aside.

In a sifter combine 2½ cups flour, 1 teaspoon baking powder, 1 teaspoon baking soda, and ½ teaspoon cinnamon. Sift onto a large piece of parchment paper (or wax paper). Set aside until needed.

Place 1 pint strawberries in a colander. Gently spray the berries with lukewarm water. Shake the colander to remove excess water from the berries. Stem and then cut the berries into ¼-inch dice. Set aside.

Place 1¼ cups sugar and 6 ounces butter in the bowl of an electric mixer fitted with a paddle. Mix on low speed for 1 minute, then beat on medium for 2 minutes until soft. Scrape down the sides of the bowl and the paddle. Beat for an additional 2 minutes on medium until even softer. Scrape down the sides of the bowl and the paddle. Add 2 eggs and the egg white, one at a time, beating on medium for 30 seconds after each addition, and scraping down the sides of the bowl once all the eggs have been incorporated.

Operate the mixer on low while gradually adding the sifted dry ingredients; mix until incorporated, about 45 seconds. Add ½ cup sour cream and 1 tablespoon vanilla extract and beat on medium for 15 seconds until combined. Remove the bowl from the mixer, add the diced strawberries, and use a rubber spatula to fold the berries into the batter until thoroughly combined.

Immediately divide the cake batter into the prepared pans (about 3 cups of batter in each pan), spreading it evenly. Bake on the center rack in the preheated oven until a toothpick inserted in the center of each cake layer comes out clean, 30 to 32 minutes. Remove the cake layers from the oven and cool in the pans for 15 minutes at room temperature. Invert the layers onto cake circles (or onto cake plates). Carefully peel the paper away from the bottoms of the cakes; then turn over the cakes, baked tops facing up. Refrigerate the cakes until needed.

Prepare the Strawberry Garnish

Place 8 whole medium fresh strawberries in a colander. Gently spray the berries with lukewarm water. Shake the colander to remove excess water from the berries. Stem and then cut the berries lengthwise into ¼-inch-thick slices. Refrigerate until needed.

STRAWBERRY CINNAMON CAKE

6 ounces (1½ sticks) unsalted butter, cut into ½-ounce pieces; plus 2 teaspoons (melted)
2½ cups all-purpose flour
1 teaspoon baking powder
1 teaspoon baking soda
½ teaspoon ground cinnamon
1 pint fresh strawberries
1¼ cups granulated sugar
2 large eggs
1 large egg white
½ cup sour cream
1 tablespoon pure vanilla extract

STRAWBERRY GARNISH

8 whole medium fresh strawberries (about 1 ounce each)

CHOCOLATE WILDERBERRY BUTTERCREAM

10 ounces semisweet baking chocolate, coarsely chopped
1 cup heavy cream
½ cup granulated sugar
¼ cup Wilderberry Schnapps
¾ pound (3 sticks) unsalted butter, cut into ½-ounce pieces

Make the Chocolate Wilderberry Buttercream

Place 10 ounces chopped semisweet chocolate in a large bowl.

Heat 1 cup heavy cream, ½ cup sugar, and ¼ cup Wilderberry Schnapps in a small saucepan over medium-high heat. When hot, stir to dissolve the sugar. Bring to a boil. Pour the boiling cream mixture over the chopped chocolate. Set aside for 5 minutes; then stir with a whisk until smooth. Pour the mixture (now ganache) onto a baking sheet with sides and spread it evenly. Refrigerate for 20 minutes until chilled, but not firm.

Place ¾ pound butter in the bowl of an electric mixer fitted with a paddle. Mix on low speed for 1 minute, then increase the speed to medium-high and beat for 2 minutes until soft. Scrape down the sides of the bowl and the paddle. Beat on medium for 2 more minutes until very soft. Scrape down the sides of the bowl and the paddle. Add the chilled ganache and beat on medium for 1 minute. Again scrape down the sides of the bowl and paddle. Beat on medium for 1 more minute. Remove the bowl from the mixer, and use a rubber spatula to finish mixing the buttercream until combined. Transfer 1½ cups of buttercream to a pastry bag fitted with a large straight tip. Set aside at room temperature until needed.

Assemble the Cake

Remove the cake layers from the refrigerator. Use a cake spatula to spread 1½ cups of buttercream evenly and smoothly over the top and to the edges of one of the cake layers. Place the second cake layer onto the buttercream-coated layer and gently press into place. Spread the remaining buttercream evenly and smoothly onto the top and sides of the cake; refrigerate the cake for 30 minutes.

Pipe a circle of buttercream teardrops (about ½ inch high at highest point, 1 inch wide, 2 inches long, and 1 teaspoon in volume), each one touching the next, along the outside edge of the top of the cake. Arrange a circle of strawberry slices, stem ends toward the center of the cake, inside the circle of buttercream teardrops. (The berry slices should slightly overlap the teardrops.) Repeat alternating circles of buttercream and strawberries until the entire top of the cake is covered, creating a flowerlike effect. Refrigerate the cake for at least 30 minutes before slicing and serving.

To Serve

Heat the blade of a serrated slicer under hot running water and wipe the blade dry before making each slice. Serve immediately.

THE CHEF'S TOUCH

Can you imagine life without the seemingly omnipresent but esteemed strawberry? We can't at The Trellis, where strawberries have adorned countless salads, brought divine juiciness to various chutneys and relishes, taken a vivid place on the plate alongside many savory foods, and, of course, imparted such bliss to the mouth in ice creams, sorbets, cookies, brownies, and cakes. Be thankful for the year-round availability of fresh strawberries, and add our Chocolate Strawberry Teardrop Cake to your list of favorite strawberry recipes.

One pint of fresh stemmed strawberries should yield about 2 cups of diced pieces. I suggest purchasing 2 pints for this recipe, to ensure that you have enough berries for the cake batter, and also broaden your opportunity to select 8 whole medium berries free of blemishes for the garnish.

Wilderberry Schnapps lends a snappy berry flavor to the buttercream. Other berry liqueurs or berry-flavored brandy could be used; or if you prefer no alcohol, you may eliminate the schnapps without adjusting the recipe.

After assembly, you may keep the Chocolate Strawberry Teardrop Cake in the refrigerator for 2 to 3 days before serving. To avoid permeating the cake with refrigerator odors, place the cake in a large, tightly sealed plastic container.

This cake may be prepared over 2 days. DAY 1: Make the Strawberry Cinnamon Cake layers. Once cooled, cover with plastic wrap and refrigerate until assembling the whole cake. DAY 2: Prepare the fresh Strawberry Garnish. Make the Chocolate Wilderberry Buttercream. Assemble the cake as directed in the recipe, then refrigerate for at least 30 minutes before serving.

COCOA BUTTERSCOTCH GOOMBAH CAKE

SERVES 12

Make the Cocoa Cream Cheese Swirl Cake

Preheat the oven to 350°F. Place 2 ounces cream cheese and ¼ cup of the sugar in the bowl of an electric mixer fitted with a paddle. Mix on low speed for 30 seconds, then beat on medium for 1 minute until combined. Scrape down the sides of the bowl and the paddle. Add 1 large egg yolk and ½ teaspoon of the vanilla extract and mix on medium for 30 seconds. Remove the bowl from the mixer and finish mixing the batter with a rubber spatula until smooth and virtually lump free. Set the cream cheese mixture aside at room temperature until needed.

Lightly coat the insides of three 9 × 1½-inch nonstick cake pans using some of the 1 tablespoon of vegetable oil. Line the bottoms of the pans with parchment paper (or wax paper), then lightly coat the paper with more vegetable oil. Set aside.

In a sifter combine 3 cups flour, ⅔ cup cocoa powder, and 1½ teaspoons baking powder. Sift onto a large piece of parchment paper (or wax paper) and set aside until needed.

In an extra-large bowl whisk together 1½ cups whole milk, the remaining 1¼ cups vegetable oil, 3 large eggs, and the remaining 1 tablespoon of vanilla extract. Add the remaining 2 cups of sugar and whisk until incorpo-

rated. Add the sifted dry ingredients; then use a rubber spatula to fold the ingredients together until combined. (Don't worry if the batter looks lumpy; the cake layers will be so fine.)

Immediately divide the cake batter into the prepared pans (about 2 cups of batter in each pan), spreading it evenly. Drizzle about 2½ tablespoons of the cream cheese mixture over the entire surface of the batter in each pan in a zigzag pattern. Marbleize the batter in each pan by using a toothpick inserted about 1 inch into the batter, and in a spiraling motion, circle around the entire surface of the cake, working from the outside edges to the center.

Bake on the top and center racks in the preheated oven until a toothpick inserted in the center of each cake layer comes out clean, about 30 minutes. (Rotate the pans from top to center halfway through the baking time.) Remove the cake layers from the oven and cool in the pans for 15 minutes at room temperature.

Invert the layers onto cake circles (or cake plates) that are covered with plastic wrap. (This keeps the cake layers from sticking.) Carefully peel the paper away from the bottom of each layer. Refrigerate the cake layers until needed.

COCOA CREAM CHEESE SWIRL CAKE

2 ounces cream cheese, cut into 1-ounce pieces
2¼ cups granulated sugar
1 large egg yolk
1 tablespoon plus ½ teaspoon pure vanilla extract
1¼ cups plus 1 tablespoon vegetable oil
3 cups all-purpose flour
⅔ cup unsweetened cocoa powder
1½ teaspoons baking powder
1½ cups whole milk
3 large eggs

BUTTERSCOTCH GOOMBAH

1 pound (4 sticks) unsalted butter, cut into ½-ounce pieces
½ cup (4 ounces) tightly packed dark brown sugar
½ cup heavy cream
½ cup Skor English Toffee Bits

Make the Butterscotch Goombah

Place 15 ounces of the butter in the bowl of an electric mixer fitted with a paddle. Mix on low speed for 1 minute; then beat on medium-high for 2 minutes, until soft. Scrape down the sides of the bowl and the paddle. Beat on medium for 2 more minutes until very soft. Scrape down the sides of the bowl.

Heat ½ cup dark brown sugar, ½ cup heavy cream, and the remaining 1 ounce butter in a medium saucepan over medium-high heat. When hot, stir to dissolve the sugar and melt the butter. Bring to a boil. Reduce the heat to medium and continue to boil the mixture, stirring frequently, for 5 minutes, until the mixture resembles a thick syrup. Remove from the heat and transfer to a medium glass bowl. (The mixture will stick to other surfaces, especially stainless steel.) Cool in an ice-water bath, stirring constantly until cold to the touch and thick like taffy, 6 to 7 minutes.

Add the cold butterscotch to the mixing bowl with the softened butter. Beat on medium for 30 seconds to combine. Scrape down the sides of the bowl and the paddle. Beat for an additional 30 seconds on medium until very smooth. Remove the bowl from the mixer, add ½ cup Skor English Toffee Bits, and finish mixing with a rubber spatula until thoroughly combined.

Assemble the Cake

Remove the cake layers from the refrigerator. Turn one of the cake layers over onto a clean cake circle. Gently pull the plastic wrap away from the marbleized surface of the cake layer. Use a cake spatula to spread 1¼ cups of Butterscotch Goombah evenly and smoothly over the top and to the edges of the cake layer. Turn the second cake layer over onto the Goombah-iced bottom layer, and gently press it into place. Gently pull the plastic wrap away from the cake layer. Spread the remaining 1¼ cups of Goombah evenly over the top and to the edges of the second cake layer; then top the Goombah with the third cake layer, marbleized side up, gently pressing the cake into place. Pull the plastic wrap away from the top cake layer. Refrigerate the cake for a least 2 hours before slicing and serving.

To Serve

Heat the blade of a serrated slicer under hot running water and wipe the blade dry before cutting each slice. Keep the slices at room temperature for 15 to 20 minutes before serving.

THE CHEF'S TOUCH

My goombah (an older friend who acts as an adviser) for many years has been Jim Seu, and for him, butterscotch is the key to an unrivaled chocolate alliance. As a retired restaurant owner, Jim had the luxury of time to visit Ganache Hill and critique the confections for this book during the long, arduous months of recipe development and testing (just kidding about "arduous"). When he obstinately opined that our recipes lacked his beloved butter-scotch, we were prompted to develop the Cocoa Butterscotch Goombah Cake in his honor.

Although Jim Seu was enthusiastic about this cake, he offered that the presence of chocolate (actually cocoa) was a bit subtle. So for Jim and all of my other chocolate depen-dent friends, a big scoop of Black Satin Ice Cream (page 184) served with this cake is the mother of all synergies.

To prevent impinging on the chocolate and butterscotch amalgamation, use a flavor-less vegetable oil like safflower or canola for the swirl cake.

After assembly, you may keep the Cocoa Butterscotch Goombah Cake in the refrigera-tor for 1 or 2 days before serving. To avoid permeating the cake with refrigerator odors, place the cake in a large, tightly sealed plastic container.

Single-malt Scotch with butterscotch? Risking the chance that you may think I have lost my marbles, I urge you to trust me. One sip and one bite will convince you of a conflu-ence beyond compare.

This cake may be prepared over 2 days. DAY 1: Bake the Cocoa Cream Cheese Swirl Cake layers. Once cooled, cover each layer with plastic wrap and refrigerate until the next day. DAY 2: Make the Butterscotch Goombah, then ice the cake with the Goom-bah as directed in the recipe. Refrigerate the cake for 2 hours before slicing and serving.

MIDNIGHT TRUFFLE CAKE

SERVES 6

Prepare the Truffles of the Night

Place 4 ounces chopped semisweet chocolate in a medium bowl.

Heat ½ cup heavy cream and 1 tablespoon sugar in a small saucepan over medium heat. When hot, stir to dissolve the sugar. Bring to a boil. Pour the boiling cream over the chopped chocolate. Set aside for 5 minutes; then stir with a whisk until smooth. Pour the mixture (called ganache) onto a dinner plate and use a rubber spatula to spread the ganache in a smooth, even layer. Place the ganache in the freezer for 15 minutes, or in the refrigerator for 30 minutes, until very firm to the touch.

Place ¼ cup cocoa powder in a small bowl. Remove the firm ganache from the freezer or the refrigerator. Portion 12 individual tablespoons of ganache onto a separate dinner plate. (About 2 tablespoons of additional ganache will remain; listen to the devil or your conscience before deciding on how best to dispatch the excess.) Wearing a pair of disposable vinyl (or latex) gloves, roll each portion of ganache, one at a time, in your palms in a gentle, circular motion, using just enough pressure to form smooth, round truffles. Roll the truffles individually in the cocoa powder. Refrigerate the truffles on a clean, large dinner plate until needed.

Make the Black Cocoa Sponge Cake

Preheat the oven to 350°F. Lightly coat the inside of a 9 × 13 × 2-inch nonstick pan with some of the 2 teaspoons of melted butter. Line the bottom of the pan with parchment paper (or wax paper); then lightly coat the paper with more melted butter. Set aside.

In a sifter combine 1 cup flour, 1 teaspoon baking soda, and ¼ teaspoon baking powder. Sift onto a large piece of parchment paper (or wax paper) and set aside until needed. Sift ¾ cup cocoa powder onto a separate piece of parchment paper (or wax paper) and set aside until needed.

Place 1 cup sugar and 2 eggs in the bowl of an electric mixer fitted with a paddle. Beat on medium-high speed for 2 minutes until the mixture is slightly thickened and light in color. Operate the mixer on medium while slowly adding ¾ cup vegetable oil in a steady stream. Mix until incorporated, about 1 minute. Operate the mixer on low while adding 1 cup boiling water in a slow, steady stream; mix until incorporated, about 45 seconds.

Continue to operate the mixer on low while slowly adding the sifted flour, baking soda, and baking powder; mix until incorporated, about 1 minute. Increase the speed of the mixer to medium and beat for 2 minutes.

TRUFFLES OF THE NIGHT

4 ounces semisweet baking chocolate, coarsely chopped
½ cup heavy cream
1 tablespoon granulated sugar
¼ cup unsweetened cocoa powder

BLACK COCOA SPONGE CAKE

2 teaspoons unsalted butter, melted
1 cup all-purpose flour
1 teaspoon baking soda
¼ teaspoon baking powder
¾ cup unsweetened cocoa powder
1 cup granulated sugar
2 large eggs
¾ cup vegetable oil
1 cup boiling water

CHOCOLATE SOUR CREAM ICING

2 cups confectioners' sugar
¼ pound (1 stick) unsalted butter, cut into ½-ounce pieces
4 ounces unsweetened baking chocolate, coarsely chopped and melted (pages 197–98)
6 tablespoons sour cream
2 tablespoons gin
1 teaspoon pure vanilla extract

Scrape down the sides of the bowl. Now operate the mixer on low and slowly add the sifted cocoa powder; mix until incorporated, about 1 minute. Remove the bowl from the mixer and use a rubber spatula to finish mixing the batter until thoroughly combined.

Transfer the cake batter to the prepared pan, using a rubber spatula to spread it evenly. Bake on the center rack in the preheated oven until a toothpick inserted in the center of the cake comes out clean, 28 to 30 minutes. Remove the cake from the oven, and cool in the pan for 15 minutes at room temperature. Invert the cake onto a baking sheet covered with plastic wrap (or onto a large rectangular platter covered with plastic wrap). Peel the paper away from the bottom of the cake. Refrigerate the cake until needed.

Make the Chocolate Sour Cream Icing

Sift 2 cups of confectioners' sugar onto a large piece of parchment paper (or wax paper). Set aside.

Place ¼ pound butter in the bowl of an electric mixer fitted with a paddle. Mix on low speed for 1 minute; then increase the speed to medium-high and beat for 2 minutes until soft. Scrape down the sides of the bowl and the paddle. Beat on medium for another 2 minutes until very soft. Add the melted chocolate and mix on medium for 15 seconds. Scrape down the sides of the bowl. Add 6 tablespoons sour cream, 2 tablespoons gin, and 1 teaspoon vanilla extract and mix on medium to combine, about 15 seconds. Add

the sifted confectioners' sugar all at once, and then mix on the lowest speed (stir) to combine, about 45 seconds. Scrape down the sides of the bowl. Now mix on medium for 1 minute. Remove the bowl from the mixer and use a rubber spatula to finish mixing the icing until thoroughly combined. Reserve ½ cup of icing in a small bowl. Transfer the remaining icing to a pastry bag fitted with a medium star tip.

Assemble the Midnight Truffle Cake

Remove the Black Cocoa Sponge Cake from the refrigerator. Turn out the cooled cake onto a cutting board, baked top facing up. Discard the plastic wrap. Use a sharp cook's knife to cut away about ¼ inch of the edges of the cake to form a rectangle approximately 11½ inches long and 7½ inches wide. Cut the rectangle in half lengthwise, creating 2 rectangles measuring 11½ inches long and 3¾ inches wide.

Pipe 24 stars of Chocolate Sour Cream Icing (measuring about 1¼ inches high and 1¼ inches wide), each star touching the next, across the top of one of the cakes—3 stars across the width and 8 stars across the length. Place the second cake layer, baked top facing up, on top of the iced cake layer, and press down gently but firmly to level the layers. Transfer the reserved ½ cup of icing to a pastry bag fitted with a medium star tip. Pipe 12 stars of chocolate icing, evenly spaced, on the top of the cake—2 rows of 6 stars—each measuring ½ inch high and ½ inch wide. Place a truffle on the top of each star. Use a utility turner (large wide spatula) to transfer the cake to a baking sheet; then refrigerate the cake for at least 1 hour before cutting.

THE CHEF'S TOUCH

Chocolate truffles have entered the American culinary consciousness fairly recently. A prized copy of *Cocoa and Chocolate*, published in 1886 by the company that manufactures Baker's chocolate, makes no mention of truffles. In Marion H. Neils's *Candies and Bonbons and How to Make Them* (1913) a confection called Chocolate Rocks bears a resemblance in ingredients—sweet chocolate and thick cream—as well as in method, "melt the mixture to a smooth paste, . . . mold it into round centers." But the appellation "rocks" probably did little to create popularity. The 1950 edition of *The Gourmet Cookbook* has a paucity of chocolate recipes, and sadly, none resembles truffles. My notes and texts from when I attended the Culinary Institute of America in the early '60's are absent of any mention of chocolate truffles. (Back in those days, it was Hershey bars and M&M's for this chocolate lover.)

Thank goodness we don't need to search far for chocolate gratification of the highest order in today's chocolate-crazed America. And if for some reason you are not able to find marvelous chocolate truffles at your favorite specialty food store, then arm yourself with just a few ingredients and our recipe for Truffles of the Night, and unrestrained intemperance is only a few motions of your hands away.

If you are a creature of the night who is compelled to spend the midnight hour with chocolate, consider eating this cake with Kremlyovskaya chocolate-flavored, triple-distilled vodka, a unique Russian beverage that is certain to soothe nocturnal desires.

This cake may be prepared over 3 days. DAY 1: Prepare the Truffles of the Night. Refrigerate the truffles in a sealed plastic container. DAY 2: Bake the Black Cocoa Sponge Cake. Once cooled, cover with plastic wrap and refrigerate until the next day. DAY 3: Make the Chocolate Sour Cream Icing. Remove the cake from the refrigerator, then ice the cake and top with truffles as directed in the recipe. Refrigerate the cake for 1 hour before slicing and serving.

CHOCOLATE CRANBERRY CONSPIRACY
with CRANBERRY APPLE TIPPLER

SERVES 12

Make the Cranberry Apple Tippler

Preheat the oven to 400°F.

Heat 1 cup dried cranberries, ½ cup of the cranberry-flavored vodka, and ½ cup dried currants in a medium saucepan over medium heat. Bring to a simmer while stirring frequently with a rubber spatula. Simmer for 1 minute. Transfer the mixture to a small noncorrosive bowl. Cover the top of the bowl tightly with plastic wrap and set aside until needed.

In a large noncorrosive bowl, add ½ teaspoon lemon juice to 1 quart of cold water to make acidulated water. One at a time, core and quarter (do not peel) the 2 Granny Smith apples and the 2 Red Delicious apples. Cut each apple quarter lengthwise in three equal pieces then crosswise in half. Immediately place the apple sections in the acidulated water to prevent them from discoloring. Set aside.

Heat ¼ pound butter, ½ cup light brown sugar, and ¼ cup clover honey in a small saucepan over medium heat. Bring to a simmer; then adjust heat so the mixture will simmer for 1 minute. Remove the saucepan from the heat.

Drain the unpeeled apple sections in a colander, rinse under cold water, and vigorously shake until almost dry. Return the drained apples to the large bowl. Add the hot brown sugar mixture and mix with a rubber spatula to coat the apples thoroughly. Transfer the apples and all the contents of the bowl to a baking sheet with sides, spreading them evenly. Bake in the preheated oven for 30 minutes until the apple sections are light brown in color. Remove the roasted apple mixture from the oven, and transfer it to a large noncorrosive bowl. Add the dried fruit and vodka mixture and the remaining ½ cup cranberry-flavored vodka. Stir to combine. Set aside at room temperature to cool; then refrigerate, covered with plastic wrap, until ready to serve.

Make the Chocolate Cranberry Cake

Preheat the oven to 350°F. Lightly coat the insides of three 9 × 1½-inch nonstick cake pans using some of the 1 tablespoon melted butter. Line the bottoms of the pans with parchment paper (or wax paper); then lightly coat the paper with more melted butter. Set aside.

Place 1½ cups dried cranberries in the bowl of a food processor fitted with a metal blade. Process the cranberries for 30 seconds until finely chopped (or finely chop by hand using a cook's knife). Set aside.

CRANBERRY APPLE TIPPLER

1 cup dried cranberries

1 cup cranberry-flavored vodka

½ cup dried currants

½ teaspoon fresh lemon juice

1 quart cold water

2 Granny Smith apples

2 Red Delicious apples

¼ pound (1 stick) unsalted butter, cut into ½-ounce pieces

½ cup (4 ounces) tightly packed light brown sugar

¼ cup clover honey

CHOCOLATE CRANBERRY CAKE

1 tablespoon unsalted butter, melted

1½ cups dried cranberries

2¼ cups all-purpose flour

¼ cup unsweetened cocoa powder

2¼ teaspoons baking powder

¾ teaspoon baking soda

1¼ cups granulated sugar

1¼ cups orange juice

2 large eggs

⅓ cup vegetable oil

1 large egg white

2 ounces semisweet baking chocolate, coarsely chopped and melted (pages 197–98)

In a sifter combine 2¼ cups flour, ¼ cup cocoa powder, 2¼ teaspoons baking powder, and ¾ teaspoon baking soda. Sift directly into the bowl of an electric mixer. Position the bowl into place on an electric mixer fitted with a paddle. Add 1¼ cups sugar. Mix on low speed to incorporate, about 15 seconds. In a large bowl, whisk together the finely chopped cranberries, 1¼ cups orange juice, 2 large eggs, ⅓ cup vegetable oil, and 1 large egg white until thoroughly combined. Add the whisked cranberry–orange juice mixture to the mixing bowl and mix on medium-low speed for 20 seconds to incorporate. Use a rubber spatula to scrape down the sides of the bowl. Add 2 ounces melted semisweet chocolate and beat on medium for 10 seconds until thoroughly combined. Remove the bowl from the mixer and use a rubber spatula to finish mixing the batter until well blended.

Immediately divide the cake batter into the prepared pans (about 1¾ cups of batter in each pan), spreading it evenly. Bake on the top and center racks in the preheated oven until a toothpick inserted in the center of each cake layer comes out clean, 24 to 26 minutes. (Rotate the pans from top to center halfway through the baking time.)

Remove the cake layers from the oven and cool in the pans for 15 minutes at room temperature. Invert the layers onto cake circles (or cake plates) that are covered with plastic wrap. (This keeps the cake layers from sticking.) Carefully peel the paper away from the bottom of each cake layer. Refrigerate the cake layers until needed.

Make the White Chocolate Walnut Icing

Sift 4 cups of confectioners' sugar onto a large piece of parchment paper (or wax paper). Set aside.

Place ½ pound butter and 6 ounces cream cheese in the bowl of an electric mixer fitted with a paddle. Mix on low speed for 1 minute, then beat on medium-high for 2 minutes until soft. (To avoid splattering the butter and cream cheese mixture, use a pouring shield attachment, or place a towel or plastic wrap over the top of the mixer and down the sides of the bowl.) Scrape down the sides of the bowl and the paddle. Beat on medium for 2 more minutes until very soft. Add 3 ounces melted white chocolate and beat on medium-high for 30 seconds. Add the sifted confectioners' sugar, all at once, and mix on the lowest speed (stir) to combine, about 1 minute. Scrape down the sides of the bowl and the paddle, then beat for an additional 30 seconds on medium until thoroughly combined. Add the chopped toasted walnuts and beat on medium for 10 seconds to combine. Remove the bowl from the mixer and use a rubber spatula to finish mixing the ingredients until well blended. Set aside at room temperature until needed.

Assemble the Cake

Remove the cake layers from the refrigerator. Use a cake spatula to spread 1 cup of icing evenly and smoothly over the top and to the edges of each of two of the cake layers. Stack the two layers, then top with the last inverted cake layer, bottom facing up. Gently press the

WHITE CHOCOLATE WALNUT ICING

4 cups (1 pound) confectioners' sugar

½ pound (2 sticks) unsalted butter, cut into ½-ounce pieces

6 ounces cream cheese, cut into 1-ounce pieces

3 ounces white chocolate, coarsely chopped and melted (pages 197–98)

1½ cups walnut halves, toasted (page 199) and finely chopped

layers into place. Spread the remaining 3 cups of icing evenly over the top and sides of the cake. Refrigerate the cake for 4 hours before slicing and serving.

To Serve

Heat the blade of a serrated slicer under hot running water and wipe the blade dry before making each slice. Place each slice onto a serving plate and keep at room temperature while heating the Cranberry Apple Tippler. Heat the tippler in a saucepan over medium heat (or in a glass bowl in a microwave oven). When warm, ladle ¼ cup of Cranberry Apple Tippler around the cake on each plate. Serve immediately.

THE CHEF'S TOUCH

We selected dried cranberries for the Chocolate Cranberry Cake and the Cranberry Apple Tippler, rather than the sassy fresh or frozen berries, not because we were intimidated, but rather for the accessibility of dried fruit. Fresh cranberries have a limited season—October to December—and frozen berries are usually difficult to locate by early summer. You will have no problem finding dried cranberries year-round in the bulk food or dried fruit sections at the supermarket.

The Cranberry Apple Tippler may be kept refrigerated for several days in a covered noncorrosive container. Heat only as much as you need, about ¼ cup per slice.

This cake may be prepared over 3 days. DAY 1: Make the Cranberry Apple Tippler. Cool to room temperature; then cover with plastic wrap and refrigerate until needed. DAY 2: Make the Chocolate Cranberry Cake layers. Once cooled, cover with plastic wrap and refrigerate until you assemble the whole cake. DAY 3: Make the White Chocolate Walnut Icing. Assemble the cake as directed; then refrigerate for at least 4 hours before serving with the Cranberry Apple Tippler.

Finlandia Cranberry-Flavored Vodka would make an intriguing beverage to accompany this dessert. Serve it directly from the freezer with the cake, and a wicked conspiracy is assured.

Chocolate
SINE QUA NONS

Essential Recipes
for the Chocophile

CHOCOLATE HONEY

¾ cup clover honey

2 ounces unsweetened baking chocolate, coarsely chopped

Heat ¾ cup clover honey and 2 ounces chopped unsweetened chocolate in the top half of a double boiler over medium-low heat. Use a rubber spatula to stir the mixture constantly until the chocolate is melted and thoroughly incorporated with the honey, about 4 minutes. Remove from the heat.

Rather than make the Chocolate Honey in a double boiler, you may prefer to use a microwave oven. Heat 2 ounces chopped unsweetened chocolate in a small glass bowl in a microwave oven set at medium power for 1½ minutes. After removing the chocolate from the microwave oven, add ¾ cup clover honey; then use a rubber spatula to stir until the chocolate is melted and thoroughly incorporated with the honey.

Transfer the Chocolate Honey to a small plastic container. Set aside to cool at room temperature; then cover and store at air-conditioned room temperature for several days.

THE CHEF'S TOUCH

Our Chocolate Honey may be used for both sweet and savory recipes that will profit from the flavor enhancement of chocolate and honey. Use it, in the quantity that is specified, in a recipe calling for honey, or experiment by using it as you would a seasoning.

Single-flower honey, such as lavender, although uniquely flavorsome, would not find synergy with unsweetened chocolate. For that reason, I recommend using a mild-flavored honey like clover or orange blossom for this recipe.

Keep the Chocolate Honey covered in a noncorrosive container at room temperature for up to a week.

In need of a soothing nonalcoholic beverage? Try chocolate milk and honey. Heat 1 cup of milk with 2 tablespoons of Chocolate Honey in a small saucepan over medium heat. When hot, stir to dissolve the honey. Bring to a simmer; then serve.

CHOCOLATE HAZELNUT CRACKLE

MAKES 2 POUNDS

2 cups skinned hazelnuts, toasted (page 199)
2¼ cups granulated sugar
½ teaspoon fresh lemon juice
4 ounces unsweetened baking chocolate, coarsely chopped

Put the 2 cups hazelnuts on a nonstick 10 × 15-inch baking sheet.

Place 2¼ cups sugar and ½ teaspoon lemon juice in a medium saucepan. Stir with a long-handled metal kitchen spoon to combine. (The sugar will resemble moist sand.) Caramelize the sugar by heating it for 11 to 12 minutes over medium-high heat, stirring constantly with the spoon to break up any lumps. (The sugar will first turn clear as it liquefies, then light brown as it caramelizes.) Remove the saucepan from the heat, add chopped unsweetened chocolate, and stir to dissolve. Immediately and carefully pour the caramelized mixture over the toasted hazelnuts, covering all the nuts. Harden at room temperature for at least 30 minutes.

Invert the crackle onto a clean, dry cutting board. (It should pop right out of the baking sheet.) Use your hands to break the crackle into pieces (as large or small as you like). Store the crackle, with parchment paper (or wax paper) between the layers to prevent sticking, in a tightly sealed plastic container until you are ready to use it.

THE CHEF'S TOUCH

The Chocolate Hazelnut Crackle may be eaten as a snack or used as an impressive garnish on cakes such as the Chocolate Porto Enchantment Cake (page 147) or the Cocoa Butterscotch Goombah Cake (page 167). To use as a garnish, insert a large piece of the crackle into the top of each slice, or sprinkle smaller pieces alongside the cake on each plate.

The Chocolate Hazelnut Crackle will keep for several days at air-conditioned room temperature if stored in a tightly sealed plastic container, or in the freezer for several weeks. Whether stored at room temperature or in the freezer, be certain to place sheets of parchment paper (or wax paper) between the layers to prevent the crackle pieces from sticking to one another.

CHOCOLATE TEMPTRESS

4 slightly heaping #20 ice cream
    scoops chocolate ice cream
    (about 9 ounces total)
1 cup Kremlyovskaya chocolate-
    flavored, triple-distilled vodka
2 tablespoons half-and-half cream
1 tablespoon Frangelico hazelnut
    liqueur
1 tablespoon Royale Chambord
    raspberry liqueur
½ ounce semisweet baking
    chocolate, finely chopped

Place 4 slightly heaping #20 ice cream scoops of chocolate ice cream in a blender. Add 1 cup chocolate-flavored vodka, 2 tablespoons half-and-half cream, 1 tablespoon hazelnut liqueur, and 1 tablespoon raspberry liqueur. Blend until smooth, about 30 seconds. Divide the blended drink equally among 4 cocktail glasses and garnish each with 1 teaspoon of finely chopped chocolate, sprinkled over the top.

THE CHEF'S TOUCH

Don't mistake the Chocolate Temptress for one of the froufrou ice cream drinks at some restaurants. This is a real cocktail; one sip will convince even the most cynical imbiber of traditional libations that chocolate has found a niche at the bar.

Crafted by The Trellis head bartender Melody Zeigler, the Chocolate Temptress has several components. Like all the cocktails I have ever enjoyed, the secret to its success is premium liquor. So take the time and the money to purchase the listed ingredients in the recipe, and you will be rewarded with a remarkably original and satisfying cocktail.

Use the best quality chocolate ice cream you can find, or use our Black Satin Ice Cream (page 184) for this recipe, and after that, my chocolate-loving friend, you are on your own!

CHOCOLAT CHAUD DE SADE

SERVES 4

3½ cups whole milk
½ cup half-and-half cream
¼ cup unsweetened cocoa powder
¼ cup granulated sugar
8 ounces semisweet baking
  chocolate, coarsely chopped
½ teaspoon pure vanilla extract
¼ teaspoon almond extract

Heat 3½ cups whole milk, ½ cup half-and-half cream, ¼ cup cocoa powder, and ¼ cup sugar in a medium saucepan over medium heat. When hot, stir with a whisk to dissolve the cocoa powder and sugar. Bring to a simmer; then immediately remove from the heat. Add 8 ounces chopped semisweet chocolate, and stir until the chocolate is melted and the mixture is smooth. Use a rubber spatula to scrape down the sides and bottom of the saucepan. Add ½ teaspoon vanilla extract and ¼ teaspoon almond extract, and stir to combine. Serve immediately in warm mugs.

THE CHEF'S TOUCH

History has recorded that the noted writer Marquis de Sade had a passion for chocolate in all forms. (No matter the subject, the marquis was nothing if not diverse in his interests.) This delicious hot chocolate beverage is dedicated to arguably the most notorious eighteenth-century chocolate libertine.

Depending upon your tolerance for decadence, you may top the hot chocolate with unsweetened whipped cream, float a marshmallow or two on the top, or even stir in a shot of your favorite brandy. One cannot help but wonder how the marquis took his hot chocolate.

BLACK SATIN ICE CREAM

MAKES 1¼ QUARTS

9 ounces semisweet baking
   chocolate, coarsely chopped
1½ cups heavy cream
1½ cups whole milk
⅓ cup unsweetened cocoa powder
¾ cup granulated sugar
3 large egg yolks

Place 9 ounces chopped semisweet chocolate in a medium bowl. Heat 1½ cups heavy cream in a medium saucepan over medium-high heat. Bring to a boil. Pour the boiling cream over the chopped chocolate. Set aside for 5 minutes; then stir with a whisk until smooth. Set aside.

Heat 1½ cups milk, ⅓ cup cocoa powder, and ¼ cup of the sugar in a medium saucepan over medium heat. Stir to incorporate the cocoa powder and dissolve the sugar. Bring to a boil.

While the milk mixture is heating, place the remaining ½ cup sugar and 3 egg yolks in the bowl of an electric mixer fitted with a paddle. Beat on high speed for 2 minutes until thoroughly combined; then use a rubber spatula to scrape down the sides of the bowl. Beat on high for an additional 2 minutes until slightly thickened and pale yellow. If at this point the milk mixture has not yet started to boil, adjust the mixer speed to low and continue to mix until it does boil; otherwise, undesirable lumps may form when the boiling milk mixture is added.

Gradually pour the boiling milk mixture into the beaten sugar and egg yolks and mix on low to combine, about 45 seconds. Return the combined mixture to the saucepan, using a rubber spatula. Heat over medium heat, stirring constantly. Bring to a temperature of 185°F, about 2 minutes. Remove from the heat and transfer to a large stainless steel bowl. Add the heavy cream and chocolate mixture and stir to combine.

Cool in an ice-water bath to a temperature of 40° to 45°F. Freeze in an ice cream freezer following the manufacturer's instructions. Transfer the semifrozen ice cream to a 2-quart plastic container, cover the container securely, and then place in the freezer for several hours before serving. Serve within 3 to 4 days.

THE CHEF'S TOUCH

The rich, velvety texture and flavor of Black Satin Ice Cream will massage your mouth with its sensuous chocolate creaminess. If the Black Satin Ice Cream is too hard to scoop when removed from the freezer, place it in the refrigerator for 25 to 30 minutes. Not only will the ice cream be easier to scoop, it will also be more pleasurable, as the taste of the chocolate becomes more intense when the ice cream is not frozen solid.

WARM DARK CHOCOLATE FUDGE SAUCE

MAKES 2¾ CUPS

1½ cups heavy cream

1⅓ cups granulated sugar

5 ounces unsweetened baking chocolate, coarsely chopped

2 ounces (½ stick) unsalted butter, cut into ½-ounce pieces

Heat 1½ cups heavy cream, 1⅓ cups sugar, and 5 ounces chopped unsweetened chocolate in a medium saucepan over medium heat. When hot, stir to dissolve the sugar and melt the chocolate. Bring to a boil. Adjust the heat to medium-low, and simmer the mixture for 20 minutes, stirring frequently, until thickened and very smooth. Remove the saucepan from the heat. Add 2 ounces butter, one ½-ounce piece at a time, stirring to incorporate the butter before adding the next piece. Keep warm in a double boiler until needed or cool to room temperature; then refrigerate in a tightly sealed plastic container.

THE CHEF'S TOUCH

Pair this glistening pool of dark chocolate sauce with almost any of the cakes in *Death by Chocolate Cakes,* and you may raise the dearly departed.

To reheat refrigerated sauce, place it in the top half of a double boiler over medium-low heat. Stir the sauce frequently while heating until warm and smooth.

Keep the sauce covered in a noncorrosive container in the refrigerator for up to 1 week.

WHITE CHOCOLATE ESPRESSO SAUCE

6 ounces white chocolate, coarsely chopped
1 cup heavy cream
2 teaspoons instant espresso powder
¼ cup Oblio Caffe sambuca

Place 6 ounces chopped white chocolate in a medium bowl.

Heat 1 cup heavy cream and 2 teaspoons instant espresso powder in a medium saucepan over medium heat. When hot, stir to dissolve the espresso powder. Bring to a boil. Pour the boiling cream over the chopped white chocolate. Immediately stir with a whisk until smooth. Cool in an ice-water bath to a temperature of 45° to 50°F. Add ¼ cup Oblio Caffe sambuca. Stir to incorporate. Transfer the chilled sauce to a plastic container. Cover and refrigerate until needed. Serve chilled.

THE CHEF'S TOUCH

Oblio Caffe sambuca, a product of Italy, gives this sauce an edge. You may omit the liqueur without adversely affecting its sublime texture, but that will make the sauce, well, less intoxicating. On the other hand, select your pour of choice. Try white sambuca, Drambuie, or even Tía Maria, in equivalent proportions, for exotically different tastes.

I think you will find the White Chocolate Espresso Sauce to be compatible with several of the cakes in this book. Do not be parsimonious when you serve it with such decadent cakes as Julia's Eighty-fifth Birthday Cake (page 91) or the Excessively Expressive Espresso Ecstasy (page 157), and you will reserve your place in chocolate heaven.

The sauce may be stored in a covered, noncorrosive container in the refrigerator for several days without any diminishment in quality.

HIGH-TEST WHITE CHOCOLATE ICE CREAM

MAKES 2 QUARTS

8 ounces white chocolate, coarsely chopped
½ cup half-and-half cream
2¼ cups heavy cream
¾ cup granulated sugar
4 large egg yolks

Heat 8 ounces chopped white chocolate and ½ cup half-and-half cream together in the top half of a double boiler over medium-low heat. Use a rubber spatula to stir the chocolate and cream until completely melted and smooth, 6½ to 7 minutes. Remove from the heat and set aside until needed.

Heat 2¼ cups heavy cream and ¼ cup of the sugar in a medium saucepan over medium-high heat. When hot, stir to dissolve the sugar. Bring to a boil.

While the heavy cream mixture is heating, place the remaining ½ cup of sugar and 4 egg yolks in the bowl of an electric mixer fitted with a paddle. Beat on high speed for 2 minutes until thoroughly combined; then use a rubber spatula to scrape down the sides of the bowl. Beat on high for an additional 2 minutes until slightly thickened and pale yellow. If at this point the heavy cream mixture has not yet started to boil, adjust the mixer speed to low and continue to mix until it does boil; otherwise, undesirable lumps may form when the boiling cream mixture is added.

Gradually pour the boiling heavy cream mixture into the beaten sugar and egg yolks and mix on low to combine, about 45 seconds. (To avoid splattering the boiling milk mixture, use a pouring shield attachment, or place a towel or plastic wrap over the top of the mixer and down the sides to the bowl.) Return the combined mixture to the saucepan, using a rubber spatula to facilitate transferring all of the mixture from the bowl. Heat over medium heat, stirring constantly. Bring to a temperature of 185°F, about 2½ minutes. Remove from the heat and transfer to a large stainless steel bowl. Add the white chocolate and half-and-half cream mixture and stir to combine.

Cool in an ice-water bath to a temperature of 40° to 45°F. Freeze in an ice cream freezer following the manufacturer's instructions. Transfer the semifrozen ice cream to a 2-quart plastic container, securely cover the container, and then freeze for several hours before serving. Serve within 3 to 4 days.

THE CHEF'S TOUCH

This High-Test White Chocolate Ice Cream would be right at home when served with almost any piece of cake in this book.

Because of the lavish use of cream and eggs, this ice cream does not freeze rock-solid, which makes it easy to scoop, never mind swallow.

Equipment, Ingredients, and Techniques

EQUIPMENT

BAKING SHEETS AND CAKE PANS

All of the baking sheets and cake pans used for testing the recipes in this cookbook were of consumer quality rather than commercial bakeware. Most of this equipment was purchased at our local Ace Hardware and Target stores. The exception was the 6 × 2-inch heart-shaped pans for the Chocolate Tender Passion. (These aluminum pans with an anodized finish were purchased from Wilton Enterprises at www.wilton.com.) The locally purchased baking sheets and cake pans were of good quality and value. All had nonstick finishes. We use only baking sheets with sides (for extra rigidity and to lower the opportunity for the sheet to warp in a hot oven). The standard size is 10 × 15 inches.

You may have noticed that even though we specify nonstick pans, I still note in many of the recipes that the pans should be buttered and sometimes lined with parchment paper or wax paper. The reason is to ensure quick release of a baked batter without fail. I can recommend the following manufacturers for quality and value: Ekco Housewares (Baker's Secret), Nordic Ware (Bundt brand bakeware), and Farberware (Professional series).

BOWLS

Although only noted in this cookbook where it was critical, the fact is that all of the bowls at Ganache Hill are noncorrosive. (The noncorrosive surface prevents the chemical interaction of the surface with food, especially acidic foods.) For years I have recommended stainless steel bowls as the bowls of choice because of their durability (they can bounce off tile floors) and ease of cleaning (no pores to get clogged up with nasty bacteria, like salmonella). Economical glass bowls are also noncorrosive and easy to clean. The following list of bowl sizes corresponds with the bowls indicated in this book.

small	= 1 ½ to 2 quarts
medium	= 2 ½ to 3 quarts
large	= 3 ½ to 4 quarts
extra large	= 6 to 7 quarts

DISPOSABLE VINYL OR LATEX GLOVES

For those who prefer not to get their hands smeared with chocolate (Freud has his theory about such types), disposable vinyl (or latex) gloves can be worn for rolling truffles. If you use your bare hands, the rolling will be easier (but not less messy) if you dust the palms of your hands with powdered cocoa. We found vinyl gloves at our local Ace Hardware store.

DOUBLE BOILER

At Ganache Hill we usually nest a stainless steel or glass bowl over a saucepan to fashion a double boiler. When using such a makeshift double boiler, be certain that about half of the bowl can be inserted into the saucepan, and that the bowl covers the entire top of the pan. Prior to setting the bowl over the saucepan, place about 1 inch of water into the pan. (Make certain that the bottom of the bowl does not touch the water in the pan.) Even if you use a real double boiler, which is comprised of two saucepans, with one pan nesting perfectly into the other, be sure that the bottom of the top pan doesn't touch the water in the bottom saucepan. This will help prevent the chocolate from scorching as it is melted.

ELECTRIC MIXER

Whenever I am queried about my favorite piece of baking equipment, I answer unequivocally that it is a table-model electric mixer. And if you are serious about baking, consider owning two mixers, each with an extra bowl. (At Ganache Hill we have two KitchenAid mixers, a model K5SS 5-quart, as well as a model K45 4½-quart.) Many, if not all, of the recipes in this cookbook can be adequately prepared using a handheld electric mixer, a whisk, a stiff rubber spatula, or even a wooden spoon (only try the wooden spoon method with a professional trainer nearby). Succinctly put, a table-model mixer has the strength and efficacy to combine ingredients thoroughly and efficiently.

If you are experiencing problems with ingredients splattering outside of the mixing bowl, I suggest using a pouring shield attachment. Or cover the top of the mixer down the sides to the bowl with a towel or plastic wrap, especially when mixing at medium speed or higher.

ICE CREAM FREEZER

Ice cream lovers can rejoice because ice cream making has never been easier or more economical due to a new generation of ice cream freezers. There are several manufacturers producing machines that are low cost ($50 to $60), easy to use (they do not require salt to freeze the ingredients), drudgery free (hand cranking is not necessary), and compact in size. Simply freeze the supplied canister insert for several hours; then place it on the electronically driven base of the machine, add the ice cream, custard, or sorbet base, turn the machine on, and in less than 30 minutes the ice cream is frozen enough to place in the freezer to harden.

When purchasing an ice cream machine, I suggest you find a model that makes from 1 to 1½ quarts. At such low prices why not purchase two? You will find these machines in kitchenware stores, department stores, and even at your local Target.

ICE CREAM SCOOPS

The ice cream scoops listed below are suggested for some of the recipes in *Death by Chocolate Cakes*.

12 scoop = 3 ounces
20 scoop = 1½ ounces
70 scoop = ½ ounce

For quicker and more effective portioning of several batters in this cookbook, use the appropriate ice cream scoop listed below rather than the measuring spoon or cup suggested in the recipe.

MICROWAVE OVEN

At last count, almost every home in America harbored a microwave oven. I must confess that I was a veritable Luddite for decades regarding this technology. I eschewed the microwave because of my inclination to be tactile with food. Seeing, smelling, and, yes, even touching ingredients while they cook is an important aspect of the way I cook. So why have I finally jumped on the microwave bandwagon, albeit in a limited fashion? Over the years, many people asked me why I did not use the microwave, if only for melting chocolate. Bowing to that oft-repeated question—and to my own curiosity—I asked Ganache Hill test kitchen chef Brett Bailey to head over to Target and purchase a microwave. Brett settled on an economically priced ($150) Panasonic, model NN-S758, 1100-watt microwave oven. I have to confess that by the time we finished testing the recipes for this book, I preferred the ease and efficiency of the microwave oven to the double boiler for melting chocolate. (See Techniques: Melting Chocolate in a Microwave Oven, page 197, for instructions.)

	ICE CREAM SCOOP
Blueberry Chocolate Chip Cakes (page 15)	# 12 level scoop
Cocoa Bourbon Cakes (page 35)	# 20 heaping scoop
Cocoa Hazelnut Cakes (page 21)	# 70 level scoop
Peanut Chocolate Chip Cupcakes (page 23)	# 20 slightly heaping scoop
Chocolate Chunk Cookie Cakes (page 17)	# 12 level scoop
Espresso Cheesecakes (page 37)	# 12 scant scoop
Lemon Poppy Seed Cakelettes (page 45)	# 70 heaping scoop
Truffles of the Night (page 171)	# 70 level scoop

OVEN

Successful baking depends on seemingly myriad factors. The quality of the ingredients, skill of the baker, atmospheric pressure, alignment of the moon and the planets, and operational equipment all play a role in the rise, and sometimes fall, of a cake. The key piece of equipment people seem to take for granted is the oven. The common assumption is that if the oven is set on 350°F, then whatever is placed in the oven will cook at that temperature. Unfortunately, this is where so many bakers go astray, because temperature-accurate ovens seem to be as rare as folks who don't love chocolate. In order to ensure that an oven is operating at a specific temperature, I recommend using a mercury-filled tube thermometer. This inexpensive piece of equipment will keep you in the know regarding the actual temperature inside your oven (versus the oven setting). I mentioned in *Death by Chocolate Cookies* that the ovens at Ganache Hill were very accurate and provided an even flow of heat. Almost four years later this continues to be true. Please E-mail me at goganache@aol.com if you are interested in knowing the manufacturer and model of our ovens.

PARCHMENT (OR WAX) PAPER

Lining cake pans with parchment (or wax) paper helps ensure that baked cake layers will easily be released from the pans. The paper is not always needed, but when it is specified in this cookbook, I do recommend its use.

Although I acknowledge a professional bias for parchment paper, I have found that wax paper can be substituted for parchment paper if it is not directly exposed to heat. The paraffin on wax paper may melt in the oven if the surface of the paper is exposed. But when completely covered, as with a cake batter, the paraffin should not melt. Remember that wax paper is not reusable. Parchment paper can stand exposure to high baking temperatures whether it is exposed or not, and in some cases, it can be reused.

PASTRY BAG

I have always found washing and then drying a pastry bag an annoyingly messy task. If you are of a similar bent, you probably will jump for joy as I did when I discovered disposable plastic bags. So if the concept of decorating and then tossing is compelling, go to Tavolo at www.tavolo.com or Wilton Enterprises at www.wilton.com, and order a bunch of disposable decorating bags. You'll thank me for it! Traditional reusable, plastic-lined, fabric pastry bags are available from King Arthur Flour's Baker's Catalogue at www.kingarthurflour.com as well as the Tavolo and Wilton Web sites.

RUBBER SPATULA

Nothing surpasses a rubber spatula for removing all of the chocolate, or whatever else needs to be completely and efficiently removed, from the inside of a bowl, saucepan, or storage container. I suggest an extensive collection of all sizes of rubber spatulas, as well as a few heat-resistant spatulas for working with very hot ingredients.

SAUCEPANS

I have never been overly particular about the pedigree of the cookware I own. At Ganache Hill we have a substantial collection of Corning Vision saucepans (sizes listed below). Brett purchased these at a local outlet mall. We particularly like these glass saucepans for cooking demonstrations. Of course, they will shatter if dropped on a ceramic tile floor (but they are inexpensive). However, after I received a piece of KitchenAid Hi-Density Hard-Anodized Clad Cookware, I became hooked. These beautiful pans may change my casual attitude about cookware purchases in the future. Below are the saucepan sizes suggested in *Death by Chocolate Cakes,* and their equivalents:

> small = 1 quart
> medium = 1½ to 2 quarts
> large = 3 quarts

THERMOMETERS

Oven Thermometer   Allow me to be redundant: The most reliable way of baking at the desired oven temperature is by utilizing an oven thermometer. Use a mercury-filled tube thermometer instead of a spring-style thermometer as your reliable guide to the actual level of heat in the oven (as opposed to the setting on the oven temperature dial or electronic readout). The thermometer can be left in the oven at all times, no matter how high the heat, with the exception of the self-clean setting, which produces high enough heat to ruin most thermometers.

Instant-Read Test Thermometer   These thermometers are not designed for oven use, but rather to get a quick reading on liquids, ice cream custards, heated vegetable oil, and other foods. Use a thermometer with a range of 0° to 200°F for the ice cream recipes in this cookbook. For the Chocolate-Dipped Orange Fry Cakes (page 27), use an instant-read test thermometer with a range of 50° to 500°F.

WHISKS

A recent article about whisks in the *New York Times* made me think that I was not getting out enough. An accompanying picture for the interesting text displayed nine whisks. (Several looked like instruments of torture or pleasure, depending upon your inclinations.) One in particular, from a major kitchenware retailer, looked like a miniature theme park ride. Inside of the wire tines was a wire ball that contained a ceramic bead. To my eye, this internal cage had the potential to create havoc if not thrills; and sure enough, the correspondent noted that "with each upward stroke, cream caught in the cage flies out everywhere." Unless you are looking for a conversation piece or two, I propose a more traditional collection of whisks. For the sake of convenience, I would suggest a few different sizes of stainless steel whisks from 6 to 12 inches in length, equally divided between light and flexible whisks (for light batters, whipped cream, and meringues) and heavier gauge, sturdy whisks (for sauces, heavily textured batters, and ganache).

INGREDIENTS

Logistically, the organization of ingredients is integral to successful baking. Whether the baking is happening at the corner bake shop or in your home, the procurement, proper storage, and eventual preparation of ingredients should be planned to maximize the enjoyment of creating compelling confections. High quality ingredients may not in themselves ensure tasty results, but without fresh ingredients, the cook or baker is doomed to produce mediocre fare.

Having said all of that, I don't want to wax too serious because, after all, cake is just cake, and just about anyone can produce delicious results. I encourage you to market shop for most ingredients. Unlike fine wine, which improves with age, eggs, butter, and even chocolate don't benefit from weeks in dark, damp storage. The following information about some key ingredients used throughout this book should guide you from the supermarket to chocolate cake heaven.
NOTE: I have listed the brands used at Ganache Hill merely to offer a benchmark for quality products, not as an endorsement.

BAKING POWDER
AND BAKING SODA

Many refrigerators contain an open box of baking soda to ostensibly mitigate refrigerator odors. You be the judge about baking soda's effectiveness in odor control, but please heed this caveat: Do not use the contents of the aroma-suppressing box for leavening a cake.

When it comes to baking powder and baking soda, a freshly opened container is best. Be sure to check the expiration date on the package, and unless you are baking for a horde, purchase small containers. Be precise in the measurement of either of these ingredients because too much can cause the cake to fall. Brand of baking powder utilized at Ganache Hill: Calumet; brand of baking soda utilized at Ganache Hill: Arm and Hammer.

BUTTER

Yes, I admit it: I am a butter lover. The rich flavor, moistness, and perfect crumb that defines an exceptional piece of cake can only be achieved utilizing real butter. Almost every recipe in this book contains unsalted butter. To achieve the same delicious results that we are accustomed to at Ganache Hill and The Trellis, purchase U.S. Grade AA unsalted butter. If you must use margarine, be prepared for uneven results, because the different proportions of fat to water in butter versus margarine can affect the leavening, texture, and taste of a cake.

Unsalted butter should be stored in the refrigerator or the freezer to deter rancidity. All of the recipes in this book, with the exception of Rose Levy Beranbaum's Marble Empire Cake, were prepared using butter directly from the refrigerator. Frozen butter should be thawed under refrigeration before using. (This may take a couple of days.)

Use softened butter if you choose to use a handheld electric mixer or a whisk, rather than the recommended table-model electric mixer. Brand utilized at Ganache Hill: Land O'Lakes.

CHOCOLATE

While chocolate is a complex food that contains a multitude of chemical compounds, you need not be degreed in pharmacology to concoct the chocolate cakes prescribed in this book. All chocolate used at Ganache Hill is manufactured right here in the United States and can be found in most supermarkets. My penchant for using American chocolate is not entirely based on patriotism. The fact is that the widely available brands that I have listed here are delicious, economical, and easy to work with, and they produce extraordinarily flavorful chocolate cakes. One note of caution: Check the ingredients list on the back of the package to verify that you are purchasing real chocolate. If the label lists any fat other than cocoa butter, it's not the good stuff. Many American, as well as European, manufacturers add palm kernel oil and/or coconut oil to their chocolates. That's because those fats cost substantially less than cocoa butter,

which is sold to cosmetic and pharmaceutical manufacturers for the big bucks.

Chocolate Chips and Mini-Morsels   I beg you, please do not substitute chocolate chips or mini-morsels for baking chocolate. Almost without exception, chips and morsels simply will not produce the desired outcome. Most chips and morsels are formulated differently than baking chocolate, and that's why they maintain their shape even after being baked. Brand chocolate chips utilized at Ganache Hill: Baker's Semi-Sweet Real Chocolate Chips. Brand chocolate mini-morsels utilized at Ganache Hill: Nestlé Real Semi-Sweet Chocolate Mini Morsels.

Milk Chocolate   If you love the smooth, creamy flavor of milk chocolate, you are not alone. Although I am a big fan of milk chocolate bars, I usually don't espouse milk chocolate in baking, and instead choose darker chocolate for more assertive flavor. Our Milk Chocolate Peach Pecan Upside-Down Cake (page 129) is an extraordinary exception to my usual dark chocolate inclination. Brand utilized at Ganache Hill: Ghirardelli Pure Milk Chocolate.

Semisweet Baking Chocolate   Almost all of the recipes in this book contain some amount of semisweet baking chocolate. If you prefer darker, more assertively flavored chocolate you may substitute exactly the same amount of bittersweet chocolate in any of our recipes. Do check the ingredients label on the packaging, which should read (in this order): chocolate (unsweetened), sugar, cocoa butter, soy lecithin (an emulsifier), vanilla extract. As mentioned previously, do not purchase chocolate that contains any fat other than cocoa butter. Brand utilized at Ganache Hill: Baker's Semi-Sweet Baking Chocolate Squares.

Unsweetened Baking Chocolate (Chocolate Liquor) Look at the packaging of unsweetened chocolate: It should list one ingredient—chocolate. Unsweetened chocolate is not palatable on its own, but it is the heart and soul of all chocolate confections. It is the juice, if you will, of the cacao plant. Unsweetened chocolate is present in some form in all other chocolate. Unsweetened chocolate is by composition more than 50 percent cocoa butter, the remaining amount being what is termed cocoa solids. Brand utilized at Ganache Hill: Baker's Unsweetened Baking Chocolate Squares.

Unsweetened Cocoa Powder Cocoa is produced by pressing almost all of the cocoa butter out of unsweetened chocolate. The flavor intensity of cocoa is diminished by exposure to air, so I recommend purchasing small containers and keeping the container tightly sealed. Look at the container closely before purchasing it to make certain you are not selecting a breakfast cocoa drink mix. The only ingredient listed should be cocoa. Brand utilized at Ganache Hill: Hershey's Cocoa.

White Chocolate It can't be chocolate—it's the wrong color! But since unsweetened choco-late contains more than 50 percent cocoa butter, then white chocolate, which is primarily composed of cocoa butter, must indeed be chocolate. It was not always that way. Only since 1998 has the FDA allowed chocolate manufacturers to label white chocolate as such. Prior to that time, only a product that contained a certain amount of cocoa solids could actually be merchandised as chocolate. The ingredients listed on a package of white chocolate should be sugar, cocoa butter, milk, soy lecithin (an emulsifier), and vanilla extract. Remember, palm kernel oil (or any other vegetable fat, for that matter) need not apply. Brand utilized at Ganache Hill: Baker's Premium White Chocolate Baking Squares.

Eggs

I cannot overemphasize how crucial fresh eggs are to a successful cake. Select fresh grade AA large eggs for all the recipes in this book. Using smaller or larger eggs may adversely affect the leavening of a cake. I recently had a friend tell me that she was not having success with one of my recipes. After much prodding, she revealed that she always uses jumbo eggs. Although the substitution of one size egg for another may sometimes work, it can't be guaranteed. Although many bakers recommend bringing eggs to room temperature before using them, I don't subscribe to that practice. All of the recipes in this book were successfully prepared using eggs directly from the refrigerator. Brand utilized at Ganache Hill: generic, direct from the supermarket.

FLOUR

Avoid generic flour. Baking results can be altered by improperly milled flour. Make sure that the flour specified in the recipe is indeed the flour that you have selected, since a substitute may result in pancakes rather than cakes. On the other end of that phenomenon, make sure you don't use self-rising flour, unless it is specified; and it's not called for in this book. Brand of all-purpose flour utilized at Ganache Hill: Gold Medal. Brand of cake flour utilized at Ganache Hill: Swans Down.

NUTS

Nuts indeed, and lots of them. Many of the recipes in this cookbook contain nuts. Whether they're pecans, walnuts, peanuts, pistachios, macadamia nuts, or hazelnuts, nuts bring flavor and texture to the party. Look for nuts in the bulk food section at the supermarket. Buy them whole (unless you need them sliced) and unsalted if you can. For long-term storage, place nuts in a tightly sealed container in the freezer. Bring them to room temperature before using. And do toast them before using (see Toasting Nuts in the Techniques section, page 199) to bring out the flavor. Brand utilized at Ganache Hill: generic, from the bulk food section of our local Ukrop's supermarket.

TECHNIQUES

CARAMELIZING SUGAR

Caramel never seems to wane in popularity. Whether it's soft, firm, liquid, chewy, or teeth shattering, the elemental confectionery flavor and aroma of sugar cooked until golden brown awakens many delicious memories. And what gets me so excited about making and working with caramel is its simplicity. Despite the caution needed when making caramel (it gets darn hot), please don't be shy about attempting the delicious caramel recipes in this book. Hopefully my directions will lessen your fears so that caramel will become part of your kitchen repertoire.

CUTTING CAKE

Because overindulgence of chocolate (an oxymoron for sure) is a legal vice, I suggest portions that are significant in size as well as height. If you espouse confectionery moderation (another oxymoron), you may cut many more slices of dessert from a cake like the Mocha Mud Cake (page 111) than the suggested 12 servings. The only downside to cutting more portions is that the slice of cake may not stand straight up but rather will need to be served on its side.

For professional-looking portions, use a 10- to 12-inch serrated slicer when cutting the cakes. Place the cake to be sliced on a sanitary cutting surface. Heat the blade of the slicer under hot running water and wipe the blade dry before making each slice.

ICE-WATER BATH

In order to quickly lower the temperature of hot ice cream custard (the base) before transferring it to an ice cream freezer, the custard should be cooled in an ice-water bath. This will facilitate the freezing process. For the recipes in this cookbook, place the hot mixture into a large bowl; then place the bowl into a sink or an extra-large bowl that has been partially filled with ice water. I recommend using a stainless steel bowl for this procedure as stainless steel is a better conductor of temperature than glass or plastic. Stir the hot mixture frequently for quick cooling. An additional benefit of cooling hot foods quickly is its suppression of bacteria growth, which can cause food to spoil.

MELTING CHOCOLATE IN A DOUBLE BOILER

Melting chocolate for baking need not spoil your day. It's actually a cinch if just a couple of precautions are employed. First, set up the double boiler as described in the Equipment section (see page 189). I recommend melting coarsely chopped chocolate slowly over medium heat while stirring frequently with a rubber spatula until the chocolate is completely melted and smooth. Melting it too quickly over high heat may render scorched, inedible chocolate. Avoid introducing any moisture into the melting or already melted chocolate; it may sieze (the chocolate stiffens into a coagulated mass, suitable only for the garbage disposal). Melted chocolate should stay that way for up to an hour, depending on the ambient temperature in your kitchen. If your kitchen is cool, keep the melted chocolate over warm water until ready to use, unless the recipe requires the chocolate to be chilled before using.

AMOUNT OF CHOPPED CHOCOLATE	APPROXIMATE MELTING TIME
1 to 2 ounces	2½ to 3 minutes
3 to 4 ounces	3½ to 4 minutes
5 to 6 ounces	4½ to 5 minutes
7 to 8 ounces	5½ to 6 minutes
9 to 16 ounces	6½ to 8 minutes

MELTING CHOCOLATE IN A MICROWAVE OVEN

I won't apologize for being such a late convert to microwaves, but I am now prepared to say that the microwave is a very efficient piece of equipment for melting and tempering chocolate. It's quick—about twice as fast as a double boiler—and it is relatively foolproof as long as you don't microwave for longer than necessary. (Just like a double boiler—too much heat, and the chocolate will scorch.)

Microwave coarsely chopped chocolate in a glass bowl. After removing the chocolate from the microwave oven, use a rubber spatula to stir it until smooth. At Ganache Hill we use a Panasonic Model NN-S758, 1100-watt microwave oven, and we always use the medium setting for melting chocolate. Melted chocolate should stay that way for up to an hour, depending on the ambient temperature in your kitchen. If your kitchen is cool, keep the melted chocolate over warm water until ready to use, unless the recipe requires the chocolate to be chilled before using. The following melting times may vary, depending on the model, wattage, and power settings available on your microwave oven.

AMOUNT OF CHOPPED CHOCOLATE	APPROXIMATE MELTING TIME
1 to 3 ounces	1½ minutes
4 to 8 ounces	2 to 2½ minutes
9 to 16 ounces	2½ to 3 minutes

MELTING CHOCOLATE WITH OTHER INGREDIENTS

Several of the recipes in this cookbook require melting chopped chocolate with other ingredients, such as butter and cream. As when melting chocolate all by itself, a modicum of attention and care is recommended, especially with regard to heat. It's always best to heat chocolate slowly rather than quickly, and over low rather than high heat.

If it seems odd that in some cases it takes less time to melt chocolate with other ingredients in the microwave oven than by itself, be aware that the combination of ingredients actually accelerates the heating and subsequent melting. The information on pages 200–201 should create smooth sailing and smooth chocolate.

MINCING AND SECTIONING CITRUS ZEST

For minced citrus zest, use a sharp vegetable peeler to remove the colored part of the fruit's skin, but not the bitter white membrane underneath, called the pith. Once the colored skin has been removed, use a very sharp cook's knife to cut the skin into angel-hair-thin julienne strips; then mince the strips.

For attractive citrus fruit sections, use a sharp serrated knife to cut away the colored skin and the pith. Then remove the sections from the peeled fruit by cutting along the membrane between the sections.

SCRAPING DOWN THE INSIDES OF A MIXING BOWL

Is it necessary to scrape down the sides of the bowl so frequently during the preparation of a cake batter? When we tested the recipes in this book, I frequently experimented with the agreed-upon techniques to determine how they affected the cakes. We found that scraping down the sides of the bowl helped incorporate the ingredients in the batter. The smoother results suggested that this simple technique was well worth the effort.

SIFTING DRY INGREDIENTS

Sifting dry baking ingredients breaks up any lumps and eliminates foreign objects from ingredients like flour and cocoa. In addition, sifting aerates the ingredients, making them easier to incorporate into the first stages of a batter, which in turn creates a smooth batter. Sift the dry ingredients onto a large piece of parchment paper or wax paper to make it easier to pick up, carry, and add the ingredients to a mixing bowl.

SKINNING HAZELNUTS

A few years ago, we had difficulty finding skinned hazelnuts at the supermarket, so we skinned them ourselves. This is not a bad job, especially if you enjoy snacking on hazelnuts. To skin them, toast the nuts on a baking sheet with sides in a preheated 325°F oven for 18 minutes. Remove the nuts from the oven and immediately cover the entire top of the baking sheet with a damp cotton towel. Invert another baking sheet with sides over the first one to hold in the steam and make the nuts easier to skin. After 5 minutes, remove the skins from the nuts by placing them inside a folded dry cotton kitchen towel and rubbing them vigorously.

TOASTING NUTS

Most nuts (with the exception of dry roasted peanuts and pistachios) should be toasted and then completely cooled before they are used in a recipe in this book. Toasting accentuates the flavor of the nuts (even nuts that were previously roasted) and dissipates any moisture the absorbent nut flesh acquired during storage.

Toasted nuts should also be completely cooled before they are chopped, especially if the chopping is done in a food processor; otherwise, the nuts may end up as a puree rather than as discernable chopped pieces. Since nuts are perishable, I recommend storing them in the refrigerator or freezer. (Refrigerated or frozen nuts should be brought to room temperature before toasting and using.)

For best results, toast nuts at 325°F. Always purchase unsalted nuts for baking recipes.

NUT TOASTING TIMES

pecan halves	12 minutes
pine nuts	8 minutes
skinned hazelnuts	12 minutes
sliced almonds	10 minutes
macadamia nuts (unsalted)	18 minutes
walnut halves	14 minutes
whole cashews	12 minutes

USING A PASTRY BAG

When it comes to filling a pastry bag, a little technique goes a long way. Turn about one-third of the large open end of a bag inside out, forming a cuff. Place the desired decorating tip inside the bag. (At least one-third of the tip should emerge from the small open end of the bag.) Fill the bag no more than half full (too full, and the contents will flow out of the top). Unfold the cuff and twist it closed. Hold the bag with one hand placed over the twisted top and squeeze the bag firmly while using the other hand to guide the tip of the bag.

INGREDIENTS	DOUBLE BOILER TIME	MICROWAVE OVEN TIME
1 ounce semisweet chocolate with 2 tablespoons unsalted butter	2½ to 3 minutes	1½ minutes
2 ounces white chocolate with ½ cup half-and-half cream	4 to 4½ minutes	1½ minutes
2 ounces semisweet chocolate and 1 ounce unsweetened chocolate with 3 ounces unsalted butter	5½ to 6 minutes	1½ minutes
4 ounces white chocolate with 1 cup heavy cream	6 to 7 minutes	2 minutes
3 ounces semisweet chocolate and 1 ounce unsweetened chocolate with ¼ pound (1 stick) unsalted butter	5½ to 6 minutes	2 minutes
4 ounces semisweet chocolate and 1 ounce unsweetened chocolate with ¾ cup heavy cream	5½ to 6 minutes	2 minutes
5 ounces unsweetened chocolate with ½ pound (2 sticks) unsalted butter, 1¾ cups brewed coffee, and ¼ cup rum	2½ to 3 minutes	2 minutes

INGREDIENTS	DOUBLE BOILER TIME	MICROWAVE OVEN TIME
6 ounces semisweet chocolate with 5 ounces unsalted butter	6½ to 7 minutes	2 minutes
6 ounces semisweet chocolate and 2 ounces unsweetened chocolate with ¼ pound (1 stick) unsalted butter	6½ to 7 minutes	2 minutes
7 ounces white chocolate with 1 cup heavy cream	8 to 9 minutes	2½ minutes
8 ounces semisweet chocolate with 5 ounces unsalted butter	6½ to 7 minutes	2 minutes
8 ounces semisweet chocolate with ½ pound (2 sticks) unsalted butter	6 to 6½ minutes	2½ minutes
8 ounces white chocolate with ¼ cup heavy cream	6 to 6½ minutes	2 minutes
1 pound semisweet chocolate with ½ pound (2 sticks) unsalted butter	7½ to 8 minutes	3 minutes
1 pound semisweet chocolate with 1 pound (4 sticks) unsalted butter	11 to 12 minutes	3½ minutes

Bibliography

Amendola, Joseph. *The Bakers Manual for Quantity Baking and Pastry Making.* New York: Aherns Publishing Company, 1960.

Ayto, John. *The Diner's Dictionary—Food and Drink from A to Z.* Oxford and New York: Oxford University Press, 1993.

Beranbaum, Rose Levy. *The Cake Bible.* New York: William Morrow and Company, 1988.

Bloom, Carol. *The International Dictionary of Desserts, Pastries, and Confections.* New York: Hearst Books, 1995.

Braker, Flo. *The Simple Art of Perfect Baking.* New York: William Morrow and Company, 1985.

Coe, Susan D., and Michael D. Coe. *The True History of Chocolate.* New York: Thames and Hudson, 1996.

Corriher, Shirley O. *Cookwise.* New York: William Morrow and Company, 1998.

Desaulniers, Marcel. *Death by Chocolate.* New York: Rizzoli, 1992.

———. *Desserts to Die For.* New York: Simon & Schuster, 1995.

Etlinger, Steven, and Irena Chalmers. *The Kitchenware Book.* New York: Macmillan Publishing Company, 1993.

Greenspan, Dorie. *Baking with Julia.* New York: William Morrow and Company, 1996.

Herbst, Sharon Tyler. *The New Food Lover's Companion.* New York: Barron's, 1995.

Knight, John B. *Knight's Foodservice Dictionary.* New York: Van Nostrand Reinhold, 1987.

Lipinski, Robert A., and Kathleen A. Lipinski. *The Complete Beverage Dictionary.* New York: Van Nostrand Reinhold, 1992.

Malgieri, Nick. *How to Bake.* New York: Harper-Collins, 1995.

Mariani, John. *The Dictionary of American Food and Drink.* New Haven and New York: Ticknor & Fields, 1983.

Medrich, Alice. *Cocolat.* New York: Warner Books, 1990.

Mimifie, Bernard W. *Chocolate, Cocoa, and Confectionary—Science and Technology.* New York: Van Nostrand Reinhold, 1989.

Ortiz, Elizabeth Lambert. *The Encyclopedia of Herbs, Spices and Flavourings.* New York: Dorling Kindersley, 1992.

Rombauer, Irma S., Marion Rombauer Becker, and Ethan Becker. *The All New All Purpose Joy of Cooking.* New York: Scribner, 1997.

Teubner, Christian. *The Chocolate Bible.* New York: Penguin Studio, 1997.

Walter, Carole. *Great Cakes.* New York: Ballantine Books, 1991.

Index